ACADEMIC LIFE

ACADEMIC LIFE

Hospitality, Ethics, and Spirituality

JOHN B. BENNETT

Quinnipiac University

Foreword by R. Eugene Rice

WIPF & STOCK · Eugene, Oregon

Wipf and Stock Publishers
199 W 8th Ave, Suite 3
Eugene, OR 97401

Academic Life
Hospitality, Ethics, and Spirituality
By Bennett, John B.
Copyright©2003 by Bennett, John B.
ISBN 13: 978-1-55635-901-9
Publication date 3/17/2008
Previously published by Anker Publishing Company, Inc., 2003

About the Author

John B. Bennett is University Scholar and Provost Emeritus at Quinnipiac University in Hamden, Connecticut. Having worked at four different academic institutions and at the American Council on Education—a national higher education association based in Washington, DC—he enjoys a wide perspective on the academy. He has been both faculty member and academic administrator, tenured full professor and chief academic officer. He has been in and out of collective bargaining—and when in, has been on both sides.

He has written and spoken extensively on the roles of department chairpersons and on other academic leadership positions and issues. He has also published widely on topics in ethics, metaphysics and process philosophy, and the philosophy of education. He is the author or editor of five previous books.

Table of Contents

Foreword

This book is a radical critique of American higher education—a profound indictment. In contrast to other biting criticisms—Sikes' *Prof Scam* or Bloom's *Closing of the American Mind* would be examples—John Bennett offers a constructive response, a new way of framing the important work taking place in colleges and universities across the country. In spite of his piercing critique, Professor Bennett obviously loves the institution, its history and purposes, and the people engaged in the work. His book models what he is advocating.

Academic Life: Hospitality, Ethics, and Spirituality orchestrates the voices of those speaking out against an academy that is disconnected from the larger purposes of an inclusive democracy: alienating, ethically challenged, and dampening of spirit. These voices, from Alfred North Whitehead to Henri Nouwen, Robert Bellah, and Parker Palmer, are drawn together here in a chorus of both protest and affirmation. The themes—hospitality, ethics, and spirituality—are thoughtfully intertwined and the central message, largely obscured in contemporary American higher education, echoes the ardent refrain from Søren Kierkegaard that "truth is relationship."

In his critique, Bennett focuses on the pernicious influence of the prestige economy that drives the pressures to rank institutions, the faculty reward system, and, particularly, the functioning of graduate education. We have all complained about the devastating impact of the hustle for prestige—the ratcheting up of pressures—as we all struggle to move up to the next level. What Bennett drives home, however, is the personal toll the prestige economy takes on the inner vitality and the self-respect of individual faculty and students. When coupled with the "insistent individualism" that Bennett finds dominating academic culture, the erosion of spirit is debilitating. I found this depiction most telling:

> Insistent individualism promotes the isolated self—it advances disconnection among faculty and staff as well as between faculty, staff, students, and institutions. It works against internal integration and separates personal from professional lives. It encourages exclusiveness rather than relationality, self-protection rather than openness to the other. It celebrates instrumental rather than relational knowledge. Insistent individualism encourages disciplinary and specialty boundaries, isolated departments, and fragmented institutions.

A major contribution of the book is the call for new metaphors to use in rethinking the academic enterprise. Bennett's exploration of hospitality and conversation are intellectually challenging and provocative. I must confess that I had trouble with hospitality when I first read it in the title. It is a word that has been seriously damaged through being commercialized, sentimentalized, and made superficial by Junior Chambers of Commerce across the country. Bennett renews the word for me by citing Henri Nouwen, the Catholic scholar who lived his faith. He contends that the hospitable works toward "the creation of space where students and teachers can enter into fearless communication with each other and allow their respective life experiences to be their primary and most valuable source of growth and maturation." Bennett deals with the strengths and liabilities of this kind of openness with intellectual subtlety and authenticity.

Bennett's exploration of conversation as a metaphor advancing our understanding of teaching and learning is especially provocative. This effort is particularly important at a time when current events have led to an increased emphasis on our ability to conduct dialogue and deliberation across differences.

This is an especially propitious time for a book of this sort to appear. As a new generation of faculty is being ushered in to replace the large cohort of senior professors moving into retirement, we have an unusually rich opportunity to shape the future of our colleges and universities. Can we cultivate a faculty, staff, and—over time—the culture of our institutions in a way that more of the values celebrated in this book are honored and fewer of the negative qualities so forcefully set forth by Professor Bennett dominate? Can we have institutions that attend to the relational aspects of teaching and learning and have the kind of connectedness that nurtures ethical integrity and attention to the interior life of students and faculty, rather than fostering individual fear and isolation? *Academic Life: Hospitality, Ethics, and Spirituality* provides us with a language and a framework for beginning the conversation.

R. Eugene Rice
American Association for Higher Education
November 2002

Preface

Three common experiences in academic life are central to this essay: Early enthusiasms about joining the community of scholars are often soon diminished by academic politics; the excitement of genuine learning seems persistently difficult to arouse and sustain in a number of students; and the challenges of leadership focus on addressing pathologies rather than on improving education. For some, the unfulfilled promises of academic life provide grist for anger or lamentation, but my interests lie in contributing to remedies. The ideal is always implicit in the actual; moments of disappointment call attention to purposes that sustain and invite us to probe their depths.

I examine these purposes by reflecting on the philosophies, ethics, and spiritualities of the academy at the beginning of a new century. Such work is often piecemeal. We reflect on the reduction of science to scientism, the brush of some forms of postmodernism with nihilism, or the many ways in which the academy is commodified and fragmented. Usually, however, we fail to connect these reflections with ethics. We leave unchallenged institutional, disciplinary, or personal behaviors about which our philosophical reflections give us both clarity and concern. And we connect neither philosophy nor ethics with spirituality, with our longings for greater inner integrity and fulfillment.

I started this project a number of years ago with various articles about academic ethics and integrity. A somewhat more comprehensive treatment appeared in *Collegial Professionalism: The Academy, Individualism, and the Common Good,* published in 1998. I continue the project here, refining and adding to earlier reflections. I find even more relevant today three framing concepts I developed over this period—insistent individualism, the relational self and its community, and the collegial ethic of hospitality that creates and supports the relational community.

Insistent individualism is my term for the excessive individualism of the academy, evident in acts of self-promotion and self-protection at the expense of a common good. It is supported by questionable models of the self, community, and nature—by atomistic philosophies that emphasize separateness, privacy, self-sufficiency, and fragmentation. Our investment in insistent individualism diverts us from a more fundamental, and spiritually fulfilling, model. This more basic philosophy calls attention to relationality and connectedness as our underlying reality—not isolation.

Practicing hospitality creates and expresses this relational community, for it involves an ethic of radical openness in sharing with and receiving from the other. Hospitality is central to the relational community most of us were seeking when we entered the academy. To be hospitable is to attend to the reality of the other—to appreciate it without preconditions and to allow it to instruct oneself. "Others" include students, colleagues, and texts—as well as the multitude of practices that constitute human living, that generate health and harmony as well as oppression and hurt. It is in relation to these others that we learn about ourselves and the world. Dwelling too much in received traditions, in comfortable routines, and in uncritical habits deprives us of gifts that the new and the strange provide.

In this book I extend these themes, adding to them the merits of conversation as the central metaphor for education. It is in conversation with each other and our traditions that we practice hospitality. Conversation is the key ingredient in teaching and learning, building community, supporting colleagues, and providing leadership. I also use the concept of covenant (rather than social contract) to describe relationships we should seek with others. In arguing for these additional concepts, I link academic ethics both to philosophy and to spirituality.

THE MANNER OF APPROACH

In what follows, research institutions, humanists, and academic leaders come in for special questions. The values of research institutions have permeated the academy, often at the expense of hospitality and conversation. The sheer size and complexity of these institutions heighten fragmentation; the specialization they encourage extends the atomistic impulse; the competition and autonomy they foster encourage entrepreneurship and academic capitalism instead of scholarly community. Other institutions seek the prestige of the research university, but often reap only its deficits and none of its virtues. In the process they neglect their own virtues.

Humanists need to play a more distinctive role in the educational conversation. They can promote reflection on the human condition, and hold up the reflexive dimension of learning—its application to the learner—so that learning makes a difference in who one is and what one does. Society looks to higher education for scientific discoveries, technological advances, and vocational training. But it also looks for the deeper insights and understandings that reflect our humanity and creativity.

However, at many institutions humanists swim against the tide—sometimes at their own doing. Their voices are confused or muffled and they become discouraged, neglecting their calling.

Practicing hospitable leadership is another theme of this book. On its face, hospitable leadership means leadership that is open, attentive, and respectful of others. The contrast is leadership that excludes, denies access to appropriate information, and misleads or treats others as means to an outcome rather than as partners in determining and achieving that outcome. This leadership severs rather than promotes the connections distinctive of a covenantal society. It models secrecy rather than sharing—controlling rather than relational power.

I argue for ways of working together that transform the deficits of institutional fragmentation and competition, that strengthen humanists in promoting greater self-understanding, and that empower educational leaders in facilitating hospitality. I develop this argument by attending to philosophy and ethics, and suggesting the importance of a fulfilling spirituality of higher education. The three are connected. Philosophy involves self-conscious thinking about the roots and goals of higher education—and the adequacy of the basic framing concepts we use. Academic ethics addresses questions of integrity—questions about how well we are educating. And the spirituality of higher education points to issues of its internal health and meaning for us.

Each area engages the other two. Doing philosophy involves questions about academic habits and acts, as well as the inner meaning of our perspectives upon academic being and doing. Reflecting upon academic ethics drives us to ask about the standing of concepts of the right and the good as well as the personal meaning inherent in our academic engagements. And pondering the authenticity of our personal and professional lives pushes us toward securing the clarity that philosophy can provide, as well as toward reflecting on the value we create for self and others by education rightly conceived and pursued.

Philosophy reminds us that we bring prior conceptual frameworks and values to our work. Some aspects of our frameworks or world views are culturally inherited; others are personal creations. Frameworks help us order the world. They also hide elements that do not fit. As a result, unexamined frameworks can lead to odd and frustrating notions of reality as well as troubling inconsistencies in our thinking and living.

Some world views dispose people to see things as separate and independent. Others promote seeing things as related, connected in complex and intricate ways. Competing for allegiance in today's academy, the atomism of the one and the holism of the other lead to different values, behaviors, and decisions. We need to examine our conceptual frameworks critically to be confident they appropriately undergird our sense of ourselves and direct our actions. We must do this work ourselves. We do not need technical philosophers, although I find the later philosophy of Alfred North Whitehead to be helpful.

Our world views, our images of reality, are connected with epistemologies and *ethics*. How we think things are implies how we should behave. Atomism upholds the "objective" or neutral point of view—but it also gives license for mistreating others. Power becomes a controlling or manipulating agency. The object of knowledge can be analyzed and dissected, taken apart and rearranged as we wish. However, if we see reality as interconnected, our knowing is itself an act of connection. We cannot stand apart from the objects we know as though our knowing had no impact upon ourselves or them.

Our philosophies are related not only to our ethics, but also to our *spiritualities*. For some, "spirituality" is a foreign term, suggesting cultism or religiosity. But the term reaches out to broader social and personal interests. Basically, it is the living out of the organizing story of one's life. In this definition everyone has a spirituality. The organizing stories of our lives turn around that to which we are ultimately loyal and which we trust for our fulfillment.

Spirituality is the lived dimension of these values and commitments—the lives that our loyalty and trust create and nourish. Spiritualities may or may not be connected with organized forms of religion, but they are certainly connected with world views. Spiritualities marked by self-preoccupation are usually characterized by atomistic philosophies and by ethics that emphasize controlling power. Other spiritualities emphasize community and relational power instead.

AN OVERVIEW OF THE CONTENTS

I consider these matters in eight chapters. Chapters One and Two examine the two sets of framing concepts—atomistic insistent individualism and relational individuality. Although prevalent in academe, insistent individualism represents a deformed development, a movement away from a more authentic type of individualism. I draw on Deborah Tannen, Julie Rivkin, Jane Tompkins, and Parker Palmer in analyzing elements of this framing concept.

Insistent individualism views persons as detached and only externally or incidentally related to others. Dwelling in this concept of selfhood reflects and creates states of alienation. Infecting institutions as well, insistent individualism represents a flawed philosophy, ethics, and spirituality. Philosophically, reality is judged not to support a prior, underlying connectedness. Opportunistic ethics flourish, since others are either potential allies or opponents. This academic spirituality glorifies self-preoccupation, for satisfaction is sought in securing sufficient power to advance one's own agenda and thwart the plans of others.

The second framing concept, relational individuality, presents a far healthier philosophy, ethics, and spirituality. Philosophically, reality is seen as a complex flow of interconnected actualities, and the self as both discrete individual and relationally constituted. Relational ethics searches for individual goods that uplift and uphold the common good. The spirituality of relational individuality celebrates learning and learnedness as shared endeavors, and finds fulfillment in practicing openness to others. Relational individuality is the more fundamental and inclusive framing concept, revealing the many ways that insistent individualism feeds upon itself.

In Chapters Three and Four I explore the virtue of hospitality as foundational to academic work. Practicing radical openness to the other is essential in efforts to protect, transmit, and extend our heritage of learning. In their different ways, Henri Nouwen, Simone Weil, and Parker Palmer instruct us that we teach and learn only by extending and sharing ourselves and our knowledge, and by attending to and receiving from the experience and knowledge of others.

Other virtues are intertwined with hospitality. I examine the scholarly traits of integrity, perseverance, and courage that a recent Carnegie Foundation report held up. I also propose several virtues of self-reflection, including how we provide testimony, exercise discernment, display humility, and extend forgiveness. Education is a profoundly social enterprise—private moments are necessary, but are preceded and followed by public moments. I suggest several spiritual practices that cultivate the habit of being hospitable—attending to the other, seeking self-knowledge, and practicing asceticism. Most of us embrace and practice hospitality gradually, and only as the communities and traditions to which we belong teach its value. However, many institutions have become captives of academic capitalism as well as insistent individualism and are inhospitable in several ways I explore.

Chapters Five and Six treat conversation as the essential metaphor for the work of the academy. However, the academy has developed a number of inappropriate metaphors for teaching and learning. "Transmitting" and "producing" are two images that highlight learner passivity. The image of battling for territory is a common metaphor used by faculty to describe the conditions in which they work.

In contrast, the metaphor of conversation calls attention to students and faculty as actively developing their own voices in relation to the voices of intellectual and humane accomplishment that constitute our civilization and our humanity. As Michael Oakeshott observes, the work of the university is to conduct this conversation and to invite others into it. Conversations of integrity acknowledge and accommodate, rather than ignore or vanquish, the interests and achievements of others.

I draw on Jurgen Habermas, George Allan, and Alfred North Whitehead to illustrate authentic uses of conversation in the academy—in teaching, scholarship, and service. Curricula should be organized so that conversations of liberal learning are included in professional studies. And institutional conversations should be marked by integrity rather than insistent individualism.

Chapter Seven identifies the collegium as a covenantal community where intellectual hospitality is developed and nurtured. Hospitable conversations involve commitments and responsibilities more adequately described by covenant than by social contract. William May and Douglas Sturm remind us that covenant relationships involve pledges to the welfare of others as conversation partners. The idea of social contract carries us only part of the way. In fact, social contracts typically emphasize individual goals and prerogatives that constrain a fuller embrace of responsibilities and obligations. Hospitality, academic ethics, and relational spirituality all point to a covenant rather than a contract as the tie that binds us together.

Chapter Eight considers the nature and role of academic leadership in promoting hospitality, conversation, and covenantal relationships. I provide suggestions for handling the challenges facing many midlevel academic leaders: department chairpersons, faculty senate members, student affairs staff, and college and school deans. I also examine opportunities that institutional presidents have to define the context within which other leaders, faculty, staff, and students work. The model of president as heroic leader seems woefully inadequate in setting the tone for hospitality, and facilitating colleague attention to ethics and spirituality.

Acknowledgments

Perhaps more than any other, Parker Palmer has in our times made the case for attending to the spirituality of the academy. In part this is because he has identified many of its present failings. But it is also because he has shown what an authentic spirituality might look like. An independent scholar and teacher, he has from time to time taught at colleges and universities, but remains unattached to any specific campus. His more distant perspective is truly valuable, one of the many needed voices in conversations about the health of the academy, and I call on his thought frequently in what follows. My own perspective is from within the academy and relies on almost four decades of service in various settings as both faculty member and administrator.

I have drawn on the work of others as well. George Allan has labored with creativity and originality in the broad field of Whiteheadian philosophy of education. Various members of the Association for the Process Philosophy of Education have heard and read some of my thinking. I am grateful to Bernard Lee and Michael Cowan of Loyola University New Orleans, Ronald Simpson of the University of Georgia, Joyce Feuchts-Haviar of California State University at Northridge, David Perrin at the University of Saint Paul in Ottawa, and James Bowler at Fairfield University for conversation at various forums at their institutions. The Yale University Whitney Humanities Center also provided a place for discussion, as did several international conferences of Improving University Teaching and Learning.

I have also drawn on some of my own recent writing. Themes from various essays in *The Department Chair* can be seen in the chapter on leadership. The concept of conversation as a central metaphor for higher education was developed in *Liberal Education.* Aspects of the notion of hospitality as a central academic virtue appeared in these and other places, noted as appropriate in the text. I am grateful to Douglas Sturm, George Allan, Bill Garland, and Victor Worsfold for their comments on the contrast between covenantal and social contract ways of thinking. Some of my other conversation partners include Gene Rice, Jerry Berberet, John Cobb, Schubert Ogden, David Stineback, and Elizabeth A. Dreyer—my wife and best colleague. Dana Green, Merritt Moseley, and Art Chickering read the whole draft and provided thoughtful suggestions.

I am grateful for the sabbatical leave Quinnipiac University provided when I relinquished the position of provost and senior vice president for academic affairs. It offered a welcome opportunity to read, reflect, and write. I also appreciate the good work of Joe Podsialdo in addressing several computer setbacks. Most of all, I agree with Parker Palmer (1997) that

> what will transform education is not another theory or another book or another formula but a transformed way of being in the world. In the midst of the familiar trappings of education—competition, intellectual combat, obsession with a narrow range of facts, credits, credentials—we seek a life illumined by spirit and infused with soul. (p. 8)

By itself this essay cannot transform anything. My hope, though, is that it will spark conversations that lead to academic lives with more spirit and greater soul.

REFERENCES

Palmer, P. J. (1997, September). The grace of great things: Reclaiming the sacred in knowing, teaching, and learning. *The Holistic Education Review, 10* (3), 8–16.

The Nature of Insistent Individualism 1

The academy has developed a reputation as both "arrogant" (Sullivan, 1995, p. 171) and a place where fierce battles are waged over small stakes. Asked why he was running for Governor of New Jersey, Princeton President Woodrow Wilson is said to have responded that he wanted out of politics!

In this chapter I look at academic politics to discern an underlying problem for academe—its insistent individualism. I am not referring to the Enlightenment celebration of the individual, rooted in the concept of critical evaluation. Autonomy in the sense of developing one's own thoughtful and critical understanding of issues of self and world is essential to an authentic individualism—informed by awareness of the primordial relationality and connectedness of life. What I call insistent individualism is the deformation of this authentic individualism into a persistent competitive and possessive individualism in which self-promotion and protection become central values.

I consider parallels between the model of "heroic" selfhood in Western films and novels, and in academe. I explore types of academic insistent individualism, examining differences between more aggressive and more passive behaviors. I trace the ceremonial contentiousness and prestige economy of education into which students are initiated. Then I examine insistent individualism at the institutional level by considering departments and institutions.

In the following chapter I consider some causes of insistent individualism and contrast it with the more fundamental and hopeful relational individualism. This chapter and part of the next focus on the "bad news." They are melancholy reports. Yet they help us to acquire self-knowledge. The chapters are themselves spiritual exercises. They reflect on some objects of our loyalty and trust—some values to which we are faithful, and some commitments that give form to the stories of our lives.

ACADEMIC POLITICS

Academic politics *can* be petty and intense.[1] Consider our struggles for computers and lab equipment, travel money, preferred courses at desired

times, and memberships on prestigious committees or the "right" editorial
boards. These are not just individual struggles. Disputes among academic
departments over resources and turf are common. Which unit teaches the
required statistics course? Gets the new building? Why is mathematics,
rather than English, getting extra lines? There are academic politics among
institutions as well. In addition to familiar athletic rivalries, serious struggles occur over enrollments, financing, and prestige. Here, too, competition can be keen and strategies both imaginative and devious.

Academics have long memories concerning defeats. Faculty and
administrators can describe in great detail hurts as though they happened
yesterday—when they actually occurred a full decade or more earlier. At
other times, when the battle is over we laugh at foibles and escapades,
perhaps incorporating them into institutional narratives. The intensity was
okay, we say, because the stakes are small. It is not as though anyone was
harmed.

However, large values may be in the balance when the hospitality and
thoughtfulness of a learned profession are absent. Not all of us are open to
debate, interested in others' ideas, or committed to honest exchange and
reasoned assessment. Some of our practices trammel the inquiry we celebrate. In the heat of political moments, well-constructed arguments give
way to clever innuendo, modest propositions are replaced by exaggerated
claims, and commitments to assessing contrary positions fairly turn into
suspiciousness and willingness to believe the worst.

These behaviors compromise the compelling purposes of the academy.
Loyalties to the heritage of human achievement we hold in trust are weakened, as is fidelity to promoting the learning of others. Speeches about the
rewards of inquiry become shallow. The inadequacy of our commitment
to critical reasoning is apparent. We lose sight of the many student futures
on the line and become numbed to our obvious responsibilities.

Almost any issue can become politicized. Budget decisions, curriculum revision, and conflicts over hiring, promotion, or merit pay are typical flashpoints. Too many or not enough students is another. Generational
differences fragment rather than complement. Long-standing personality
conflicts explode: colleagues' repeated grandstanding and bombast become
too much to endure. Intrusive trustees, regents, or legislators are also classic catalysts of trouble.

These are not just faculty problems. Administrators face these challenges too, and add their own. Some hoard institutional information
from fear that sharing will cause them to lose control or be unfairly criticized. Such apprehension is widespread and misguided. Failing to attend

to others' broader needs, many administrators create the very problems they want to avoid. Stanley Fish (2001) observes,

> bad news is better than no news; faculty imagination, like nature, abhors a vacuum, and in the absence of information the faculty will fabricate it, moving easily and imperceptibly from rumor to conjecture to hypothesis to undoubted (and completely unsubstantiated) fact. (p. B13)

Problems spread when colleagues refuse to check excesses: polarizing rhetoric and arrogant speeches escalate or are ignored rather than challenged; outright absenteeism from common responsibilities is unquestioned; and being candid only when personally convenient becomes acceptable. Adversarial energies—as well as indifference and fatigue—overcome collegial instincts. Posturing and intimidating behaviors increase, as do acts of belittling others, keeping score, and indulging in resentment.

Insistent Individualism

These things happen when insistent individualism takes over. The quality of conversation becomes cheapened, interest in collaboration diminished, and the satisfactions of working together reduced. Narrow distinctions in professorial standing are subtly enforced. Precisely when leadership is most important it becomes least evident. People of courage and integrity are silent, and individuals turn against colleagues, faculty against administrators, and vice versa. Institutions lose interest in cooperation and retreat into secrecy or espionage. Standards to which we hold ourselves accountable are relaxed, and individual isolation and institutional fragmentation are heightened.

Some justify this self-indulgence in terms of the pedagogical value of idiosyncrasy. We are told faculty are *supposed* to be different, since their behaviors challenge traditional ways of thinking. Undergraduate studies initiate students into the variousness of the world, including unusual professors. Graduate programs build on this foundation. Under the cover of academic politics, we excuse ourselves from rules and expectations that govern other enterprises. We lack effective peer challenge, critics suggest, and we permit ourselves behaviors we would camouflage in other settings.

For instance, we pronounce intellectual work as beyond precise measurement—even as we insist upon measuring and criticizing others' activities. We resist applying outcomes assessment to our work, becoming less accountable to the public—although we insist upon evaluating other industries. We tolerate misbehaving colleagues well beyond what we accept in business or government. We label as consensual, intimate relationships with students and others we supervise—rather than acknowledge that such relationships are inherently compromised by power differentials.

Those who could challenge these self-serving and contradictory positions often don't—leaving others to drift deeper into self-protective silence and cynicism. That we only fitfully acknowledge that academics can abuse society's trust is at odds with our professed belief in self-examination, and exposes us to charges of hypocrisy. Without careful assessment, we have little support for our claims to know what we accomplish in the classroom and laboratory. And our penchant to examine others rather than ourselves gives rise to the understandable charge of arrogance.

The Public Trust

Questions are also raised outside the academy. Greater participation in higher education has brought greater public awareness of its workings. Frank Rhodes (1998) calls attention to this external criticism: "America's universities are caught in a paradox: public expectations have rarely been higher; public confidence and support rarely lower. . . . universities are perceived as self-indulgent, arrogant, and resistant to change" (p. 4). The public judges accountability a moral, not just a managerial, matter. When it learns of failed civility and rationality as well as other forms of inadequate self-regulation, the public comes to doubt connections in the academy between knowledge and character, between learning about the human condition and interest in improving it. These are fundamental challenges before the academy. We are often unsuccessful even in naming, much less in addressing, them.

Surely this picture is overdrawn, some will say. Granted, there are bad apples. But most of the time we are responsible, committed to open, civil, and productive education. And this is largely correct. Unfortunately, though, a majority of good apples may not compensate, given our emphasis upon individual prerogatives. It is the few who tarnish the many. Perhaps earlier they were among the many, but along the way they changed. We have not done well in engaging them or in addressing issues they create.

Simply put, we do not work together very well. Academic politics and insistent individualism *do* infect our collective work. As a philosophy, ethic, and spirituality, insistent individualism has deep roots in our academic culture. We elevate those who stand apart—those who think otherwise—even when they injure the community we seek. Popular images of combat and solitude suggest some of our entrenched values.

ACADEMICS AND THE WESTERN: PARALLEL MODELS OF "HEROIC" SELFHOOD?

A colleague observed that when she thinks of the academic star, the rugged and solitary cowboy of conventional Western movies comes to mind.[2] Both are heroic individualists who define themselves against others. Sitting straight in the saddle, standing tall at the lectern, or enjoying top billing in the prized periodical or press, they celebrate self-reliance. Each appears remarkably self-contained, betrays few doubts in his or her cause, and evidences little essential dependence upon others. The one performs primarily in open spaces, the other on campus, but both value control, if not domination.

Both are known for endurance. The academic persists through numerous competitions, garnering credentials from the "right" institutions, identifying a cutting edge dissertation topic, securing the patronage of influential figures, finding good institutional appointments, publishing in the right places, as well as presenting at major meetings. The journey to status is often graced by good fortune, but also marked by toil and stamina. The cowboy traces no such complicated path; the test is physical rather than mental, but it can be brutal. Weather is blisteringly hot or numbingly cold, sleep deprivation is frequent, thirst and hunger are regular companions, and some form of pain is a constant. In both cases, the hero prevails through endurance. The weak fall by the wayside, give out, or otherwise give up.

Even obvious differences between cowboy and academic point to underlying commonalities. The Western protagonist is a man of few words. Silence is both a virtue and a means of control. Loquaciousness expresses weakness. The contrast with rich academic discourse appears stark, but misleads. Verbal sophistication is often used to limit connectivity between self and others, not facilitate it. Academic wordiness can have the same effect as Western laconicism. In both cases discourse is used to differentiate, separate, and exclude—to distance, not connect.

Another apparent difference is that cowboys are ascetics. They renounce companionship and civilization—hearth, children, community, and culture. In contrast, few academics suffer pain without flinching; few deliberately renounce comfort or perquisites. Nevertheless, academic individualists can also become ascetics. The hardships associated with the lonely scholar's life in the depths of the library or laboratory are deemed both necessary and virtuous (Damrosch, 1995). Self-imposed austerity is willingly borne as the cost of academic achievement and of Western manhood.

In both cases, the ideal life is marked by sufficient power to keep it independent. Yet the life of the academic insistent individualist seems no more spiritually fulfilling than that of the typical Western cowboy. Both equate with integrity and authenticity the isolation they deem necessary for control. The self is defined against the other. Exclusion rather than inclusion is the norm. Genuine freedom, liberation, and independence seem forever elusive. And yet in academe, as in Western film and fiction, the image continues to attract.

TYPES OF ACADEMIC INSISTENT INDIVIDUALISM

The most conspicuous academic insistent individualists develop skills in self-promotion and self-protection.[3] They construct self-referential frameworks that associate increase in personal standing with self-sufficiency and independence. They use verbal agility and knowledge to manipulate and control. They select few compatriots, distancing and excluding others. They invest in careerism, regardless of a more fulfilling selfhood for students, colleagues, or themselves. In a variety of ways, insistent individualists cultivate personal identity through using others. Examples are seen on every campus. Two types are quite familiar: those who pursue self-promotion and those who seek self-protection.

Self-Promotion

These faculty include the stars and the wannabes, those skilled in self-display and self-advancement. They need to be prominent in the discipline, or at least on campus. Ample and well-placed publications, favorable reviews, grant successes, and endowed lecture invitations are important, desirable currency. Academic administrators often come from the same mold, using their power to control events and secure standing. Some presidents and academic vice presidents are deeply rooted in the "command and control" mentality. A favorite administrative ploy is to claim confidentiality—particularly on financial matters—since faculty and staff cannot mount intelligent challenges to practices hidden from view. Combat with other administrators over spans of control and access to influence can be pervasive and sophisticated.

Whether faculty or administrators, aggressive insistent individualists enjoy intellectual combat, jockeying for privilege and control—for having and getting the last word, however fleeting. They are interested in scoring points, one-upsmanship, counting coup, and avoiding defeat. Delicate rules of engagement are often unimportant and interactions with colleagues and students can be abrasive and bruising. Their goal seems to be to talk and to be heard. At times, one might say of them, "there but for the grace of God goes God."

Style counts in academe, and these insistent individualists appear in many guises. Not all are abrasive. Some are slick masters of court intrigue, displaying little apparent ambition for control or standing. However, they too can be opportunistic and wage skilled combat, though in subtle, sometimes underhanded, ways. These individualists see the academy as a contest of wills and attempt to heighten their power through appearing pliable and cooperative. Differences with others are not honestly presented in open combat, but neither is combat abandoned. Dealing with the covertly aggressive can be extraordinarily difficult.

Academic violence. Among others, faculty member Jane Tompkins (1996) has described the academic violence when aggressive insistent individuals "perform." Imposing one's own construction of reality becomes the overarching objective. In countless academic papers and conferences, Tompkins (1992) suggests, professors perform this way: they ridicule opponents' gaffes, deplore efforts to be innovative as abandoning standards, and excoriate appeals to tradition as mindless repetition. They give a terrible overtone to some academic publications and conferences. Neither the politics nor the stakes are small. Others agree. "Anyone who has spent any time at all in a University knows that it is not a model community, that few communities are more petty and vicious than University faculties" (Readings, 1996, p. 190).

Former faculty member Patrick Henry (1999) makes a similar point about academic enculturation:

> Academic training infects conversation itself so that surprise, even change, gets muted, stifled. The presenter strives to be so brilliant as to forestall criticism, while the listeners lie in wait for the weak points in the presenter's argument so that they can pounce and show their superiority. (p. 69)

The conservative effect is ironic, given the reputation of academics as socially liberal. Yet, the infection is widespread and Henry includes himself: "After faculty meetings I found that I often meditated more on the clever things I'd said than on the provocative ideas of others" (Henry, 1999, p. 69).

The ethical and spiritual toll can be substantial. Pressures to perform oppress and block the natural, original thirst for learning and knowledge, substituting fear of reproach and desire for approval. They stunt and warp human creativity; they lead to narrow specialization and focus; they neglect imagination and intuition; they reinforce self-preoccupation and self-promotion. In short, they impoverish the self—and the broader community.

The radically disaffected. Every campus has a small number of radically disaffected faculty. These are the hostile cynics who have deteriorated into the incurably aggrieved. They value their isolation and negativity as virtuous. They master the rhetoric of polarization and denounce with certainty what others treat with caution: The barbarians are at the gate, students are not even minimally prepared, the curriculum proposal is completely unworkable, the grant concept is "naïve" (the ultimate condemnation), the administration is both corrupt and incompetent, other faculty are blind, etc.

These critics refuse to believe conflicting evidence. They cannot accept that things are better than they declaim, for then they lose their martyrdom. They defend their low class enrollments and high dropout rates as evidence of high standards. Alternatively, they present their abusive behaviors as pedagogical gambits, bold devices to shatter student preconceptions and lethargy. The shallowness of these descriptions is transparent, yet the records of these faculty prevent them from finding new positions that might revitalize their careers. They are trapped and drain energy and vitality from the rest of us.

Self-Protection
By far the greater number of academic insistent individualists are neither overtly nor covertly aggressive. They are of a second type—more passive, perhaps deploring the unattractive behaviors of aggressive colleagues, but unwilling to confront them. The second type retreat, practicing their insistent individualism through withdrawal. They include the private souls who follow their own path, rather than community guidelines, in developing course and grading objectives. For most, though, days of protest never came, or are long over. They are seeking solitude and escape from dealing with problem faculty or calling them to accountability. Self-protection rather than self-promotion is the primary objective.

Some go further by throwing up by their hands and withdrawing altogether. They shrug their shoulders, resign from committees, flee from campus, and so become physically as well as psychically unavailable. Now in self-imposed exile, they ignore faculty meetings and neglect office hours. They become minimalists, adept at calculating the least of themselves that must be made available to others.

Others won't withdraw at all, such as senior faculty who refuse to retire. Some seem frightened at the loss of the only world they know—full-time teaching, comfortable routines, and controlling power. Others just never step aside—hanging on rather than graciously giving way to the next generation of academics. Colleagues cannot summon courage to tell them that it's time to go. Institutions contribute, failing to provide retired faculty with affiliation relationships that many desire—access to secretaries, modest research funds, laboratory space, etc. With such arrangements, retired faculty could continue teaching and research—but on a different scale, allowing room for the next generation to revitalize the profession.

As Eugene Arden (2001) notes, the elimination of mandatory retirement for faculty has been a mixed blessing, "preventing young scholars who are at the beginning stage from entering the pipeline [and delaying] colleagues already in the system from moving up in rank when they should" (p. 8). Those who refuse to retire are costly to institutions, accelerate the use of adjunct professors, and create additional questions about the value of traditions such as tenure.

Academics can also check their commitment to impartial and critical reason. Lennard Davis (1999) acknowledges the central role of emotions in academic life: "the public tends to think of academics as hyper-rational creatures, but the fact is that they live their careers through their emotions" (p. B8). Many are consumed by the politics of academe. Davis also notes that to achieve *real* academic victory, "it's not enough to succeed; one's colleagues must also fail" (p. B8). What the Germans call *schadenfreude* is part of the shadow side of the academy, rarely publicly acknowledged but often privately enjoyed—hardly a desirable model of either ethics or spirituality. That some of the deepest satisfactions in academe occur only when others fail suggests an egocentric, self-serving spirituality where the object of loyalty is the self narrowly defined.

Insistent individualism prevents mutually fruitful, sustained colleagueship in pursuit of common goods. Social interactions turn on self-interest: "What is your rank, and is there anything I can gain from associating with you?" (Simpson, 1999, p. 238). In order to advance my career, whom should I cultivate and whom avoid? Genuine academic community is scarce among insistent individualists. Institutions become aggregations of soloists. The ties that bind are the happy moments when self-interest aligns with self-interest. But such coalitions change quickly and close associates one day become opponents the next. A deeper contentiousness replaces superficial agreements.

Some hold that behind this self-aggrandizement and violence lurks a deeper spirituality of fear. From this perspective, it is fear of change and loss of control that fuels insistent individualism. The other is seen as competitor, not colleague—one who challenges our identity and accomplishments, rather than offers opportunities mutually to grow and create a common good. As Parker Palmer (1997) observes, "in academic culture, I am carefully buffered, carefully walled off, through systematic disrespect, from all of those things that might challenge me, break me, open me, and change me. It is a fearful culture" (p. 11).

In sum, whether pursuing self-promotion or seeking self-protection, insistent individualists neglect a common academic good. Unable or unwilling to practice openness with others, they create a tone that permeates the academy. Doubtless Palmer (1993) speaks for many when he notes, "we have a hard time talking to each other without falling into competition and even combat, into an unconscious rhythm of defense and offense that allows for little openness and growth" (p. 13). There is a bit of insistent individualist in each of us and, when pressed, we find it easier to make excuses than to change—or challenge—colleagues.

INSISTENT INDIVIDUALISM, TEACHERS, AND LEARNERS

As a result, our insistent individualism interferes with both teaching and learning; a kind of ceremonial contentiousness seems deeply embedded in them. This agonism is reinforced by the prestige economy of much graduate education, where student self-understanding and identity are linked to specific faculty—attachments that often create unhealthy student dependence.

An Agonistic Culture

Several decades ago, the cultural linguist Walter Ong observed how, over the centuries, formal education had involved learning through ceremonial combat—rituals of contest conducted by males to initiate younger males. Learning was achieved, tested, and displayed in oral disputation, with public humiliation a constant risk. The object of debate was to overwhelm the opponent (Ong, 1981).

Influenced by Ong, Deborah Tannen suggests that academic contentiousness not only continues, but is more open than hidden, and is bad for us. She points to endemic ritualized oppositions and adversarial patterns in higher education. She observes that war metaphors frame our thinking, pervade our speech, and overshadow alternatives. She defines agonism as "a kind of programmed contentiousness—a prepatterned unthinking use of fighting to accomplish goals that do not necessarily require it" (Tannen, 1998, p. 8). For example, she suggests that "the way we train our students, conduct our classes and our research, and exchange ideas at meetings and in print are all driven by our ideological assumption that intellectual inquiry is a metaphorical battle" (Tannen, 2000, p. B7).

Surely Tannen is on track. The academic as a kind of Western gunslinger *does* engage us. We disguise feelings of vulnerability by combating the influence of others rather than absorbing it. We attack their positions, hoping to explode or shoot them down—while defending and shoring up our own. We speak of border disputes, skirmishes, and all-out wars. We treat meetings as trench warfare, or free-fire zones. When the battle goes against us, we go underground to join the resistance. Or we choose a strategic accommodation. Our opponents range from colleagues, students, and administrators through regents, trustees, legislators, and competing institutions, to a flagging secondary school system and an unsupportive public.

Like Tompkins on academic violence, Tannen reminds us of the expense of agonism. Scholarly papers usually follow the "conventional framework" of opposition—tempting faculty to oversimplify and misrepresent others' positions, ignoring their complexity and nuance. Following faculty, graduate students learn to tear apart and simplify works they read rather than also to integrate them. Perhaps unintentionally, we *do* educate our students for analysis and critique rather than also for sympathetic and balanced synthesis. And we may confuse heated debate with education—admiring hard and challenging questions, ignoring complexity and nuance, and slighting genuine educational conversation. Ironically, the cumulative effect is often conservative, "nearly everyone feels vulnerable and defensive, and thus less willing to suggest new ideas, offer new perspectives, or question received wisdom" (Tannen, 2000, p. B7).

Academic agonism becomes a way of life for insistent individualists. These educators struggle to master the subjects of their inquiry, to subdue and dominate them. In the process they form themselves. As Parker Palmer (1983) reminds us, each epistemology entails its own ethic: "Every way of knowing tends to become a way of living" (p. 22). As a way of knowing, insistent individualism reduces others to objects for utilitarian manipulation. These objects are held at a distance to prevent any possible personal impact, especially any need to change our ways. As a result, the professional knower is divided from the personal self. The knower is an objective spectator—manipulating and controlling the known, but allowing it no entrance into the self.

The ethical outcome tends toward opportunism and unrestrained competition. But the most damaging aspect of agonism is its impact on a healthy spirituality:

> Living, working, and thinking in ways shaped by the battle metaphor produces an atmosphere of animosity that poisons our relations with each other at the same time that it corrupts the integrity of our research. Not only is the agonistic culture of academe not the best path to truth and knowledge, but it is also corrosive to the human spirit. . . . We need new metaphors through which to think about our academic enterprise, or to conceptualize intellectual interchange. (Tannen, 2000, p. B7)

In the chapters that follow I propose hospitality and conversation as alternative metaphors and keys to healthier academic ethics and more authentic spiritualities.

A Prestige Economy, Fragmentation, and Alienation

Insistent individualism also characterizes groups. For example, graduate students may find their most reassuring identity as students, disciples even, of select faculty members. Julie Rivkin (1993) calls our attention to the multiple deficits—indeed, the "pernicious influence"—of the "prestige economy" of graduate education (p. 16). Part of what she says applies to undergraduate studies and junior faculty as well. The prestige economy often means a profound sense of powerlessness—until one becomes a protégé. One's identity, value, and agency are mediated by and through "the 'proper names' of famous professors. To be a student of X or Y is the only way to have any value or identity" (Rivkin, 1993, p. 16).

Some faculty and students *are* well matched in terms of intellectual interests and professional values. All too often, though, the consequence for the student is a lack of agency and self-control. He or she is vulnerable to even slight fluctuations in professorial approval. The prestige economy can also dangerously inflate the student's sense of authority and value.

The protégé can identify "with the accomplishments and professional rank of the mentor, thus experiencing a falsely aggrandized sense of importance" (Rivkin, 1993, p. 17). When such individuals are finally on their own, they lack the personal authority and judgment needed to function well in a new setting.

Of course, we are speaking of students fortunate enough to enjoy the protectorship of a powerful professor, interested in opening doors and mentoring. However, "some students never seem to find a protector; they remain unadopted, unprotected, within a system in which one actually needs protection" (Rivkin, 1993, p. 17). The issues they face are readily recognizable to anyone familiar with graduate education. They range from simple accessibility to a thesis director to the need for protection from other "famous professors" who do not approve of one's dissertation topic or methodology. Junior faculty face parallel problems. Education is already permeated by multiple sources of anxiety. The prestige economy simply adds to these burdens.

Since most faculty are initially socialized into higher education at research and doctoral-granting universities, these institutions exercise influence well beyond their borders and their numbers. Even close-knit, small liberal arts institutions have a share of insistent individualists: in these settings where one would least expect it, the positive role of the other as constitutive of self (and vice versa) is neglected. Hospitality as genuine openness to others is devalued and contrasted with academic rigor and the hardnosed demands of serious academic work. Likewise, the natural rhythm of movement from academic community to solitude and back is often skewed toward a more permanent solitude and isolation. Increasingly one hears the image of "silos" used to describe where and how academics work—psychologically, if not also physically and structurally, separated from others. Silos suggest both isolation and embattlement. As containers for storage, their walls ensure purity. When used to house missiles, they are designed to attack and resist counterattack.

Self-preoccupied individualists leave common tasks to others. Excuses include higher obligations elsewhere: consultancies, invited essays, addresses to national meetings. These behaviors result in a pretty thin "community"—the faculty as an aggregation of individualists with minimal reciprocity, historical continuity, or intellectual interaction. Deficient in mutual respect and support, aggregations embody a negative form of belonging—what Douglas Sturm (1998a) defines as the objective meaning of alienation considered as a condition of deprivation. It is an inherently contradictory relationship. Alienation is interaction through which an individual is constrained to act against his or her own good, to the advantage of another (Sturm, 1998a).

Familiar examples of alienation include the exploitation of graduate students by supervising senior faculty, similar treatment of probationary faculty, and the marginalization of everyone in disciplines out of favor. The dynamic extends to those at institutions considered second or third tier. Patricia Plante (1990) correctly calls this arrangement rigidly hierarchical: "Any college or university is as class conscious as a British social club. Hierarchical thinking unapologetically reigns, and intellectual meritocracy orders the ranking of everything from graduate schools to profiles of entering freshmen" (p. 28). Fragmentation and alienation are inevitable. "The class system places the Ivy Leaguers in the aristocratic box seats, the community colleges in the second balcony, and all others here and there in the orchestra and mezzanine" (Plante, 1990, p. 28).

Implicated in this alienation are the guilds that define intellectual inquiry by excluding others, award tenure and promotion on the basis of selective tests of purity rather than contributions to a larger common good, and attend to narrow disciplinary self-interest. Bruce Wilshire (1990) identifies these sad behaviors as typical expressions of what he calls the academic professionalism of the academy. In the end, all are impoverished, both dominant and subordinate—those who control and those controlled.

Academic insistent individualism is not new. Clark Kerr (1994) notes that ethical lapses have a long history, citing Adam Smith's complaint about Oxford professors who "make a common cause to be all very indulgent to one another, and every man to consent that his neighbor may neglect his duty provided he himself is allowed to neglect his own" (p. 9). Even so, Kerr himself confesses that "I once looked upon the colleges and universities as the purest ethical institutions on earth. I regret to say that I have observed what I consider to be a partial disintegration since about 1960" (p. 15). A culture of fierce academic independence has defined much of the later 20th century—perhaps more than Kerr had in mind, with a spiritual consequence he failed to note.

DEPARTMENTS AND INSTITUTIONS AS INSISTENT INDIVIDUALISTS
The academy also has abundant *organizational* and *institutional* forms of insistent individualism. Curricula are fragmented and whole fields of learning lack integration. For some time, increasing specialization has been the order of the day and an agent of insistent individualism. Over 75 years ago, Whitehead (1967a) observed the liabilities of specialization

and increasing professionalization, noting that the latter "produces minds in a groove. Each profession makes progress, but it is progress in its own groove" (p. 187). Everything outside the groove is treated superficially and "there is no groove of abstractions which is adequate for the comprehension of human life. . . . the whole is lost in one of its aspects" (Whitehead, 1967a, p. 187). Of course there is no vision of the whole apart from some perspective. But Whitehead is lamenting the loss of balance and coordination among these perspectives at the very time they have multiplied. His comments apply directly to the university.

Disciplines, Specialty Fields, and Departments

Reflecting on the academy's involvement with, and reaction to, the Enlightenment, Edward Farley (1988) notes that "the systematic exclusion of imaginative, tradition-oriented, and praxis perspectives has helped produce a contemporary scholarship that is specialized to the point of triviality, preoccupied with technologies of method and with reworking already surfeited subjects with ever more ingenious procedures" (p. 15). Everyone is poorer for this miniaturizing of knowledge. The fragmentation of curricula is a consequence, and the development of specialty fields plays a special role.

Some knowledgeable critics of higher education link specialization to the failure of the academy to address societal ills. As he thinks of the burgeoning environmental stresses that educational research and practice might address, John Cobb's (1991) distress is unmistakable:

> The specialty fields constitute self-contained communities of research whose selection of topics is little affected by any needs but their own. As one who finds the decent survival of humanity in the context of a healthy biosphere a matter of almost ultimate importance, I am appalled. (p. 243)

Society has created institutions of higher learning and provided scholars with resources and time, encouraging them to pursue truth. The public has every right to ask that they

> offer us guidance as to how to respond to the urgent issues of the day, issues that threaten to make this very nearly the last day. And we are told, implicitly at least, that these are not matters of interest to the university, that it has organized its life to other ends. (Cobb, 1991, p. 243)

More inclusive paradigms of learning are needed to correct the abstractions of specialty fields.

> It is in the world of the larger learning that one confronts the complexity, mystery, and dimensionality of reality. . . . there must be a constant correction of one's focused specialty, a restoring of the abstracted subject matter to its concreteness and contextuality. (Farley, 1988, p. 48)

And then, as Cobb (1991) implores, universities need to apply the fruits of this broader learning to the urgent needs of humankind and the world. However, the self-preoccupations of personal and institutional insistent individualism stand in the way.

Administrative structures are often obstacles. Departments, schools, or colleges can fall victim to protracted internal struggles. Departments that fall into extreme dysfunctionality or even receivership illustrate the high cost of insistent individualism and its associated social contract. Competition and conflict become so pronounced that administrators desperately seek alternative arrangements. Sometimes an interim arrangement of governance by committee is attempted. At other times, an outsider is appointed to keep things going. The Yale philosophy department was a classic example of extreme conflict, resulting in an extended period of receivership with two successive chairpersons appointed from outside the department. Columbia University's English department is another example—so badly fragmented for over a decade that new senior faculty appointments were made by a committee of outside senior scholars selected by the university from five *other* institutions (Arenson, 2002). These are celebrated examples because the departments had once been known for energy and excellence. The extent of their decline suggests the instability of an aggregation of individualists held together by conflict and a social contract.

But even peaceful departments and schools often struggle to increase bonds, to create forms of connectivity and togetherness amidst the plurality they also value. Too often, other departments are seen as competitors—ready to pounce upon students, facilities, and budget. Securing budgetary acknowledgment of current credit-hour production is a common concern, and disputes about how to credit crossdisciplinary courses or programs work against interdisciplinary initiatives. It is no surprise that faculty may know little of what colleagues are doing educationally. As a result, ownership of the collective enterprise is spotty and institutions appear inefficient and self-indulgent.

Indeed, institutions themselves are often excessively individualistic, competing against each other for more or better students, faculty, and funding. Friendly critics such as Alexander Astin (1991) regularly remind the higher education community of the expense of chasing reputation and resources—instead of attending more directly to the advancement of individual learning. His message has yet to gain adequate purchase. Rather than cooperating with contiguous institutions and creating sensible and effective consortia to advance learning and other shared purposes, most colleges and universities operate autonomously, targeting their energies on higher standings in the polls and comparative rankings.

INSTITUTIONAL BEHAVIORS

In competing for resources, departments, colleges, and universities chase after prestige. And prestige is often measured in terms of expert scholars, sporting reputations created by publications and grants that establish their authority in a field or, frequently, a subspecialty. Through adroit public relations strategies, organizations attribute the characteristics of parts to the whole—those of individual faculty to the department, college, and university—in order to enhance the institution's competitive standing. Other institutional behaviors also contribute to insistent individualism. I consider four: misrepresenting things, depending excessively on part-time faculty, separating or unbundling faculty functions, and creating for-profit subsidiaries.

Misrepresentations

Many institutions see other institutions as rivals not just in athletic contests, but in cutthroat competition for students, faculty, and prestige. Indeed, the very depth of these rivalries is sometimes presented as an excuse for misrepresenting one's institution in data provided to news media, university-ranking publications, and popular college guidebooks. The misrepresentations include "rounding up" institutional data to present the most attractive face to potential students, their parents, and other members of the public. Questionable self-reported data include number of faculty, student credentials, ratios of applicants admitted to those enrolling, numbers actually enrolled, the percentage of those who leave within their first year, and the ratio of graduating to entering students (Stecklow, 1995).[4]

Nor have the misrepresentations been restricted to numbers. Admissions offices sometimes advertise new programs that have not yet received state or accrediting agency approval, but, we are told, the programs will eventually get it and in the meantime why let a competitor get ahead?

Additionally, photographs of a smiling, diverse student body have been used in admissions materials even though the pictures were doctored (Clegg, 2000; Jacobson, 2001). One campus strategy involved using agency models rather than students to depict an attractive student body. Other institutions simply recomposed existing authentic photographs, using photodesign software to achieve desired racial and gender balances.

When questioned about these breaches of integrity, institutional spokespersons often respond that they suspect or even "know" that "everyone else is doing it"—an argument that would fail in any introductory ethics course. These institutional behaviors do not help form moral citizens. They reek of institutional self-interest, not broader civic responsibility. They reveal preoccupations with competitive success that fly in the face of promoting enlarged student competencies and humane sensitivities.

Perhaps a broader form of institutional misrepresentation is practicing habitual secrecy—withholding information that would assist students and parents in evaluating institutions. One example is the refusal of almost all the 470 four-year institutions that participated in the National Survey of Student Engagement (NSSE) to disclose any of their own data—insisting that only average national data be released (Bartlett, 2001). Designed to gauge how well colleges encourage learning, NSSE was conceived and initiated as a better alternative to the *U.S. News & World Report* rankings. The questionable reliability of those rankings together with the secrecy surrounding individual institutional NSSE results suggests how insistently individualistic institutions are when it comes to public accountability. Yet colleges and universities are supported by society and exist to promote its good. The public should have access to accurate information about their activities.

Excessive Adjunct Dependence

An additional problem is the rapidly growing dependence of institutions upon temporary, adjunct, or part-time professors. Of course there are good reasons to hire them. Replacing full-time with temporary or adjunct faculty avoids institutional commitments to tenure-track faculty in areas of limited student interest. Adjunct or graduate assistant faculty are certainly less expensive. And from a pedagogical point of view, some part-time faculty are excellent resources—bringing fresh hands-on experience in rapidly developing fields.

However, the liabilities of turning over significant (and growing) chunks of the curriculum to adjuncts are worrisome. Although there are few studies of the teaching effectiveness of part-time faculty, other critical issues are clear. Part-time faculty are less available to students for advising—a situation aggravated by little office space for meeting students. In addition, part-time faculty are rarely available to each other or to full-time colleagues for discussion of pedagogical issues. Teaching initiatives and progress reports cannot be pursued in systematic fashion. As a result there is no ordered information that can be used collectively to improve teaching. Further, even long-term part-time faculty are rarely included in institutional discussions about hiring and promoting where pedagogical issues could be related to program mission and curricular directions and used to evaluate candidate credentials. Similarly, few part-time faculty are involved in other governance activities that bear on curriculum development or planning.

As a result, large numbers of instructional staffs are excluded from full participation in the conditions that make for effective education. Shrinking percentages of full-time faculty carry the brunt of attending to overall educational integrity. Relying upon increasing numbers of part-time faculty is ineluctably changing the culture of higher education and jeopardizing its educational mission—even as institutions continue to market their campuses as intimate places characterized by low student-faculty ratios and by personal attention to student needs.

Unbundling

An increasing display of insistent individualism appears in the unbundling of faculty roles in instruction. Unbundling is the separation of three functions traditionally united in one faculty member—course construction, teaching, and advising. Unbundling isolates these three functions from each other and from scholarship or research. Although long practiced with graduate teaching assistants and adjunct faculty, unbundling is now associated with the staffing of much distance delivery of education, particularly in for-profit institutions or subsidiaries.

Perhaps assisted by an external advisory board, a handful of full-time faculty develop the courses, an activity presumably enhanced by their record of relevant scholarship. Other instructors are hired to deliver the courses. These are part-time or adjunct faculty who have no direct, systematic interaction with the full-time course developers and perhaps no ongoing relevant scholarship. A third cadre of individuals, also usually part-time, is composed of student advisors. They too have little direct interaction with either instructor or course designer. Instead of the constant interaction among content, delivery, and reception envisioned in the traditional model (and promoted organizationally by locating these

three functions in one person), unbundling virtually guarantees fragmentation.

This fragmentation of roles and functions is often hailed as an
advance in productivity rather than as a retreat into pedagogical fragmentation and atomism. However, unbundling *is* a mechanistic act
reflecting atomistic presuppositions. It subdivides teaching into its small-
est components, seen as independent of each other. It marks a return of
time-and-motion studies. Unbundling neglects the relational contribution of each function to the other. Teaching is presented as though it
were independent of research, and vice versa. Both teaching and research
are presented as independent of decisions about modes of delivery. And
everything is separated from advising. Unbundling exacts a large toll on
academic community.

For-Profit Subsidiaries

In a quite recent development, mainline institutions are establishing for-
profit instructional subsidiaries in spite of inevitable conflicts of interest.
After decades of deploring proprietary post-secondary institutions—on
grounds that student learning takes second place to profits in these busi-
nesses—major traditional universities are now rushing to create their
own units. These are hard times for higher education, we are told, new
sources of revenue must be exploited, and competitive responses developed to full-scale, for-profit institutions. The grounds for original suspicions about proprietary institutions remain, however. It is difficult to
secure the primacy of student learning when investor returns must also
be considered.

Of course, seeking increased revenue streams and facilitating student
learning need not be completely mutually exclusive. But mainline institutions inevitably sow confusion among their publics when they trade on
their traditional reputations in establishing markets for these new
ventures. Fidelity to their basic mission is at risk. Their constancy of
character turns on serving the common good through honoring
covenants to promote, protect, and extend learning—not to generate
investor interest and return. In sum, providing fudged information,
creating misleading advertising, relying on adjunct instructors to do the
work of full-time faculty, and creating potentially massive conflicts of
interest in instructional programs embody institutional insistently individualistic behaviors. Intercollegiate athletic abuses are another cause of
concern. These behaviors imply that public misrepresentations are
acceptable, that even outright fabrications can be justified by some

higher end, and that the slow evisceration of academic substance through the decreasing use of full-time faculty is permissible. Many institutions have abandoned other aspects of a moral role they once played. Few are providing adequate moral leadership by analyzing and speaking to issues of environmental abuse, the economics of global warming, exploitation of developing nations, urban decay and poverty, drug addiction, domestic abuse, illiteracy, inadequate primary and secondary schooling, teenage pregnancy, crime and incarceration, etc. Nor are many providing needed leadership on local issues, such as adequate compensation for their janitorial staff—or even for their own graduate students. Only when publicly pressed by student demonstrations have some institutional leaders finally shown the moral awareness that educational institutions should both illustrate and promote in their students.

The broader educational community could also benefit from greater moral reflection. Licensing and accrediting agencies that provide public assurances that institutions and their programs are in order are widely viewed as weak and having low standards. As Robert Atwell observes, "basically, the bar isn't very high" (McMurtrie, 2001, p. A28). And in the rare cases when they actually impose sanctions, agencies are reluctant to share reasons with the public, thereby decreasing opportunities for informed judgments. There are alternative configurations of accrediting agencies that could strengthen the self-regulation of higher education, but little progress has occurred even in considering them (Bennett, 1998).

CONCLUSION

Thus, we see that there are significant proclivities toward individualism across the higher education world. The disposition to behave in self-absorbed and self-protecting ways and to put narrow self-interest ahead of the welfare of others or a broader common good is widespread. Individual and institutional identity, worth, and fulfillment are understood in terms of power to shape and control others, and to resist their power.

Detached selves construct ties with others for individual advantage in a process of constant renegotiation and compromise. The formation of an underlying, supportive intellectual community seems at best a secondary goal. Calculations of individual advantage predominate. Openness to others, what I call hospitality, is diminished by concern that it will heighten one's vulnerability. Healthy academic ethics and spiritualities struggle for breath. Instead, what Bernard Loomer (1976) termed "unilateral power" prevails—the desire to achieve influence and control over others while resisting their influence and control.

The model of insistent individualism has a long history, but in recent years it has gained vigor and eclipsed the standing and strength of a relational model. Insistent individualism promotes the isolated self—it advances disconnection among faculty and staff as well as between faculty, staff, students, and institutions. It works against internal integration and separates personal from professional lives. It encourages exclusiveness rather than relationality, self-protection rather than openness to the other. It celebrates instrumental rather than relational knowledge. Insistent individualism encourages disciplinary and specialty boundaries, isolated departments, and fragmented institutions.

In the next chapter I consider why insistent individualism is so prevalent in the academy. In the final analysis, I think, insistent individualism is built on a faulty philosophy and generates inadequate academic ethics and a spirituality that fails to nourish. In subsequent chapters I suggest alternatives that our tradition contains. Chief among them are hospitality and conversation.

REFERENCES

Arden, E. (2001, October). When it's time to leave—leave! Mandatory retirement is good for higher education. *AAHE Bulletin, 54* (2), 8–9.

Arenson, K. W. (2002, March 17). Columbia soothes the dogs of war in its English Dept. *The New York Times*, pp. A1, 43.

Astin, A. (1991). *The unrealized potential of American higher education.* Athens, GA: The University of Georgia Institute of Higher Education.

Bartlett, T. (2001, November 23). Colleges praise new source of data, as long as their scores stay secret. *The Chronicle of Higher Education*, p. A31.

Bennett, J. B. (1998). *Collegial professionalism: The academy, individualism, and the common good.* Phoenix, AZ: American Council Education/Oryx Press.

Clegg, R. (2000, November 24). Photographs and fraud over race. *The Chronicle of Higher Education*, p. B17.

Cobb, J. B., Jr. (1991). Theology against the disciplines. In B. G. Wheeler & E. Farley (Eds.), *Shifting boundaries: Contextual approaches to the structure of theological education* (pp. 241–258). Louisville, KY: Westminster/John Knox.

Damrosch, D. (1995). *We scholars: Changing the culture of the university.* Cambridge, MA: Harvard University Press.

Davis, L. J. (1999, June 11). The uses of fear and envy in academe. *The Chronicle of Higher Education*, p. B8.

Farley, E. (1988). *The fragility of knowledge: Theological education in the church and the university*. Philadelphia, PA: Fortress Press.

Fish, S. (2001, October 19). To thine own faculty be truthful. *The Chronicle of Higher Education*, pp. B13–B14.

Henry, P. (1999). *The ironic Christian's companion: Finding the marks of God's grace in the world*. New York, NY: Riverhead Books.

Jacobson, J. (2001, March 16). In brochures, what you see isn't necessarily what you get: Scandals raise larger issues about how diversity is portrayed. *The Chronicle of Higher Education*, p. A41.

Kerr, C. (1994, January/February). Knowledge ethics and the new academic culture. *Change, 26* (1), 8–15.

Loomer, B. (1976, Spring). Two kinds of power. *Process Studies, 6* (1), 5–32.

McMurtrie, B. (2001, January 12). Regional accreditors punish colleges rarely and inconsistently. *The Chronicle of Higher Education*, pp. A27-A28.

Ong, W. J. (1981). *Fighting for life*. Ithaca, NY: Cornell University Press.

Palmer, P. J. (1983). *To know as we are known: Education as a spiritual journey*. San Francisco, CA: Harper and Row.

Palmer, P. J. (1993, November/December). Good talk about good teaching: Improving teaching through conversation and community. *Change, 25* (6) 8–13.

Palmer, P. J. (1997, September). The grace of great things: Reclaiming the sacred in knowing, teaching, and learning. *The Holistic Education Review, 10* (3), 8–16.

Plante, P. (1990, Winter). An administrator will yearn for the classroom: Myth or reality? *Educational Record, 71* (1), 27–30.

Readings, B. (1996). *The university in ruins*. Cambridge, MA: Harvard University Press.

Rhodes, F. H. T. (1998). The university and its critics. In W. G. Bowen & H. T. Shapiro (Eds.), *Universities and their leadership* (pp. 3–14). Princeton, NJ: Princeton University Press.

Rivkin, J. (1993, Spring). Beyond the prestige economy of graduate education. *Liberal Education, 79* (2), 16–19.

Simpson, R. D. (1999, Summer). The importance of being a nobody in higher education. *Innovative Higher Education, 23* (4), 237–240.

Stecklow, S. (1995, April 5). Cheat sheets: Colleges inflate SATs and graduation rates in popular guidebooks. *The Wall Street Journal, CCXXV* (66), pp. A1, 8.

Sturm, D. (1998a). *Community and alienation: Essays on process thought and public life.* Notre Dame, IN: University of Notre Dame Press.

Sullivan, W. M. (1995). *Work and integrity: The crisis and promise of professionalism in America.* New York, NY: HarperBusiness.

Tannen, D. (1998). *The argument culture.* New York, NY: Random House.

Tannen, D. (2000, March 31). Agonism in the academy: Surviving higher learning's argument culture. *The Chronicle of Higher Education,* p. B7.

Tompkins, J. (1992). *West of everything: The inner life of westerns.* New York, NY: Oxford University Press.

Tompkins, J. (1996). *A life in school: What the teacher learned.* Reading, MA: Addison Wesley.

Whitehead, A. N. (1967a). *Science and the modern world.* New York, NY: The Free Press.

Wilshire, B. (1990). *The moral collapse of the university: Professionalism, purity, and alienation.* Albany, NY: State University of New York Press.

ENDNOTES

1. For an extended treatment of this point see my "Academic Politics, Leadership, and Hospitality," *Academic Leadership, the Online Journal,* (Fall, 2000), 1 (1), www.academicleadership.org.

2. In what follows I draw upon elements of the Western that Jane Tompkins provided in her analysis of the genre (Tompkins, 1992).

3. Portions of the material that follows appeared in "Hospitality and Collegial Community: An Essay." *Innovative Higher Education,* (Winter 2000), 25 (2), 85–96. Other portions appeared in "The Academy and Hospitality," originally published in *CrossCurrents: The Journal of the Association for Religion and Intellectual Life,* (Spring/Summer 2000), 50 (1 & 2), 23–35.

4. Some of this misrepresentation is now being addressed by new regulations at the US Department of Education, but full implementation will take time and some institutions will look for loopholes.

Why the Prevalence of Insistent Individualism? 2

We have seen how we pay dearly for insistent individualism. Its values and commitments adversely affect relationships among faculty and staff. They are evident in atomistic and unconnected curricula, isolated disciplines, and fragmented departments. They show themselves in protracted and wasteful competition among institutions of higher education. Insistent individualism underwrites a philosophy of education that highlights separation; it invites the ethical charge that the academy does not practice the self-examination it preaches; and it glorifies a spirituality of self-preoccupation. I argue that insistent individualism does not present a compelling picture of higher education. It should not command our attention and support. Yet we seem reluctant to acknowledge its abundant presence—or to change things.

Why is insistent individualism so prevalent? Since our behaviors reflect prior patterns of feeling and thinking, I suggest that insistent individualism reflects a philosophical atomism—our tendency to regard individuals as self-enclosed and unconnected in deep, constructive ways to others. Our institutions help by reinforcing atomistic assumptions in their reward systems and in their own competitive behaviors. Individuals both contribute to and internalize these institutional values. When we are disposed and taught to see others as potential threats, it seems natural to seek self-protection.

In this chapter I also contrast the self-preoccupation of insistent individualism with relational individualism—a way of thinking and being that is better grounded philosophically, more faithful to our calling as educators, and more fulfilling ethically and spiritually. In the remainder of the book I argue for relational individualism as it is expressed in hospitality, conversation, and covenantal connections.

FAULTY PHILOSOPHIES AND EXPERT PERFORMANCE

Over two decades ago, John Smith (1982) wrote of "the narcissism, both intellectual and personal, that has become widespread in academe" (p. 448). He did not analyze the phenomenon further, nor did he indicate when he thought it began to grow. But self-preoccupation seems deeply rooted in us. Our consumerist culture nourishes excessive attention to self and our prevailing concepts of reason emphasize utilitarian calculations rather than intrinsic values. We often hold others to a higher standard and we are prone to make exceptions for ourselves from public expectations and norms. Although the current climate of narcissism certainly accentuates it, this proclivity toward insistent individualism seems in some ways to transcend times and cultures. In the broader context of spirituality, various religious traditions do remind us of the universal pull of self (the *curvatus in se*) or the grip of attachments that generate suffering, including attachment to self. From these points of view, we may seem to be victims of our history and nature as well as our culture.

Philosophies of Atomism

Insistent individualism is also fostered by faulty philosophies—by our ways of thinking that include deformed concepts of self and world. Individuals are judged basically self-enclosed and separate, related to others only externally and incidentally. The implicit metaphysics is that reality does not support a prior, underlying connection of selves. Whatever connectivity insistent individualism can muster is radically unstable, perhaps ultimately illusory. As a result, atomism supports competition and struggle as typical ethical modes of relating. Judgments of significance are private, not public; matters of value remain internal perceptions, not something intersubjectively available. Almost inevitably, the resulting spirituality glorifies self-preoccupation. Thomas Hobbes lurks in the background of this kind of thinking.

Philosophically, insistent individualism appears when strict self-determination is judged the essential characteristic of an individual, the indispensable key to his or her integrity. Given such a strong sense of self-determination, substantial dependence upon others is seen as a denial of one's essence and integrity. As Rowan Williams (2000) presents the point,

> it is as if the standard form of relation between human agents is a temporary agreement by independent partners to do something together, something which could be done by others and done without substantially changing the identity and position of the contracting parties. (p. 83)

Personal identity is not deeply affected by these arrangements with others—in this sense they are superficial matters, relating to surface appearances, not internal realities. Relations with colleagues and students may carry prudential importance but little moral urgency. Realistic, clear thinkers in this tradition hold that persons are appropriately self-regarding and interested in others' welfare primarily as means to their own. Communities are simple sums of their parts, not objects of loyalty in their own right. Their real worth is their instrumental contribution to the good of the individual, a position that unites easily with concern for self. And as John Smith observed, this way of thinking and behaving seems to describe much of the academy. It is not difficult to identify some of the ways.

As graduate students we learned that success meant making names for ourselves, even at the expense of others. Protecting our own initiative took precedence over defending the initiatives of others or promoting fidelity to the inquiry. And our initiatives were often solitary. Thinking of the university's responsibilities to those considering an academic career, Jaroslav Pelikan (1992) suggests

> it will always be necessary in the university for us to counsel those students who think that they would like to become scholars to find out early for themselves whether they can bear to be alone as much as a scholar must be alone. (p. 65)

The academy selects for, and then favors, rugged individualists.

After we became full partners in the enterprise, we learned the value attached to expert performance. Faculty are to display their authority at every point—in teaching, scholarship, and even service. The expectation is internalized, and anxiety about meeting the expectations of colleagues and students can be high. In a memoir that describes her painful experiences in education, Jane Tompkins (1996) observes the unhappy consequences of expert performance when it becomes an institutional, guild, and personal expectation. What is at stake is not the need for skills in teaching large classes. Rather, she is questioning a widespread culture that places primary value on "appearing smart" and validates personal worth through what one displays, rather than who one is or can become.[1]

Appearing Smart

Inadequate self-knowledge plays a role in fostering a performance mentality. We often shield ourselves from fully realizing these prevailing academic expectations. For instance, despite thinking for decades that she had been helping students to understand material, Tompkins (1996) states she finally realized that

> what I had actually been concerned with was showing the
> students how smart I was, how knowledgeable I was, and how
> well prepared I was for class. I had been putting on a perfor-
> mance whose true goal was not to help the students learn . . .
> but to perform before them in such a way that they would
> have a good opinion of me. (p. 119)

These pressures to perform block the natural, original thirst for learning and
knowledge, substituting fear of reproach and desire for approval. They stunt
and warp; they lead to specialization and narrowness of focus; they neglect
imagination and intuition; they reinforce self-preoccupation and self-
promotion.

We pay a steep personal price for trying to "perform" expertly. There is
little room for bad days, for moments of forgetfulness or inattentiveness, or
for the truthful admission that one simply does not know. The image of
performer heightens the vulnerability every educator feels, even though
performing well also provides the occasional moments of welcome adula-
tion. This emphasis upon performance neglects the whole person. Tompkins
uses words like "spirituality," "self-understanding," and "inner life" to
describe what she thinks academics sacrifice. Self-understanding is not a
priority. Head and heart are divided, leaving competitive performance as the
sole measure of worth. The result is narrowly channeled energies, isolated
learners, incomplete self-understandings, and neglected education.

By contrast, Tompkins calls for education of the emotional, creative, and
spiritual side of students and teachers, as well as of their intellect. She urges
an education that facilitates growth in personal insight and self-understanding. Such education

> would address the need for purpose and for connectedness to
> ourselves and one another; it would not leave us alone to wander
> the world armed with plenty of knowledge but lacking the skills
> to handle the things that are coming up in our lives. (Tompkins,
> 1996, p. xvi)

But this kind of education seems all too rare and faculty are often poor
models.

After all, good teaching is difficult. Julius Getman (1992) notes that
many faculty create artificial personalities to cope:

> Unsuccessful teachers develop personalities to protect them-
> selves and shift responsibility for their failures to the students
> or the system. Many attempt to develop a role that suggests
> that they are too brilliant to be understood by the students
> they teach. The insecure merely develop a style that suggests
> greater success, importance, and originality than they feel
> entitled to. (p. 27)

Playing a role or creating a persona impedes communication with
colleagues and students and one must then protect the projected self-
image. Often these personae cease being temporary stratagems to get
through challenging and difficult times. They take hold and perdure.
Uncovering and modifying them involves substantial work and risk.
Many are unable to see the task through.

We have noted some of the philosophical, atomistic liabilities involved in
this expectation of performance—individuals locked inside themselves, self-
absorbed and preoccupied, linked with others only through transactional and
superficial relationships. Fear becomes a primary emotion when others
remain strangers, always able to threaten our standing. We then seek power
for control rather than collaboration. When educators dwell in the image of
performance, community is reduced to a utilitarian convenience for an aggregation of rugged individualists, reflecting the notion of self as a substantial
entity that *has* relationships rather than emerges *from* them.

And yet, the role of authority that lies behind the image of expert
performer cannot be eliminated. Though she may not have recognized its
full import, Tompkins (1996) suggests as much:

> when I embarked on my experiments in teaching, I thought I
> was putting the performance mentality behind me by putting
> students at the center of things. But now I see that the experi-
> ment itself became my performance. . . . The ego's need to be
> reflected *one way or the other* intrudes everywhere. (p. 162f.)

Only if we move to a larger concept of the self and recognize it as essentially relational and as requiring hospitality to the needs of the other, can we
address the issues that Tompkins raises. But this requires moving to more
hospitable resources, such as those that Whitehead and other relational
thinkers provide. Seeing selves as social and connected, not separate and
isolated, is the philosophy we need.

INSTITUTIONS AND ATOMISM

Universities contribute to the problem by the way they elevate competition. Results, not efforts, count. Individual stakes are high. Faculty have positions, tenure, and promotion to secure. Administrators have careers to consider. And institutions have created a lot of competitors. Despite the suffering that academic insistent individualism creates, those seeking academic jobs outstrip available positions in all but a few fields. This oversupply highlights colleagues as competitors. As May (2001) observes, "the social style remains one of friendliness, but an inner wariness . . . takes possession of the soul" (p. 11). The consequences are natural and foreseeable. "As colleagues turn into teeth-clenching competitors, the capacity for mutual nurture and renewal diminishes, and service to the common good yields to the necessities of survival" (May, 2001, p. 11).

In a variety of ways, campuses also teach insistent individualism to students. Colleges and universities market themselves primarily as purveyors of instrumental goods, rather than as engaging the human condition. Each "sells education not as the pathway to truth, but as the ticket to an escape route from poverty and insecurity" (May, 2001, p. 63). It draws its power and authority from playing on fears of defeat in the marketplace rather than on desires to learn. "It dangles before all takers an expansion of power, control, and opportunity" (May, 2001, p. 63). It does so while engaged in fierce competition with other institutions.

Presidents and other chief administrators set a tone of insistent individualism when they plan ways to increase institutional prestige, prominence, and comparative rankings. Deborah Tannen's images of the fighter and the battlefield often provide the backdrop for institutional planning sessions. Strategies to shore up weaknesses and exploit strengths are developed in secrecy. The work of competitors is closely watched and plans to be the first with a new program, secure favorable or forestall harmful legislative initiatives, or promote an ambitious development or capital campaign may take on overtones of a battle—as the term campaign itself suggests.

Problematic Behaviors

The questionable institutional practices noted in the last chapter both illustrate and exacerbate insistent individualism. A philosophy of atomism undergirds fabricating or withholding public data, providing misleading advertising, expecting adjunct instructors to do the work of full-time faculty, and creating institutional conflicts of interest. Perhaps the apparent separateness fostered by philosophical atomism shields institutions from recognizing the full implications of their acts. Institutions assume that manipulating data and claiming possibilities as actualities are separate from teaching and learning.

Institutions whose actions contravene fostering truthful conversation fragment their educational role and forget that they teach through actions. But their actions teach very well. What students, faculty, and staff learn is that the pressures of competition are taken to justify ways to "round up" the numbers of graduating seniors, as well as to "round down" the percentage granted admission—or to misrepresent new programs. And they learn that there is as yet little collective attention to these practices as ethical issues with significant consequences. There is no adequate self-regulation—"No institution is known to have suffered sanctions for falsely reporting information to a guidebook or ranking source or for intentionally fabricating data reported to the public" (Corts, 1997, p. 7).

Likewise, institutions that claim part-time faculty are interchangeable with full-time faculty obscure the circumstances in which education occurs. They suggest that instructional piece work is fully equivalent to coordinated education—delivered by full-time faculty in regular conversation with each other about curricular relevance and adequacy, about research implications for teaching and vice versa, about department mission, about student advising and faculty evaluation. They imply that course construction can be separated without expense from course instruction and from traditional student advising, curricular oversight, and instructional ownership by full-time faculty. They suggest that the intellectual life and conversation of a campus are unaffected by this "outsourcing" of its teaching.[2] These institutions separate issues of public representation from those of instructional integrity. They presume one has nothing to do with the other.

Similarly, mainline institutions assume that for-profit activities can be adequately isolated from traditional activities. Yet, the emergence and expansion of for-profit institutions and instructional subsidiaries convert education from a social institution into a consumer industry. Developing corporate subsidiaries within the institutional structure introduces conflicts of interest and time. It creates conditions for enormous tensions between maximizing investor wealth and facilitating student learning. It presupposes a kind of atomism, for no traditional institution that creates a profit center wants to lose its nonprofit status—its exemption from taxation or its appeal to donors (not just investors). So it is happy to compartmentalize its operations, in effect attesting that one has nothing to do with the other. Critics say institutions want things both ways—to enjoy tax-exempt benefits and also to hold their proprietary units exempt from intrusive public scrutiny.

Finally, the movement toward unbundling throws into question the very definition of a faculty member as well as the meaning of education. In the traditional concept, a faculty member has one job with three mutually-related dimensions—teaching, scholarship, and service. Each of these dimensions bears on the other. Teaching uninformed by relevant scholarship is inadequate, if not actually fraudulent. Students are deprived of seeing the instructor model the pursuit of learning—showing the tenacity and creativity that is required and the values and fruits that ensue. Likewise, scholarship that is not conducted with an eye toward teaching is incomplete. And service that is inattentive to the requirements of teaching and scholarship as well as the relevant needs of the public is hardly professional by any definition. In sum, the traditional faculty role is a shorthand description of three interrelated activities—not the three isolated and separable activities suggested by unbundling.

These institutional understandings and behaviors are rooted in philosophical mistakes. Atomism views parts of the whole as self-contained. It separates what cannot be divided without expense to the activities sundered. Atomism is also a moral mistake, for isolating matters provides misleading information about how things are. Its atomism often misleads the institution itself—in its more overt representations such as fudged data, though, the institution simply assumes that it won't get caught by authorities. However, it may easily get caught by its own faculty and students, thereby sending the message that a spirituality of deception is acceptable.

The inability or unwillingness of many universities to work toward intellectual unity and integrity leads them to seek "nonsubstantive" activities as a surrogate. William May (2001) offers one example: "A new class of specialists, athletes, provides the university with liturgical forms that gather the community together and thereby substitutes for the unity it lacks at more substantive intellectual and spiritual levels" (p. 250). Other efforts to promote school spirit often pursue the same surrogate objectives. That athletic programs are often atomistic seems obvious. "We can no longer deny that college sports, particularly big-time college sports, are in direct conflict with virtually every value an academic institution should stand for" (Gerdy, 2002, p. 33f.).

Academic capitalism exacerbates these mistakes. Robert Bellah (1998) notes that in education, as elsewhere, the disintegration of the post-war institutional order has meant that the primary relationships "between universities and students are being stripped of any moral understanding other than that of market exchange" (p. 93). Higher education is certainly big business (in the size of its budgets, numbers of employees, extent of facilities, etc.), but is the business of higher education just business or entertainment? Does it exist to make a profit or to maximize wealth for investors? Should it be measured primarily in terms of market share or annual growth rate? Nomenclature like customers, market analysis, student headcount (or, worse, body count), and credit hour production advances this mind set. After a certain point, higher education turns itself into a commodity.

PROTECTION FROM PERSONAL ANXIETIES AND FEAR

Yet, despite its liabilities, we also know that insistent individualism helps shield us from fear and anxiety. Most academic jobs are replete with opportunities for failure. Expectations for tenure and promotion seem constantly to escalate. Scholarly work is fragile; the effect of teaching is uncertain; and few triumphs today guarantee success tomorrow. It is natural that others appear as threats to our intellectual safety. Aggressive domination or passive retreat then seem understandable strategies, despite the fragmentation and isolationism they create.

There are other reasons why insistent individualism is prevalent. The academy naturally attracts incipient insistent individualists. The calendar leaves large parts of the year free of institutional obligations. Long-standing traditions provide individuals extraordinary freedom and incentives to direct their teaching and research, and to put a personal stamp on them. Problems and topics for investigation are usually freely selected, not assigned. Approaches to teaching and interactions with students are personal choices.

Likewise, stringent accountability is rarely enforced. Once the hurdle of tenure has been crossed, there may be no significant evaluation of performance for years, if not decades. More than one faculty member has acknowledged, "I have not been evaluated in more than 20 years!" Overall, teamwork is hardly a key professional requirement, is rarely rewarded, and, accordingly, is not a strength of many. Anxious grasping after individual status is far more deeply ingrained, and letting go is not easy.

Indeed, some critics of higher education put the blame for insistent individualism squarely on faculty grasping for standing. For instance, Martin Anderson finds *self-indulgence* to be the most prominent feature of the academy. Anderson (1992) diagnoses the key problem as professorial hubris, and suggests that it is simply "unchecked intellectual arrogance" (p. 124). Faculty see themselves as intellectual elites, morally superior to others. This elitism is a "virulent phenomenon, shared by a group of people who feel superior to others solely by virtue of their higher intelligence and learning" (Anderson, 1992, p. 124). Under the guise of higher-order values, academics permit themselves the pursuit of personal privilege, prestige, and reputation no matter the expense to teaching, collegiality, or student learning.

However, critics like Anderson ignore how hard and risky good teaching can be. Insistent individualism seems to be more deeply rooted in a culture of fear than in elitist forms of self-indulgence. The classic expression of professorial anxiety is the tormented dream about teaching failures and inadequacies. Michael Berube (2001) comments on

> the psychic landscape: the mysterious building, the spectral students, the surreal classroom, the sheer suffocating terror. *This is the class that will expose me as a fraud,* you think. Or: *This time they'll know I didn't prepare all summer.* Even: *When this is over they'll fire me on the spot.* . . . it doesn't matter how experienced or accomplished you are: If you care at all about your teaching, you are haunted by teaching-anxiety dreams. (p. B20)

We know that many faculty struggle with similar apprehensions about their scholarship—forever delaying publication because further data might emerge or the perfect expression found.

A Culture of Fear

The nightmares of which Berube writes point to a perverted level of anxiety and fear that creates the need for control. We seek power to shore up ourselves against colleagues and their challenges to our way of doing things, to the knowledge we claim and accomplishments we value. Many of us work to keep colleagues out of our classrooms, holding that they are an intrusive rather than natural, helpful presence. We shelter our scholarship because others are unqualified to evaluate it. In fact, it is fear more than elitist self-aggrandizement that fuels insistent individualism. And it is painful. Palmer (1992a) terms it "the pain of disconnection . . . [the] sense on the part of faculty of being detached from students, from colleagues, from their own intellectual vocation and the passions that originally animated it" (p. 3f.).

And it is not just colleagues who can appear as threats to our self-image. Students are a potent force, wielding more power than they realize. Insistent individualism closes us off from the vitalities of youth. Our faculty identity is under assault when students don't share our intellectual passions. Because students have the power to wound, we teach defensively—spurning our students before they have an opportunity to spurn us. This dynamic leads to stagnation. Palmer (1992a) observes that it is "an occupational hazard of the professoriate, often taking the form of cultured cynicism, of an attitude toward students that says, 'I have a Ph.D., I write books, I travel to conferences, and I get paid for it. Who needs you?'" (p. 4). As a result, instead of belonging to a community of scholars, academics "find themselves in distant, competitive, and uncaring relationships with colleagues and students" (Palmer, 1998, p. 20f.).

Thus, a deeper diagnosis of the dissatisfactions within higher education points toward a widespread culture of fear. "The teaching and learning enterprise in our society is riddled with fear. Fear, not ignorance, is the enemy of learning, and it is fear that gives ignorance its power" (Palmer, 1992b, p. 2). Fear comes to characterize classrooms, teachers, and administrative structures.

> As a teacher, I am at my worst when fear takes the lead in me, whether that means teaching in fear of my students or manipulating their fears of me. Our relations as faculty colleagues are often diminished by fear; fear is nearly universal in the relations of faculty and administration. (Palmer, 1998, p. 36)

For these reasons, dwelling excessively on self may be less the result of an inflated ego than an effort to mask the fear that one might be less than others think. Status is a relative thing, uncertain and fleeting. It must be constantly defended. Worries about vulnerability and insecurity abound and take their toll. Writing about professionals in a broader sense, May (1983) notes the centrality of "the fear that our competitors will do us in or that we will slide into the vortex of decay and death with the powerless if we get too close to them" (p. 126). Despite the protections that tenure provides, academics are not immune. Even the serene can be pulled down and exhausted. There must be a better way.

ACADEMIC PROFESSIONALISM

Yet even the concept of professionalism in the academy betrays elements of insistent individualism. What ought to bear signs of community has marks of exclusion. In his analysis of the professional ideal in America, Bruce Kimball documents the shift in the 20th century from a stress on knowledge and selfless service to an exclusion rooted in socioeconomic factors. Maximizing prestige and income has replaced an earlier emphasis upon the utility of expertise. Lawyers and physicians come immediately to mind, but are professors far behind? Surely speaking for more than himself, Kimball (1992) asks: Has the isolationism of increasing academic specialization inverted "the ethic of selfless service?" (p. 314f). Has specialization been used "to deflect criticisms of professionals' power and prestige by disguising their self-interest?" (Kimball, 1992, p. 314f.).

Some entrepreneurial academics invite this question by openly pursuing new global economic opportunities. Many seek to retain the salaries and other resources of the academy while also functioning as free agents in the market place. Some scholars put this development in the best light, suggesting that entrepreneurial science faculty, for instance, have "elided altruism and profit, viewing profit making as a means to serve their unit, do science, and serve the common good" (Slaughter & Leslie, 1997, p. 179). Perhaps more realistically, though, Slaughter and Leslie observe that market-oriented faculty "justified their emerging commitment to entrepreneurship in terms of saving their units. . . . they seldom spoke about students, undergraduate educators, education in general, or the institution as a whole" (p. 201). Academic capitalism raises large questions about the fidelity of academics and institutions to the good of their students.

Presenting a more philosophical analysis, Bruce Wilshire argues that the very status and authority of even the traditional academic professional seems to require exclusion of outsiders. Esoteric language and arcane publications inhibit communication. The prevailing culture encourages faculty to feel primary obligations to disciplines and disciplinary colleagues—not to students, institutions, or the broader public. Even graduate students and junior faculty have but marginal claims. It is the professional society and fully credentialed members that count. Academic disciplines provide the recognition that creates the professional self. And this is just the problem, for the "professionalizing" of the academy, together with the institutional separation of disciplines, has served no one's *real* interests. Indeed, Wilshire (1990) writes of the educational "bankruptcy" of the university, holding that it "has failed to provide a matrix within which our common concerns for meaning and being, and for humane and ethical knowledge, can thrive" (p. 34).

Instead of this type of academic professionalism, we should pursue *collegial* professionalism. In the latter, "professionalism is converted *from* credentialism and exclusivity, protectionism, and isolation from others, and it moves *to* an emphasis upon connectivity and imaginative empathy, competence and dedication to the learning needs of the other" (Bennett, 1998, p. 52). Practicing hospitality and conversation provides the way to collegial professionalism—as we explore in later chapters. Yet we often persist in excluding others. Barabara Herrnstein Smith reflects on how we construct and enshrine sharp divisions between professional roles and responsibilities, maintaining archaic hierarchies of academic caste and privilege. Indeed, we not only perpetuate but elevate these distinctions through displays of "extraneous clubbiness and exhibitions of arrogance that add insult to injury for a considerable body of *internal* 'outsiders,' that is, people in the academy who lose in the related status wars" (Smith, 1989, p. 291). Perhaps the worst example is attitudes toward adjunct faculty—even as we move toward ever greater dependence upon part-time faculty, we persist in ways of excluding them.

The ironies are rich. Compared with physicians, lawyers, and others, academics have but a tenuous claim upon professional status. Many academic areas have no licensing requirements. For them, graduate school provides the sole certification of expert knowledge. With no industry-wide requirement of continuing education for academic professionals, the graduate degree also serves for most of us as the perennial credential—revocable only in the most extraordinary of circumstances. There is no national membership organization committed to clear standards of self-regulation, including discipline or expulsion of those whose behavior falls short. We in higher education have large amounts of autonomy and individualism; we lack sustained, exacting peer review or other forms of public, professional accountability after the tenure award.

INSISTENT INDIVIDUALISM SUMMARIZED

The atomism of insistent individualism undermines good teaching and research. Faculty attempts to control learning create student dependencies, instead of student confidence in their own abilities. In research, faculty perceptions of self-worth and self-identity are often rooted in assessments of relative standing and strength rather than in joint insight and discovery. Gain by one professor seems to require loss by another. Attitudes of insistent individualism plague the whole academy, but since competitiveness requires time and chutzpah, these attitudes are often more visible among tenured professors beyond formal evaluation activities. Institutions cooperate by front-loading evaluation processes, focusing on the probationary period—suggesting that the tenured professor is the measure of his or her own value and promoting aloof and self-absorbed behaviors.

Eventually alienation is the outcome. When individuals are regularly separated from the common ground of shared experience, they are left without legitimate connection to each other—without reciprocity, collaboration, and mutual enrichment. Others are seen as competitors, not colleagues. But constant competitiveness generates fatigue and self-doubt. Insecurity about self-worth leads some to posturing and self-promotion—others to withdrawal and self-protection. All see personal failures only as negativities—signs of personal inadequacies—for they lack the transformative possibilities that supportive communities can provide.

For these and other reasons, too many educators work in isolation and do not express genuine interest in others, pay careful attention to their perspectives and needs, or share freely and sensitively from a personal stock of learning. Rather than practicing hospitality, some are actively hostile. Long-time Michigan professor Ejner Jensen (1995) holds that

> many faculty members in our colleges and universities are embittered to a quite surprising degree. . . . the very real losses caused by their feelings of regret, envy, frustration, betrayal, and isolation constitute one of the continuing unresolved problems in higher education. (p. 8)

Indeed, Jensen finds the more virulent forms of faculty disaffection and alienation to include "mean-spiritedness toward colleagues, contempt for students, and a strong condemnation of the whole academic enterprise" (p. 8). To the extent that he is correct, experiencing the satisfactions of mutual interaction and reciprocity, and enjoying a healthy and nourishing spirituality become a remote ideal rather than the rule in the academy.

As communities of individualists, colleges and universities mirror these liabilities. Teaching and learning are seen as individual rather than shared activities. Organizational structures divide and isolate rather than facilitate interaction and conversation. Institutional behaviors teach the acceptability of insistent individualism by modeling it in their marketing and their increasing reliance upon adjunct faculty as stewards of the core academic enterprise. Despite their public representations—and perhaps their inner intentions—these institutions offer a philosophy of atomism, an ethics of opportunism, and a spirituality of self-preoccupation.

However prevalent, insistent individualism is inadequate and cannot stand alone. It suggests an enduring substantialist self, with an invulnerable core of free selfhood, one internally unaffected by others and only externally affected by learning. These are hardly the marks of the thoughtful, educated person that college catalogues and mission statements celebrate. These attitudes of insistent individualism seem to heighten, rather than protect us against, the anxieties and vulnerabilities associated with educating others. And, ironically, insistent individualism presupposes a shared understanding that worth is achieved and displayed in competitive victory—that is, that personal standing and identity *are* relational. Since we need recognition by the other, individualism presupposes community. Even the language and knowledge in which individualists dwell are public or social, not private, achievements—they are constituted by rules that are community, not individual, accomplishments. In short, insistent individualism by itself is ultimately logically and descriptively inadequate, unable to account for the conditions of its applicability. The model of the person or institution as self-contained undercuts itself.

Critical reflection on these liabilities is in order. We know that insistent individualism is the dark side of the academy, not the whole picture. But practicing self-knowledge and naming, not ignoring, the negative is essential to restoring health and pursuing a more vibrant and hospitable academy. Wilshire (1990) reminds us of the primal and abiding experience that is the essential foundation for our sense of self and other:

> despite confusion, distraction, and a strange kind of loneliness, there is a vague but fundamental level of experience in which we directly and pre-critically experience ourselves to be one self, to be in a community, or set of communities, and also, of course in a world. . . . It is the deepest, if most obscure, source of authorization of self. (p. 44)

Insistent individualism ignores or forgets the context from which individuality emerges. We are left with what Whitehead calls the fallacy of misplaced concreteness—treating an abstraction as a concrete reality. The true concrete reality is the nexus of a pregiven wealth of relationships and interactions from which a narrow portion is removed and treated as the whole.

RELATIONAL INDIVIDUALISM:
A BROADER PICTURE AND A BETTER WAY

As a philosophy, an ethic, and a spirituality, insistent individualism constrains individual and communal satisfaction. It rejects a deeper understanding of the conditions under which our lives are lived. It obscures a more generous, indeed compelling, sense of what education and educators should be. Fortunately, insistent individualism is but part of a larger story.

We have seen that insistent individualism ignores the important contributions that others make in our lives—roles they play in who we are and in the experiences we treasure. It ignores as well the contributions we make to the inner lives of others. Philosophically we can speak of these roles in terms of the underlying and normative import of internal relations and the relational self. John Smith (1982) underscores the importance of community: "the primordial fact of experience in any form is *individuals together* in some network of relations" (p. 448). Insistent individualism seems so unfulfilling precisely because it contradicts the deepest principles of reality—that selves are inescapably constituted by others and by a public life. Indeed, it is because we are fundamentally relational selves that we recognize insistent individualism as deficient.

So behind or underneath academic insistent individualism—and holding it up, so to speak—is a more fundamental and desirable philosophy and spirituality, with a broader ethical appreciation of connections and collaborative work. Sharing with and learning from each other are seen as primary values. Competition is understood in terms of value added. Others are viewed as bearers of intrinsic value that can enrich the self, and vice versa. Relational power is honored and celebrated—the ability to incorporate and reflect contributions from others is judged a mark of strength, not a lack of power. In short, self and others are known to be in mutual relationships that can be ignored or abused, but never eliminated. As a better way, this second view is more than just a lingering piety—it is essential to the individual and collective work of the academy.

Internal Relationships and Power

In this more fundamental view, community is recognized—even celebrated—as necessary for individual freedom and creativity. Far from simple collections or aggregations of independent selves, communities constitute the many-layered contexts within which individuals dwell and grow—and to which they contribute. Our freedom emerges from this relationality—it emerges with, and out of, the actualities and possibilities that others provide us, and we them. The greater the diversity of our relationships, the more potentiality they represent for our growth and enrichment.

This points to the importance of internal relationships, those in which we are truly inwardly affected by others. Bernard Loomer (1981) suggests that because of our connectedness with others, "the term 'relations' is [actually] a way of speaking of the presence of others in our own concrete actuality" (p. 151). Influence and presence of this sort always flows in both directions. We use our freedom to make community possible, but we also presuppose community in acting freely. According to Loomer, "we are related to be free, but more profoundly we are free in order to enter more fully into those relationships by which our own stature is enhanced" (p. 151)—those relationships in which we find ourselves fulfilled.

In this relational view, the concept of power is transformed. It no longer means only the unilateral exercise of force to achieve one's objectives in relationship to the other. Power is now recognized as the capacity to be influenced and affected as well as to influence and affect—it involves both giving and receiving. Relational power means allowing the other to make an inner difference. In Loomer's (1981) words, "the size and worth of an individual or a group is measured and created by the range, intensity, and concreteness of the relationships that can be sustained" (p. 149). As we examine in the next chapter, this kind of power involves *attending* with disciplined openness to the other—receiving as well as sharing. However, unilateral power will never be eliminated. Relational power is a vehicle for understanding and for progress, not for utopia. "This kind of power will not obliterate the inequalities of groups or individuals. . . . But it can so function that these inequalities may become mutually fructifying" (Loomer, 1981, p. 149).

Using Robert Bellah's image, we can speak of this relational way as a "second language" of academic community—in contrast and prior to the "first language" of competition and individualism. It is what we mean when we speak of the community of scholars or talk about the importance of collegiality. Far from being outdated, this second language is foundational. We rely on underlying communities for our work even when we fail to nourish them. Through this second language we understand and articulate our mutual connectedness. It gives us vocabulary and a grammar for moral reasoning and action. It provides a basis for connecting our private and our public lives.

Courageous Individualism

Understanding the self as relational affirms a healthier kind of individualism, one that suggests maturity and emancipation. This individualist thinks for himself or herself, takes personal initiative, has a singular view of the world, and a distinctive personality and character. This individualist is not captured by the crowd and is liberated from those who are. This kind of individualism is a precious achievement, an outcome of the Enlightenment. With Robert Bellah we can identify what we call relational individualism as "courageous."[3] A courageous individualist chooses to work for the common good, even when opposed by others. A courageous individualist is a relational individualist, fully appreciative of the constitutive roles of others but not reducible to them.

Bellah opposes "courageous" to "indifferent" individualism—an attitude and behavior characterized by self-preoccupation and withdrawal from society. In its extreme form, this type of individualism is not just deformed, but depraved. "A conception of the individual as fundamentally isolated and utterly selfish cannot but give rise to an indifferent, I would argue even a vicious individualism . . . [and] vicious individualism produces a vicious society" (Bellah, 1998, p. 97). Both terms—Bellah's indifferent individualist and our insistent individualist—name those who assume that meaningful lives must be built independent of others, since others are competitors. For them, educational community is a smokescreen behind which potential threats hide. It follows that problems of the broader community are for others to address.

For the courageous and relational individualist, however, identity is rooted in social interaction and cultural context. Community provides the opportunity for one's own work and entails duties and obligations to others. Educational politics is part of an essential process for making decisions that affect the common good. Loomer (1976) helps us strike the right balance—"we are at once both communal and solitary individuals. But the solitariness of individuality is lived out only in the midst of constitutive relationships" (p. 20).

Insistent individualism is an inadequate account of the facts of human experience. It abstracts excessively from the thickness and richness of personal existence. It can cost dearly, for the self-promotion and detachment of the insistent individualist become forms of self-renunciation and impoverishment. Since the self is not only constituted, but finds fulfillment, in relationship, to ignore or abuse the other is to diminish the matrix of which one is a part and from which one draws benefit. The insistently individualistic self suggests the thinness and unidimensionality of a life spent in aggressive combat and defense against others. When community is seen as something to which one contributes only for individual advantage, when there is more combat and competition than cooperation—then the self *is* diminished and experiences of estrangement and alienation dominate.

We go to great extremes to justify our insistent individualism, disguise it from ourselves, and prevent ourselves from being reminded of it. And for good reason. Insistent individualism is poisonous. One becomes enslaved by the need to appear independent. The relational self can be hindered, even ignored—but in the end it can't be denied. We need others because we can never know enough. What we do know is always partial and reflects limited perspectives and values. We also need others to keep us honest, to help us correct personal distortions and rationalizations. In a relational view, there is no individual independence apart from intrinsic connection with others. Selves are enriched by relationships with others and contribute their uniqueness in return. At the most fundamental level, this is who and how we are. Education rightly conducted requires relational thinking—reminding us of our debts to others as well as the gifts only we can provide others. Relational thinking impels us to develop habits of practicing hospitality, engaging in conversation, and developing covenantal ties with others—students, colleagues, and the broader public and world.

CONCLUSION

Insistent individualism and the relational self display different philosophies about human character, identity, and fulfillment. They are two different social ontologies. They generate two different ethics and spiritualities.

One directs us toward detached lives, the other toward a common humanity. For the insistent individualist, community is really a pseudo community, a conglomerate or aggregation of solitary egos linked to each other through instrumental relationships—relationships that in the heat of competition threaten individuality and autonomy.

The ontology of the social self points to the indispensable rootage of the self in a multitude of communities. Douglas Sturm (1998a) describes the organic nature of the self: "our identity, while bearing the stamp of our own agency, is nonetheless contingent on an organic inheritance the full depths of which we cannot pretend to comprehend fully" (p. 9).

In the following two chapters, I turn to an essential virtue for the work and well-being of the academy—hospitality. Practicing hospitality expresses the ontology of the social self, gives direction to an academic ethic, and provides content to an authentic, fulfilling spirituality.

REFERENCES

Anderson, M. (1992). *Imposters in the temple: American intellectuals are destroying our universities.* New York, NY: Simon and Schuster.

Astin, A. (1997, September 26). Our obsession with being 'smart' is distorting intellectual life. *The Chronicle of Higher Education*, p. A60.

Bellah, R. N. (1998). Courageous or indifferent individualism. *Ethical Perspectives, 5* (2), 92–102.

Bennett, J. B. (1998). *Collegial professionalism: The academy, individualism, and the common good.* Phoenix, AZ: American Council on Education/Oryx Press.

Berube, M. (2001, September 21). Dream a little dream. *The Chronicle of Higher Education*, p. B20.

Corts, T. E. (1997, January/February). Let's stop trivializing the truth. *Trusteeship,* 6–10.

Gerdy, J. R. (2002, January/February). Athletic victories, educational defeats. *Academe, 88* (1), 32–36.

Getman, J. (1992). *In the company of scholars: The struggle for the soul of higher education.* Austin, TX: University of Texas Press.

Jensen, E. J. (1995, January/February). The bitter groves of academe. *Change, 27* (1), 8–11.

Kimball, B. A. (1992). *The 'true professional ideal' in America: A history.* Cambridge, MA: Blackwell.

Kirp, D. L. (2002, March 15). Higher ed inc.: Avoiding the perils of outsourcing. *The Chronicle of Higher Education*, p. B13f.

Loomer, B. (1976, Spring). Two kinds of power. *Process Studies*, 6 (1), 5–32.

Loomer, B. (1981). Theology in the American grain. In J. B. Cobb, Jr. & W. W. Schroeder (Eds.), *Process philosophy and social thought* (pp. 141–152). Chicago, IL: Center for the Scientific Study of Religion.

May, W. F. (1983). *The physician's covenant: Images of the healer in medical ethics.* Philadelphia, PA: The Westminster Press.

May, W. F. (2001). *Beleaguered rulers: The public obligation of the professional.* Louisville, KY: Westminster John Knox Press.

Palmer, P. J. (1992a, September). Community and commitment in higher education: An interview with Russell Edgerton. *AAHE Bulletin, 45* (1), 3–7.

Palmer, P. J. (1992b). *Reflections on a program for 'the formation of teachers.'* Kalamazoo, MI: The Fetzer Institute.

Palmer, P. J. (1998). *The courage to teach: Exploring the inner landscape of a teacher's life.* San Francisco, CA: Jossey-Bass.

Pattyn, B. (1998). Introduction: Courageous or indifferent individualism. *Ethical Perspectives, 5* (2), 85–88.

Pelikan, J. (1992). *The idea of the university: A reexamination.* New Haven, CT: Yale University Press.

Slaughter, S., & Leslie, L. (1997). *Academic capitalism: Politics, policies, and the entrepreneurial university.* Baltimore, MD: Johns Hopkins University Press.

Smith, B. H. (1989, May). Presidential address 1988. Limelight: Reflections on a public year. *Publications of the Modern Language Association of America, 104* (3), 285–293.

Smith, J. E. (1982, Winter). Community, cooperation, and the adventure of learning. *Soundings, LXV* (4), 447–455.

Sturm, D. (1998a). *Community and alienation: Essays on process thought and public life.* Notre Dame, IN: University of Notre Dame Press.

Tannen, D. (1998). *The argument culture.* New York, NY: Random House.

Tompkins, J. (1996). *A life in school: What the teacher learned.* Reading, MA: Addison Wesley.

Williams, R. (2000). *Lost icons: Reflections on cultural bereavement.* Edinburgh, Scotland: T & T Clark.

Wilshire, B. (1990). *The moral collapse of the university: Professionalism, purity, and alienation.* Albany, NY: State University of New York Press.

ENDNOTES

1. Alexander Astin (1997) has also commented on the expense associated with higher education's attachment to "smartness." He observes that "my many years as a scholar of higher education and as an employee of a large university convince me that some of higher education's most serious problems can be traced to our uncritical acceptance of this value, and to the fact that most of us are not even aware of the power and scope of its influence on our lives and institutions" (p. A60). Like Jane Tompkins, he argues that we should pay far more attention to the development and cultivation of intellect broadly understood than to its mere demonstration.

2. David Kirp (2002) makes the point well: "'Outsourcing' isn't the word usually applied to the practice of hiring part-timers. But adjunct instructors—recruited on a fee-for-service basis for a single course or, at best, to teach full-time for a few years—are the academic equivalent of temp-agency fill-ins or day laborers" (p. B14).

3. See (Pattyn, 1998). The reference is to the title of a conference at the University of Leuven at which Robert Bellah was the main speaker.

Hospitality— *An Essential Virtue* 3

What does it mean to say that hospitality is a cardinal virtue in our work as academics? First, I illustrate what hospitality involves by contrasting it with insistent individualism. The openness of hospitality stands over against self-preoccupation and concern with controlling power. Second, I propose that the manner in which we *attend* to others is a basic element in practicing hospitality. Third, I look at a number of virtues associated with hospitality.

SOME FEATURES OF HOSPITALITY

Practicing the radical openness of hospitality means extending self in order to welcome the other by sharing and receiving intellectual resources and insights. Both an intellectual and moral virtue, hospitality is essential to the work and success of the academy. This is not a common view. Some may find it bizarre. Others understand hospitality as a superficial congeniality, a warm, shapeless softness—the very opposite of the rigor for which the academy should be known. Henri Nouwen (1975) notes that for many of us, hospitality suggests "tea parties, bland conversations, and a general atmosphere of coziness" (p. 66). Hospitable individuals within the academy are often regarded, and scolded, as "soft" on standards and inclined toward compromise rather than standing for intellectual rigor and excellence.

Organizationally, hospitality fares no better. Faculty and administrators associate it with recreation, tourism, or hotel/restaurant management programs rather than with goals for every program, school, and institution. As we saw in Chapter One, departments and schools often struggle over resources and prestige, and quite a few disciplines and departments house deep ideological and personal divisions. Entire institutions are locked in competition for students and standing. The insistent individualism traced earlier is like kudzu, growing by leaps and bounds. As a consequence, the concept of hospitality in academe has lost much of its original power. But as Nouwen (1975) observes of its broader importance, "if there is any concept worth restoring to its original depth and evocative potential, it is the concept of hospitality" (p. 66).

An Ancient Tradition

Hospitality has a long and honorable lineage going back to Homeric and biblical times. Once an ideal for nomadic people, being hospitable in the academy points toward companionship with colleagues in promoting and advancing learning. The etymology of "companion" directs us to one with whom we eat bread. Likewise, "colleague" means one with whom we are linked. Companions and colleagues are those with whom we seek mutual openness and intellectual reciprocity.

In academe, companion and colleague point to collegia, the learning communities we jointly create and to which we belong. As our Homeric and biblical heritages suggest, hospitality carries a sense of abundance and attentive presence to the other. They remind us that hospitality should extend to the stranger as well as the neighbor. Both traditions call for taking in the other and offering oneself and one's goods. Who is not moved by the welcome given Odysseus in his travails, by the stories of Joseph hosting his faithless brothers, by the good Samaritan, or the prodigal son? Translated to the academy, being hospitable means being radically open to others, sharing resources, and receiving with care the new and the strange, as well as critically reviewing the familiar.

Hospitality is not simply generic openness. It recognizes the particularity of others as part of the broader interdependence of being and the interconnectedness of learning that characterizes the depths of our reality. As openness to particular others, hospitality requires careful attention to who and what is really there, as opposed to what we might wish. Carefully attending and listening to the other are acquired skills, often more difficult to master than the talking that comes naturally to the professoriate. But with desire, discipline, and careful attention to others, learning and knowledge become gifts to be exchanged, no longer possessions to be hoarded and controlled.

Practicing hospitality involves awareness that new and surprising value may reside in the other, once seen with fresh eyes. We learn to welcome the roles others play in our learning since it is easy to overlook adverse evidence and we are always potential victims of self-deception. We need others to protect us from skewing and slanting our teaching and research. Their ideas provide ballast and balance to our work—perspectives that may lead to changes or even breakthroughs. We can play the same role for others. As hosts we extend hospitality to our guests—be they students and colleagues or strangers. We share our learning and offer comparisons on common topics and concerns. As Nouwen (1975) reminds us, hospitable educators work toward "the creation of space where students and teachers can enter into a fearless communication with each other and allow their respective life experiences to be their primary and most valuable source of growth and maturation" (p. 67).

Hospitable Sharing and Receiving Are Inseparable

In authentic hospitality, sharing and receiving are not seriatim, unconnected moments. To practice hospitality is to share with others in ways that involve receiving. Consequently, practicing hospitality can threaten our stability and control. Truly to share is to invite others into our world, eventually allowing their strangeness and unfamiliarity to affect and engage us. Sometimes the other is literally a stranger, but it may also be someone in our midst whom we have ignored. In either case, hospitable engagement can be threatening as well as enriching—challenging our comfortable truths, but also enlarging them and compensating for limitations in our understanding. When sharing is accompanied by receiving, the host becomes guest, one who receives the bounty of the other. Sharing the riches of my world becomes receiving as I enter into aspects of the other's world. A new, jointly constructed world may then emerge. In its fullness, hospitality bears the fruit of reciprocity, an ongoing dialectic of host and guest.

As part of this process, practicing hospitality means relinquishing protective mechanisms and refusing to insist woodenly upon one's own terms. It requires letting go the armor and weapons of insistent individualism. It means breaching the tight boundaries that encircle the correctly credentialed and the top-ranked institutions. It involves abandoning careful calculations respecting the quantity of good one decides to extend, based on what one anticipates receiving. To practice hospitality is to share experience, insights, and resources without imposing conditions that demand a return, or asking what is the least we have to offer in order to secure what we want.

Being academically hospitable means letting others know they matter as fellow inquirers, and inviting them to mutual interaction and reciprocity. It opposes the insistent individualism that throws up barriers to respect, even in familiar settings and classrooms. Too often

> we do not grant respect to students, to stumbling and failing. We do not grant respect to tentative and heartfelt ways of being in the world where the person can't quite think of the right word or can't think of any word at all. We don't grant

> respect to silence and wonder. We don't grant it to voices
> outside our tight little circle. (Palmer, 1997, p. 11)

To practice hospitality is to acknowledge the intrinsic value of the other, to treat him or her as potentially authoritative, and through interaction to discover and promote fitting and harmonious outcomes. It is to provide an appropriate response to what is, to bequeath one's moment of individual insight to the future.

To practice hospitality is to hope for reciprocity, knowing it cannot be commanded, only invited. Genuine hospitality means sharing something that isn't required with someone who doesn't have to receive it. It is neither involuntary self-sacrifice nor coerced acceptance. Sharing and receiving arise out of freedom and engender freedom, not dependence. One can but offer one's own learning without stipulations as to its use. According to Nouwen (1975), "hospitality is not a subtle invitation to adopt the lifestyle of the host, but the gift of a chance for the guest to find his own" (p. 72). The reciprocity of hospitality means drawing out from each other capacities and gifts that otherwise lie dormant. Nouwen reminds us of the centrality of hospitality to the spiritual health of academe: "If there is any area that needs a new spirit, a redemptive and liberating spirituality, it is the area of education in which so many people spend crucial parts of their lives, as students or teachers or both" (p. 84). Openness to the other is essential in an academic ethic, a philosophy of integrity, and a healthy educational spirituality.

SOME CAUTIONS

Insistent individualism can be wily, sometimes masquerading as hospitality, and several more distinctions may be helpful. Intellectual hospitality is not simply a matter of manners, etiquette, or decorum. It is not primarily about being genteel, polite, civil, or even just nice or decent. These concepts are important, particularly in pluralistic and diverse communities, but they are not sufficient. Hospitality can be counterfeit, presenting the appearance but not the reality of openness. After all, one can be polite and mannerly without really being open. Discussions can be civil but superficial—sometimes veneers of politeness covering unrelenting contentiousness.

Civility

Appeals to civility can retard discussions on important, long-overdue initiatives. The real risk may not be incivility, but inaction. Familiar examples include the "civil" refusal to review curricula or even traditional course assignments, for fear of upsetting accepted arrangements and reigniting turf wars. Educators enter into tacit agreements to isolate and ignore rather than confront colleagues who shirk service obligations, neglect students, or abandon the ongoing scholarship that informs teaching. Civil truces amongst warring parties are important, but they can deny the greater good that comes only with efforts to address the common welfare.

Student incivility is another area where hospitality can be overlooked. A number of faculty understandably protest incivility in the classroom. They are dismayed by disruptive and rude student behaviors (Schneider, 1998)—behaviors that seem to be increasing and intensifying. One study arrayed uncivil student behavior on the following continuum: disengaged, disinterested, disrespectful, disruptive, defiant, and disturbed (Gonzalez & Lopez, 2001). In increasing degree, each type undermines classroom teaching and learning. A sense of entitlement to high grades compounds matters. Of course, some of these behaviors may be responses to faculty incivility: "Teachers can be overbearing. They can adopt behavior that can mortify students. They can exhibit a purported intellectual superiority, belittle students, use sarcasm in a way that's hurtful" (Schneider, 1998, p. A12). Faculty may come late to class, introduce irrelevant material, or skip office hours. Students may simply copy their insistent individualism.

However, the basic problem may be the inhospitable conditions in which education is offered. Huge classes are inherently dehumanizing. Unclear course expectations can worsen a situation for which students have been inadequately prepared. As one observer notes, "to a degree, classroom incivility is the way some students protest an alien academic culture that they deem onerous and unfair" (Trout, 1998, p. A40). Surely the hospitable response is not to dumb down material but to work toward classes with more humane numbers where knowing students by name is possible, to explicate clearly the course and classroom expectations, to clarify and show personally why they are appropriate and fair, and to devise evaluation forms that suggest courses *should* be demanding. This can mean openly challenging the equation of learning with high grades, valued because economically marketable.

Charity and Intimacy

Hospitality is not the same as charity—dispensing intellectual goods to the less fortunate. Charity in that sense is a substitute for hospitality, a means of continuing self-preoccupation. At best, it is superficial hospitality, control masquerading as generosity. It maintains, rather than overcomes, barriers between selves. Because real intellectual hospitality leads to a critique of the self as well as the other, some academics may commit acts of charity because they find it less threatening to be hosts rather than guests. They want to be benefactors, not also beneficiaries—dispensers, not also recipients. These acts continue the structures of separation that hospitality is attempting to bridge. Hospitality honors interdependence; charity reinforces dependence.

Neither does hospitality require intimacy or close, personal relationships. Some speak of familial relationships as a relevant standard of excellence without recognizing its limitations—families themselves often fail to exhibit close-knit relationships, the academy is not something into which one is born, affiliation with the academy is voluntary in a way that family membership is not, and faculty have different obligations to colleagues than family members do to each other.[1] Academic affiliations can be severed in a way family connections cannot—a faculty member may not be renewed, a program and its instructors can be discontinued, and an instructor can disenroll a student; only in hyperbole can a parent disown a child. The goal is not intimacy, but accountability and reciprocity in sharing concerns and resources.

Far from hospitality requiring intimacy, members of a healthy collegium need not even be friends in the sense of sharing company outside the work of the collegium. What is important is that they maintain interest and a capacity for distance in evaluating what they receive in mutual openness. In the rare relationship of intimacy, hospitality in its fullness involves learning in depth about what motivates and sustains the other, as well as sharing cherished fundamental beliefs and commitments that give form and sustenance. However desirable, these exchanges are infrequent and often not sustained, but their absence is no excuse for inhospitality.

True academic hospitality is centered in the relationship between self and others on matters of learning—a relationship marked by genuine openness and respect, not necessarily by unbounded care for the other. Indeed, there may be no promise of intimacy at all. Sometimes being hospitable may support being a curmudgeon as the most fitting way of attending to the other. Certainly, hospitality is not mere chumminess, nor is practicing it simply being polite. David Damrosch (1995) makes a similar point respecting collaborative work when he observes that any requirement that the collaborators be friends eliminates most of the potential combinations that can be found on a typical campus. Academics simply aren't nice enough, to enough of their colleagues, enough of the time, for this to be a general basis for academic life. (p. 194).

Issues of Language

How we use language can block as well as nurture hospitality. Inherited patterns of expression may transmit derogatory and oppressive concepts. Like organizations, language can create and perpetuate inequities and deformations of genuine community. Yet, we must be careful. For instance, the recent, widespread shift from the inclusive use of the masculine pronoun to more gender-neutral constructions is now a common practice. Failure to appreciate that the shift is recent can result in unfair judgments of earlier writing and speaking governed by a different grammar. Charitableness and generosity of spirit, if not acts of charity, are always in order.

The use of ample questions and the subjunctive rather than the descriptive promotes hospitality in conversation. These linguistic patterns convey interest rather than presumption; they speak of considered possibility rather than assumed fact. Indeed, these uses of language can prepare the way for practicing hospitality. One can still be a self-centered individualist, but take baby steps to anticipate becoming hospitable. Desiring to change can generate stage directions for learning to practice hospitality—for acquiring the dispositions, outlooks, inclinations, and patterns of interaction in which hospitality is embedded.

A broader point is that no single position is exhaustive. Formulations are forever provisional—awaiting revision, correction, and expansion as the ongoing fruits of intellectual hospitality suggest. This is not an argument for relativism or the abandonment of standards. It is an argument for rigor, but hospitably, rather than negatively, construed. The search for truth and knowledge is never concluded.

A Matter of Respect

Authentic hospitality is marked by respect. The respectful reception and use of intellectual gifts from others is not an invasion of their privacy. Heightened competitiveness and multicultural tensions can give rise to a conviction that hard-won perspectives on the oppressiveness of privileged positions or persons are private property, off-limits to those lacking first-hand experiences. Such absolutist stances create further division rather than mutual receptivity, reflection and understanding. We do not need hard lines of separation but bridges that enable experiences to be shared, received, examined, and pondered—and then shared again.

The manner in which one receives the hospitality of another is also important. For instance, sensitive awareness of others' contributions allows one to express gratitude without embarrassing those who are shy or withdrawn. Likewise, a hospitable receiver extends courtesy and graciousness toward even the tactless and insensitive giver. These can be difficult challenges and success is usually partial. But overall, in the best of hospitable interactions, each returns to the other what he or she has received, now enriched and enhanced by the fruits of personal reflection—a potentially endless process of reciprocity, limited only by patience, time, and energy.

In sum, being hospitable involves treating others at least initially as worthy of intellectual attention, letting them know they matter as fellow inquirers, and working toward mutual interaction and reciprocity. It eschews quick dismissal without thoughtful efforts to learn—no judgments already, and irrevocably, formed. It means recognizing that each could supplement or correct the other's work and self-understanding. Hospitality points toward active sharing and a willingness to learn from others. Being hospitable is adverbial in character. It refers to *how* one relates to others.

ATTENDING TO THE OTHER

The adverbial character of practicing hospitality demands that we attend to the other with care and respect, while honoring differences and disagreements. Hospitality involves intellectual curiosity—interest in the other, the unknown, and the foreign. It stands over against indifference to new ideas, ideological rigidity, and refusal to reexamine the familiar. But practicing hospitality is never risk free. It makes one vulnerable to being misunderstood, ridiculed, and attacked. Practicing hospitality involves exposing one's faults and deficiencies. It is not simply that one's ideas may be proven deficient. It is also that one may jeopardize the appearance of self-confidence and competence that our individualistic society admires.

Respectful engagement requires suspending initial skepticism about the other as well as putting one's own cards on the table. The hospitable scholar does not shrink from allowing his or her inadequacies, frailties, and other personal weaknesses to surface. Yet he or she does not dwell in these frailties, self-consciously calling attention to them. Energies are directed toward attending to the other. This does not require surrendering to the other, to manipulation, or to acquiescing in an identity that the other creates for oneself. It certainly does not mean gullibility. Hospitality requires critical examination of all positions as well as scrupulous honesty about who one is and the standards one honors.

We can use the image of "passing over" to characterize hospitable efforts to understand the other as a concrete individual, rather than an abstraction or projection. The point in passing over is imaginatively to see things from the other's perspective. It is to suspend assimilating the other to our frame of reference or projecting our frame upon the other. It is to immerse ourselves in the other's culture and concepts, to learn the other's standpoint and intent. To pass over is to adopt for a time this different perspective and the insights it offers—and then to come back with an enriched understanding about ourselves.

Passing over to respectful engagement with the other—practicing neither indifference nor aggressive attack—requires suspending initial suspicions and attending in order to hear, not to devise a clever or argumentative response. Feigned openness does not work—others see through that pretty quickly. But respectful engagement can be difficult, requiring courageous honesty about our own position and its support. Letting go of uncritical loyalty to our own habits is essential. Bernard Loomer (1976) observes that the authentically relational self "makes his claims and expresses his concerns in such a style as to enable the other to make his largest contribution to the relationship" (p. 27).

Dwelling in the narratives and artistic images of the other can be helpful in securing imaginative access, in challenging evasions, and in generating recognition of commonalities without sacrificing respect for separateness and privacy. Throughout, the attitude we display toward the other helps create his or her response to us. As Nouwen (1975) reminds us, "a good host is the one who believes that his guest is carrying a promise he wants to reveal to anyone who shows a genuine interest" (p. 87).

Attending

The work of Simone Weil is notable for its explanation of what it means to attend. Paying attention, she says, involves putting to the side the presentation and defense of our own position in order truly to hear the other.

> Attention consists of suspending our thought, leaving it detached, empty, and ready to be penetrated by the object; it means holding in our minds, within reach of this thought, but

on a lower level and not in contact with it, the diverse knowledge we have acquired. (Weil, 1951, p. 111)

This kind of attention requires what Parker Palmer (1983) calls "the discipline of displacement" (pp. 115–116). It involves holding one's own position in abeyance, while listening intently and receptively to the other. It
means letting go our inner preoccupations as well—developing an inner
silence that allows the other to be heard.

Of course, we cannot literally leave our experiences behind. They are
part of who we are. But we can work to keep them on a lower level—
suspending, not suppressing, what we think. The point is to understand
the other in his or her terms, not our own. Attending is not a debate,
where one seeks to uncover weakness in order to attack. Agonism and
oppositional thinking are antithetical to genuine attention. The objective
is to grasp the inner rationale, to see in new ways what commends the
other's way of thinking and doing. In both teaching and scholarship, we
need to see the other not as a pristine object, but rather as an "other" with
whom we are in relationship. The person is not at our disposal. We recognize the polyvalence of this process—the multiplicity of meanings it
bears—as well as the variety of possible perspectives upon it. And we ask
about our own openness to this wealth of perspectives—our willingness
to enter into genuine conversation rather than to project our position or
to remain indifferent.

A Shallow Inclusivity

We must attend to the other's particularity before thoughtlessly appropriating symbols or ideas. Without taking time to study and understand the
other, borrowing really is a form of theft (Hunt, 1994). It fails to show
respect for the integrity of the experiences in which the borrowed symbols
and ideas are embedded. Hunt distinguishes between petty theft, "the use
of materials and sources without contextualizing or nuancing," and what
she calls "grand larceny, the wholesale taking over of people's ideas without any regard for the integrity of the work itself" (p. 106). Among the
examples of the latter that Hunt provides is "the endless repetitions of the
name and work of Alice Walker, as if somehow just quoting Alice Walker
will chase away the problem of racism" (p. 106). This kind of borrowing
is a "misuse of another's intellectual property" (Hunt, 1994, p. 106). It is
a violation of academic ethics. It turns an authentic pluralism into a shallow inclusivity and spirituality.

An important part of attending to the other is determining what is potentially worthy of respect. We must open ourselves to claims that the humanity of others lays upon us, but practicing openness to everyone means dwelling in superficialities. Refusing to recognize our own limits and finitude—trying to be open to everything and everybody at all times—is a form of arrogance and insistent individualism. Here too letting go our need for control is essential. In both teaching and learning, attending can mean listening and waiting for something—not treating it as an object to be analyzed and dominated, but as something that may stand as teacher in relation to us. When this happens, attending to the other may reveal value where we had not seen or known it before. Attending may also help us hold on to values when our grip is loosening.

Critical Evaluation

Being hospitable does not mean dwelling in heightened self-consciousness. It *does* require abandoning the protective personas and shrillness that often characterize debate. Intellectual hospitality also calls for clear and thoughtful articulation of standards, both as a courtesy to others and to determine our faithfulness to such norms—even as it prompts consideration of their adequacy. Indeed, practicing hospitality involves presenting the best defense we can of our own position—out of respect for ourselves as well as the other.

We are responsible for our own actions, endorsements, and criticisms. Hospitality demands that reasonableness, not social status or power, determine conclusions and decisions. But part of our evaluation of what we bring back could well include precisely what the other has taught us about how to judge. Unless it is mere carping, difference or dissent is always in the service of a view that is potentially more fruitful, cogent, coherent, or in other ways more satisfying. For that reason, an important part of practicing hospitality is listening to others who have had our otherness imposed upon their self-understanding. Many in majority or privileged classes have now (finally) come to see the importance of allowing women, non-Europeans, and others to speak for themselves. When this happens, we may be chastened by the other, becoming more aware of the complexity of the human condition.

Only after this initial process of sharing and receiving is under way is it appropriate to provide feedback and critical comment on the positions exchanged. This second stage presupposes the first and intends neither destruction of a position nor conversion of the other, but rather joint testing with the expectation that insights new to both parties may emerge. It is in subsequent dialogue that the rights of the self and the other are clarified and adjudicated. Critical reasoning is required of all participants in the conversation. A major question is whether what is believed is *worthy* of belief. We must evaluate the standards of others, but also engage the difficult task of questioning our own preunderstandings, standards, and behaviors. Most of the time, more precise agreements will eventually emerge, perhaps only after considerable exchange and searching examination.

Disagreements

In passing over we may discover deep-seated disagreements. When this happens, we need to fashion ideas about common purpose in the midst of conflicts over meaning. The point is not that all cultural values are equal—or incomparable. In reflecting on multiculturalism and the imperative of a scholarship of dialectical reconciliation, Charles Taylor (1992) observes that "real judgments of worth suppose a fused horizon of standards. . . . they suppose that we have been transformed by the study of the other, so that we are not simply judging by our original familiar standards" (p. 66).

Our goal should be to identify "certain norms and procedures as imperative to a life in common, norms and procedures that do not stipulate a purpose, but that provide a just procedure for arriving at a common purpose" (Anderson, 1993, p. 143). This may not be possible in some cases. Deep cultural differences may mean that we do not yet have a life sufficiently in common, and may not for the foreseeable future. At other times, our disagreements are about the nature of things. Here too the path of hospitality is commitment to further deliberation and investigation, seeking agreement on procedures that might allow us to come to a common view on the relevant nature of things—though also knowing that the time or circumstances may not yet be ripe.

Of course, in passing over we must be prepared not only for a lengthy process of interaction but also for the possibility that self-giving will be met not by reciprocal self-giving, but by refusal. Sometimes the invitation to reciprocate will be met by anger and resentment at having been ignored, marginalized, or manipulated in the past. Sometimes, too, when we share hospitality we do receive it—but not as we expected, and perhaps not from those to whom we extended it. In any case, "coming back" means returning to one's original standpoint, enriched now by the perspective of the other. In a literal sense, one's original standpoint is no more, or at least no longer the same, for it has been altered by the new understanding.

Unless one is able to seek and receive from the other, all that remains is simply a display of unidirectional power. At its worst, this is rightly seen as ugly and arrogant—refusing to allow another to help, or even to acknowledge the capacity of another to help. These are forms of control. For the hospitable scholar, however, coming back means that a new perspective on the humanity one shares with the other is now available. Since the humanity is at least partially shared and common, one now knows more about oneself in knowing more about the other. Something has been added to the original standpoint, extending and potentially transforming it. The limits of the original understanding have been transcended.

Genuine hospitality stands in contrast to the domesticated version wherein the other to whom we extend openness is already well-known. Our canon is sometimes domesticated in this way—reflecting both appropriate celebration *and* unimaginative exclusions of human excellence. At other times we pay attention to what we do *not* know, and neglect a searching examination of the familiar. The foreign and esoteric challenge us, whereas that which we think we already know may not—unless we see it from a different perspective, such as trying to explain it to the stranger. However they occur, such acts are always forms of recognizing and affirming the worth and humanity of others and expressing commitment to an enlarged common good.

As the cardinal virtue for the academy, hospitality is required, independent of personal generosity. Rosemary Haughton (1997) reminds us that the concept of hospitality

> codifies the human desire to cross boundaries, to meet, to experience compassion and act on it. The codification is important because it does not negate the generosity, but removes it from the sense that the human acceptance, the sacrifice, the *giving* are one-sided and greatly to the moral credit of the giver. There is no special moral credit in doing what a common humanity requires and the human soul naturally craves. (p. 144)

This takes the issue of practicing hospitality away from the narrow frames of moralistic preoccupations and locates it as a way of proving and keeping oneself worthy of his or her humanity.

SOME ASSOCIATED VIRTUES

Without an ethic of hospitality (and the community of inquiry which it makes possible), scholarship borders on parochialism, teaching is reduced to credentialing, and learning comes close to the receipt of information without internal impact. Education resembles a mechanical interaction— an exchange of information and credentials for tuition dollars. But hospitality hardly stands alone as a necessary academic virtue. Related virtues complement and fill it out. Three in particular have been held up for attention by the Carnegie Foundation for the Advancement of Teaching. These are the scholarly virtues of integrity, perseverance, and courage. They provide additional perspective upon the complexity of educating, even though they seem inadequate apart from the context that hospitality provides.

After considering them, I explore four additional practices that link the academy to traditions emphasizing self-reflection. These are the practices of providing testimony, exercising discernment, displaying humility, and extending forgiveness. None of these virtues is independent of hospitality or stands over against it. Rather they are implicit within the practice of hospitality. Depending upon the context and the issue, they become prominent elements.

The Carnegie Foundation Report

Glassick, Huber, and Maeroff's (1997) *Scholarship Assessed: Evaluation of the Professoriate* reviews the qualities as well as the character of a scholar. The authors note our common professional expectations that competencies be maintained, neglect of duty rebuked, and misconduct censured, but they go further by suggesting the importance of coherence between the professional and personal lives of scholars. They argue that more attention should be paid to identifying and cultivating personal qualities important to being scholars.

In particular, they hold up integrity, perseverance, and courage— three virtues characteristic of any scholar/teacher we admire. In emphasizing them as critical personal qualities, the report provides a breath of fresh air and a significant reminder about the importance of ethics and spirituality for the academy. Glassick, Huber, and Maeroff (1997) do note that linking scholarship and personal qualities "invites the possibility of bias" (p. 61). And, unfortunately, some personnel decisions have in fact involved elements of racial, gender, religious, or political discrimination. But, by definition, those decisions were biased because they included inappropriate personal considerations that had no connection with the merits of instructional accomplishment. The personal virtues and practices we are considering *are* connected with educational achievement. Far from being inappropriate or irrelevant, they underlie education. Despite insistent individualism, the scholarly community has at base always agreed that integrity, perseverance, and courage are foundational.

For example, prior to the Carnegie report, Wayne Booth (1988) argued that various personal qualities are at the heart of a scholar's professional life; namely, honesty, courage, persistence, consideration, and humility. These virtues or traits are essential to the scholar's intellectual calling. Far from opening the work of the academy to bias, fidelity to them combats bias and assures that the trust society invests in the academy is well placed. We could name and number these virtues differently, but they are all related to hospitality, giving it definition and character. Thus, hospitality involves integrity, for its very practice requires trustworthiness, sincerity, and honesty. It entails perseverance, for to be hospitable is consistently rather than episodically to commit to intellectual openness. And it requires courage, for being hospitable means accepting vulnerability, and in some situations risking embarrassment and ridicule.

Integrity. Integrity involves harmony between how I present myself and who I actually am. The point is not to craft *personas* for teaching, scholarship, and leadership that I then abandon as cost and convenience suggest. Nor, in other situations, do I accept *personas* fashioned for me by others who also change as winds shift. Rather, as a result of my honesty, others can trust what I say and do. I practice hospitality in ways that are fair in my dealings with others and neither manipulate nor dissemble. Without integrity, hospitality deteriorates and becomes a façade of openness and fidelity. The sciences illustrate how deeply integrity is embedded in the protocols employed for replication of announced findings. Fabrication and falsification compromise and corrupt the process, but eventually so do even slight embellishments or omissions.

Practicing integrity requires not only being trustworthy and having the courage to present oneself honestly, but also may demand openness about relevant uncertainties and anxieties. This commitment foils the self-protection ingrained by insistent individualism. When integrity and courage are present, even adversity can make us more honest. Most of us, though, are tempted to dwell in the values we espouse rather than address the differences between them and our behaviors. Gaps between what we tell others (and ourselves) about who we really are, and what our behaviors disclose about us, signal a lack of integrity. Others are needed to help us see these gaps and summon the fortitude to correct them.

Perseverance. Likewise, perseverance is a fundamental academic virtue, necessary for the scholarly life and the advancement of learning. Glassick, Huber, and Maeroff (1997) rightly observe that "colleges and universities cannot afford to waste valuable appointments on people who abandon scholarship once they win long-term employment" (p. 64). Tenure suggests a position of sinecure—literally a position "without care." It presupposes a tenacious commitment to continued learning. The report cites with approval Booth's (1988) observation that in an ideal university, there should be only one criterion in considering applicants for tenure or promotion: "Is this candidate *still curious*, still inquiring . . . and is it thus probable that at the age of forty, fifty, or sixty-six, he or she will still be vigorously inquiring?" (p. 329).

There is a connection between perseverance and faith. One needs to trust that the conditions for sustained inquiry will continue, that hospitality will be practiced, and community deepened. Supported by this faith, persistence in improving teaching and in pursuing new inquiries becomes possible. The surrounding culture can either help or distract us from the single-mindedness that commitment to learning requires. Booth's (1988) observation of years ago still applies:

> living in a world increasingly jumpy—a hopping, a salutatory world where everyone changes neighborhoods, spouses, professions, and crises almost as fast as she can flick the dial to a new program—the scholar necessarily digs in deep and long. (p. 70)

But both Booth and the Carnegie Report fail to emphasize the centrality of perseverance in the *collective* support of learning. For instance, current movements toward periodic review of tenured and long-term faculty need to place greater emphasis upon this commitment to the communal aspect of the academy. Although individual tenacity is important in making one's own contribution, tenacious and hospitable support of the learning of others is equally essential. Indeed, a key service responsibility of educators is to support the collective effort, acknowledging that one's own contribution is only a part.

Courage. In a similar way, courage in the pursuit of learning requires the strength to risk the disapproval of less imaginative colleagues. Courageous individuals review familiar knowledge and traditions, and examine novel, even alien, approaches. Booth notes two kinds of threats that courageous scholars and teachers face. On the one side, "the scholar must be willing to face conclusions that destroy her own intellectual comfort—conclusions that she 'personally' would rather not believe" (Booth, 1988, p. 70). These conclusions may run against longstanding political or religious convictions. They may push one from membership in some postmodernist clique into the conservatism of the National Academy of Scholars—or vice versa. Second, in addition to facing threats to intellectual comfort, a scholar needs courage to "profess conclusions that go against her interests in the world" (Booth, 1988, p. 70). These conclusions may upset the laboriously constructed corpus upon which a scholarly reputation rests.

The authors of the Carnegie Report also suggest that courage in academe requires the willingness to share ideas in the public arena. "Scholars must possess the courage of their convictions so that their work ends up feeding the debates of the day" (Glassick, Huber, & Maeroff, 1997, p. 66). Although the report does not push the point, sharing ideas more publicly requires a willingness to write for the public—to abandon the comfort of familiar, but exclusive, jargon and to pursue the task of finding a broader, more accessible vocabulary. And the virtue of courage also extends to supporting others who pursue unpopular, controversial, or nontraditional approaches or topics. The advancement of learning is a profoundly social enterprise and the practice of hospitality as openness in sharing and receiving is fundamental in all one does as scholar and teacher. Integrity, perseverance, and courage are important parts of hospitality, not substitutes for it.

The strength of the Carnegie Report is its forthrightness in identifying the moral foundations of higher education. The report reminds us in fresh ways that in addition to competence, and inseparable from it, is conscience. "Scholarship has a moral aspect that should figure in all of its dimensions: discovery, teaching, integration, and application" (Glassick, Huber, & Maeroff, 1997, p. 67). And beyond scholarship itself, there is service and teaching with their multiplicity of forms and ethical dimensions. "The university, for all of its concern about the intellect, must never lose sight of the ethical imperative by which it should be guided" (Glassick, Huber, & Maeroff, 1997, p. 67).

The weakness of the Carnegie Foundation report (and to a lesser degree Booth's work) is that the virtues of integrity, perseverance, or courage—individually or collectively—do not go far enough in pointing to the prior hospitality and openness to others essential for a community of learners. After all, one might display integrity with respect to one's own work and yet be complacent and uninterested in others'. One can be scrupulously trustworthy in respecting findings reported and methods utilized, and still be a reluctant participant in wider discussions. And critics hold that the sad mark of much academic writing is a restricted discourse that excludes a wider public.

The incompleteness of *Scholarship Assessed* and other reports like it is evident in the potential individualistic uses of the virtues upheld. Integrity, perseverance, and courage can be used instrumentally to advance the well-being of the individual or his or her community at the expense of others. This tacit instrumentalism of the virtuous character is especially ironic given the broader communal context necessary for the advancement of learning. In a time of radically increased pluralism, we need to identify common resources for our work—not ones that separate and isolate us.

What we need is clearer recognition that these virtues, and the character they describe, promote the well-being of others as well as that of the self. What we need is a deeper awareness and statement of the important connection of integrity, perseverance, and courage to hospitality and the academic life. And we need more attention to actually practicing hospitality. Only then do we advance the ethical grounding of the academy and the more holistic spirituality associated with it.

Virtues of Self-Reflection

Healthy, hospitable collegia also engage practices that have been hallmarks of religious traditions of both East and West. Among these practices are virtues such as providing testimony, exercising discernment, displaying humility, and extending forgiveness.[2]

Providing testimony. Both teachers and researchers provide testimony about what is reliable and trustworthy. They attest to the importance of their intellectual methods and subjects. Their stamina and persistence, as well as passion and commitment, speak volumes. Academic testimony is linked to hospitality when it combines authentic expression of personal commitments with sensitivity to the positions, experiences, and preoccupations of others.

Testimony in the academy must be supported with evidence, and offered with the expectation that others will respond through questions, criticism, validation, and expansion of the points at issue. Because most faculty like to talk, some of their testimony can be tiresome.[3] But at its best, academic testimony is hospitable, forthright, and complete. It identifies levels of support and separates settled from disputed issues. It acknowledges opposing positions rather than hiding adverse evidence. It is generous as well, displaying charitableness on disputed issues and imputing to others positive rather than negative motives where the available evidence is ambiguous. And it invites others to reciprocate.

Some academic testimony remains slanted toward our insistently individualistic needs for self-inflation. We know about the tendency of some to exaggerate their research or job prospects. Manuscripts can remain in preparation, being fine-tuned, or "under review" someplace almost in perpetuity. And a colleague can report turning down an endowed chair elsewhere—when in fact all that was rejected was an invitation to be a candidate. This immodesty flies in the face of the academy's proclaimed dedication to truth. And it reflects the unhealthy pressures to perform about which Jane Tompkins wrote.

The academy is rich in other forms of testimony—particularly about colleagues. Confidential peer review can provide frank, fair, and balanced judgments, though it can also be used in partisan ways, reflecting contentious disputes or personality conflicts. Likewise, the language of deans and other administrators can be exemplary or it can mirror the unhealthy devaluation of academic administrators by faculty. As Patricia Plante (1990) describes the latter,

> one will claim that he did not really seek to be a dean, but agreed to bear this cross for the sake of his beloved college. Another wishes that the cup of the vice presidency had not been offered, but will drink it to the dregs since she made the mistake of lifting it to lips that were reluctant to begin with. (p. 27)

This is ironic testimony that the core of an institution *is* its teaching and research activities, not its administrative functions. Yet, it is poignant that administrators feel it necessary to apologize for a function essential to the success of the educational core.

Exercising discernment. Academic testimony also involves discernment by those providing and receiving it. Much of this relates to self-examination. Do I desire to offer edification to others—or to promote myself under the guise of humility? Am I hearing rather than imposing patterns of meaning? Am I prepared to credit and nourish another's idea or truth claims, even when poorly expressed or when I am vested in a contrary position? Am I prepared to attend to the other as Simone Weil suggested—am I willing to hold my own position in abeyance?

This kind of self-examination prompts me to attend to the sources of my sensibilities. Where did I get my sense of virtue and vice? What roles were played by my family and friends, by teachers I had, by the literature and philosophies I studied? How have my experiences within the academy formed me for good and for ill? Discernment requires testing my behaviors and examining whether my sense of right and wrong is sound. It involves what is often called contemplation.

Discernment also calls educators to reject often unquestioned, but patently inadequate mythologies about academic leadership, such as the following:

> Those who choose to devote their professional lives to teaching and research do so for motives that transcend the self. Those who decide to spend their careers engaged in management, broadly defined so as to include leadership, do so for reasons that center on self. (Plante, 1990, p. 28)

Likewise, class consciousness and hierarchies among disciplines and institutions beg for sober introspection. There is more than a grain of truth in the comment that "mathematicians sneer at the work done by recreational therapists; epidemiologists refuse offices in the school of nursing; industrial engineers speak patronizingly about the research of industrial technologists; and philosophers question the propriety of giving academic rank to ballet masters" (Plante, 1990, p. 28). Discernment requires that judgments be based on the quality of reasoning and learning, not on social reputation, discipline, or standing.

Accordingly, discernment presupposes adequate understanding of an area of inquiry and its connections with other subjects. It requires familiarity with established protocols, and the ability to judge whether received methodologies are adequate to the material at hand—and vice versa. Exercising discernment entails judging what counts as relevant support and what does not. The reflexive character of learning is always in play. How in this context am I to use my skills and my learning to practice openness to others—to their perspectives, ideas, and concerns? What kind of testimony is appropriate in order for me to act with integrity and courage?

Displaying humility. Unfortunately, academics are known more for arrogance than humility. Exaggerated self-esteem blocks awareness of the need to wear our knowledge lightly—to cultivate the virtue of humility and to see its links to both testimony and discernment. We violate this virtue by making overreaching or inadequately substantiated claims, as well as by refusing to admit contrary claims and positions as potentially authoritative. We violate it with customs that credit coauthorship when all that is warranted is a simple acknowledgement of assistance. Humility involves rejoicing at others' successes, perhaps declining to claim credit even where warranted, admitting past mistakes, and attending to neglected or marginalized colleagues. It means enlisting the other in collaborative pursuit of truth. Humility is part of the openness of hospitality—attending to the other rather than dwelling on the self. It has nothing to do with self-abasement.

The humble person knows that the strangers to whom hospitality should be offered may be the "undocumented" workers—at the margins of the academic enterprise, colleagues who lack prestigious credentials or belong to the "wrong" group, as well as the legions of adjunct and part-time professors. Stories of the oppression of graduate students are too common—the good of the supervisor rather than the student prevails. Other examples of academic marginalization feature disciplines consigned to the bottom rung of the hierarchy of prestige—often those that stress application rather than theory, or pedagogy rather than content. As noted, educators at teaching rather than research institutions often carry burdens levied simply by their location. And at almost all institutions the full protections of academic freedom granted by tenure shield some senior oppressors, but may be denied adjunct and junior faculty.

Extending forgiveness. Persons who practice hospitality are also likely to forgive and to ask for forgiveness from others. All of us can be trapped by history's burdens—by what we have done and what has been done to us. Forgiveness is not forgetfulness of the past, but imaginative identification of new ways to live into the future. When we fail to release anger and resentment over past injuries, we give those who hurt us inappropriate and unnecessary power. And we continue to hurt ourselves, for the ongoing denial of past realities requires the denial of these past denials—compounding our burdens.

Practicing forgiveness means refusing to dwell in the past, choosing rather to embrace a new future. Giving and receiving forgiveness brings healing and new hope amidst the ashes of defeat and pain—through reclaiming, reframing, and revisioning fundamental values. The academy is not known for ready forgiveness. In some circumstances time seems only to have heightened hurt feelings, not reduced or relieved them. Resentments over past conflicts and perceived injustices linger for years and then suddenly surface.

In sum, it requires discipline and effort to acquire and practice these virtues. By definition, success is always partial. However, practicing the full range of hospitality is life-giving. It takes us beyond the routine and the narrow. It delivers us from the fear of the other as well as the conflict and protectionism that sap the vitality of the academy. It takes us out of the fear of failure as well—the fear of repeating past disappointments and remaining trapped in combat. Of course, I am describing the ideal— something that by definition is never fully met. Hospitality will always be a goal. But without such a standard of excellence, we have only the deceptive attractions of insistent individualism. Given the connectedness and relational character of reality, denial of hospitality in one arena ripples out with negative effects elsewhere.

CONCLUSION

The concepts I have been urging highlight the self as relational rather than autonomous. Who we are is a function of relationships that constitute us rather than of the controlling and distancing barriers we erect. The relational self reminds us of the richness that others can contribute and teaches us how important the academic community can be as a context in which we contribute to and receive from others. When the community to which we belong is healthy, when there is mutual interaction and support, when there is hospitality in sharing and receiving resources, insights, and criticism—then the good of the whole is pursued in ways that embrace the goods of the member selves in a quest for mutual fulfillment.

The virtues we have examined promote this openness, but they have to be learned, cultivated, and shared. They are not mere expressions of feeling. They have cognitive significance, are important guides to learning, and correlate importantly with the increase of knowledge. Equally, they have ethical punch and give shape and texture to our spiritualities.

Relationships that approach the level of mutuality and reciprocity of intellectual interest and exchange for which I am calling may be rare. But with desire, discipline, and effort more could occur. Despite its marginalization, academic hospitality remains fundamental to the work of the academy—to the pursuit, enlargement, and sharing of learning.

REFERENCES

Anderson, C. W. (1993). *Prescribing the life of the mind: An essay on the purpose of the university, the aims of liberal education, the competence of citizens, and the cultivation of practical reason.* Madison, WI: University of Wisconsin Press.

Bass, D. (Ed.). (1997). *Practicing our faith: A way of life for a searching people.* San Francisco, CA: Jossey-Bass.

Bennett, J. B. (1998). *Collegial professionalism: The academy, individualism, and the common good.* Phoenix, AZ: American Council on Education/Oryx Press.

Booth, W. C. (1988). *The vocation of a teacher: Rhetorical occasions 1967–1988.* Chicago, IL: University of Chicago Press.

Damrosch, D. (1995). *We scholars: Changing the culture of the university.* Cambridge, MA: Harvard University Press.

Glassick, C. E., Huber, M. T., & Maeroff, G. I. (1997). *Scholarship assessed: Evaluation of the professoriate.* San Francisco, CA: Jossey-Bass.

Gonzalez, V., & Lopez, E. (2001, April). The age of incivility: Countering disruptive behavior in the classroom. *AAHE Bulletin, 53* (8), 3–6.

Haughton, R. L. (1997). *Images for change: The transformation of society.* Mahwah, NJ: Paulist Press.

Hunt, M. E. (1994). Commentary. In L. K. Daly (Ed.), *Feminist theological ethics* (pp. 104–107). Louisville, KY: Westminster John Knox Press.

Loomer, B. (1976, Spring). Two kinds of power. *Process Studies, 6* (1), 5–32.

Nouwen, H. M. (1975). *Reaching out: Three movements of the spiritual life.* Garden City, NJ: Doubleday and Company.

Palmer, P. J. (1983). *To know as we are known: Education as a spiritual journey.* San Francisco, CA: Harper and Row.

Palmer, P. J. (1997, September). The grace of great things: Reclaiming the sacred in knowing, teaching, and learning. *The Holistic Education Review, 10* (3), 8–16.

Plante, P. (1990, Winter). An administrator will yearn for the classroom: Myth or reality? *Educational Record, 71* (1), 27–30.

Rosovsky, H. (1990). *The university: An owner's manual.* New York, NY: W. W. Norton.

Schneider, A. (1998, March 27). Insubordination and intimidation signal the end of decorum in many classrooms. *The Chronicle of Higher Education,* p. A12.

Taylor, C. (1992). The politics of recognition. In A. Gutman (Ed.), *Multiculturalism and the politics of recognition* (pp. 25–73). Princeton, NJ: Princeton University Press.

Trout, P. A. (1998, July 24). Incivility in the classroom breeds 'education lite.' *The Chronicle of Higher Education,* p. A40.

Veysey, L. (1965). *The emergence of the American university.* Chicago, IL: University of Chicago Press.

Weil, S. (1951). *Waiting for God* (E. Craufurd, Trans.). New York, NY: Harper and Row.

ENDNOTES

1. For an example, see Henry Rosovsky's (1990) argument. A former Harvard Dean, Rosovsky speaks of the tenured faculty as an "extended family" (p. 184) and suggests that "a good academic department should resemble a family: supportive, guiding, and nurturing" (p. 176). For the reasons I suggest, "family" seems a misleading metaphor in this context. In addition, see my earlier book for comments on Rosovsky's appeal to entertainment and business metaphors and his comparison of university faculty to a sports team (Bennett, 1998, pp. 86–88).

2. Dorothy Bass (1997) has edited a collection of essays on selected Christian religious practices. Many of the virtues applauded in her volume are also embraced in other religious traditions.

3. One is reminded of William James' observation: "What an awful trade that of the professor is—paid to talk, talk, talk! . . . It would be an awful universe if *everything* could be converted into words, words, words" (Veysey, 1965, p. 420).

Self, Others, Institutions, and the Common Good 4

Being hospitable is cooperating with what we most deeply are—interconnected. It is acting in accordance with our ontological reality—recognizing, admitting, embracing, and celebrating our relatedness. It is accepting and dwelling in the richness and the vulnerability that comes from our deepest reality, rather than wasting ourselves in ironic self-renunciation.

This chapter explores specific ways of becoming more hospitable. The first section considers the relationship between the professional and the personal. I examine several ways of understanding this connection, and I explore the importance of recovering our personal past. Healthy academic spiritualities involve living out of hospitality, and I propose several additional spiritual practices that strengthen hospitable living.

In subsequent sections, I consider the relationship between the self and others in terms of implications for the common good and the nature of academic citizenship and collegial professionalism. This in turn brings us to institutional hospitality and I present suggestions on how it can be strengthened in a time of rapid technological and socioeconomic change.

UNCOVERING DEEPER SELFHOOD

If education is more than transmission of information, must not the educator be more than transmitter? Should not educators order their lives differently precisely because of being educators—of being called, not simply recruited, to *this* vocation? Indeed, must we not move closer to the notion that *who* educators are and how they integrate their personal and professional selves affect how well they educate? Should we not only develop appropriate character but also hire and evaluate others for character as well as for content mastery and delivery skills? These are large and complex issues rarely addressed by the academy. But reflecting on the nature of authentic and integrated character is especially important today given the variety of educators and the pervasiveness of the market ethos.

I am not proposing a litmus test for educational integrity—there is no one uniform to wear or ritual to observe. Hospitable educators come in all sizes and shapes. However, academic work cannot be a matter of personal indifference. Since we form ourselves through work, one job is not as good as the next. The centrality of the market orientation obscures this reality. As Robert Bellah (1998) notes,

> not long ago professions were understood as the social roles in which occupation and vocation combined. One committed one's whole self to the profession. Character and spirit were as relevant to professional practice as knowledge and technical skills. . . . [A] profession was what one was as much as what one *did.* (p. 94)

Now, however,

> professionals are viewed as vendors of highly specialized services. The profession is considered not an identity but a marketable capacity, to be sold to the highest bidder. A person's character and commitments and the larger purpose of his or her life are irrelevant. . . . vocation and commitment have been uncoupled. (Bellah, 1998, p. 95)

This uncoupling, this disconnecting, is another expression and consequence of insistent individualism.

To separate the personal from the professional sequesters the gifts of practicing hospitality, preventing them from internal impact on the self. It also keeps personal talents and experience from enriching professional activities or providing them unique expression. These are educational liabilities. Divorcing professional learning from self-understanding and personal identity reduces learning to something mechanical, a procedure for credentialing. Learning is valued for its utility but not inwardly treasured. It is not something with inherent significance for the questing, wondering inner self, or vice versa.

Two Examples

James Elkins provides one example. He reports on surveys asking whether art historians are moved to tears by paintings they study. Many seem unable to encounter paintings "with full emotion and an open heart" (Elkins, 2001, p. B7). Some art historians regret this situation, but most consider it professionally necessary or inevitable. Elkins himself suggests that the accumulation of theories and facts stands in the way. Studying the ideas and theories of other art historians can bring broader understanding, but it does so only by taking "the rough edges off of experience" (Elkins, 2001, p. B7). Doing research before looking at an image is like taking tranquilizers—it inserts buffers between person and image, dulling the encounter and altering the relationship. Theories and facts become "shields against first-hand experience" (Elkins, 2001, p. B7).

Many art historians, and Elkins includes himself, are keeping their tears at bay. As a consequence, his profession produces "students who think crying is more or less out of the question, an embarrassment, an irrelevancy, something for neophytes, a breach of decorum, a sign of immaturity" (Elkins, 2001, p. B10). Pictures can be fascinating and challenging—but they matter to one's work, not one's life. This diminishing effect does not occur all at once. It is a slow process.

> By imperceptible steps, art history gently drains away a painting's sheer wordless visceral force, turning it into an occasion for intellectual debate. What was once an astonishing object, thick with the capacity to mesmerize, becomes . . . the object of a scholar's myopic expertise. (Elkins, 2001, p. B8)

Elkins is not happy with this state of affairs and with good reason. Something is wrong. We should distinguish in order to unite—attend to the other in order to return to an enriched self. Informed attention to the other ought to *increase* sensitivity, not "smother our capacity to really *feel*" (Elkins, 2001, p. B8). The theories and facts of the academy should assist, not impede, attention to the other. By fostering atomism and fragmentation, the academy has encouraged the smothering and dulling of experiences. Only by separating the professional from the personal could the majority of Elkins' respondents have led him to conclude that "tearlessness is a criterion of good scholarship" (p. B8).

It may be that Elkins is being ironic—perhaps spoofing his profession, and the broader academy. There are passages suggesting an indirectness, even a tongue-in-cheek posture. The broader point, though, is whether academic professionals can (or should) experience strong emotion in front of significant art. Whether serious or ironic, Elkins' essay illustrates the importance of putting personal and professional, inner and public, lives into relationship.

There are other species of tearlessness within the academy. Viewing literature solely through the lens of theory is a prominent example. Lisa Ruddick (2001) notes that "for years, literary scholarship has been refining the art of stepping away from humane connection" and its sustaining values (p. B7f.). She thinks other academics also judge intellectual life to be "dry and unnourishing" (Ruddick, 2001, p. B7f.). But they do so privately. They are reluctant to write or speak on the importance of sustaining humane values for fear of breaching professional norms, thus "courting disgrace" (Ruddick, 2001, p. B7f.). Like the art historians Elkins writes about, English and comparative literature professors often separate their personal and professional lives. Ruddick reports: "[I had] to hide or smuggle in my convictions about what sustains people—my faith, for example, in some quality of shared humanity that makes literary experience meaningful" (p. B8). She was afraid of being attacked by colleagues for violating prevailing taboos against subscribing to "shared features that constitute the essence of being human" (Ruddick, 2001, p. B8). The ultimate result, is a "self-loss," a kind of "systematic demoralization" (Ruddick, 2001, p. B8).

This pattern occurs throughout the academy. The student of law can, without professional expense, be inwardly indifferent to matters of justice; the Holocaust scholar, personally unshaken by the human capacity for evil; the ecologist, indifferent to his or her own patterns of consumption; the musicologist, intellectually engaged but personally unresponsive when listening to music. Separating the personal and the professional can lead instructors to claim that intimate relations with students do not compromise the trust involved. Dividing things in this way does not uphold objectivity—the judicious perspective for which scholars aim. Rather, it suggests a personal indifference to the very values at issue.

A bifurcated self induces what Ruddick (2001) terms "a subtle spiritual depletion" (p. B8). Persons as unified moral and intellectual agents are ill-served by separating work and self. Our vocations are integral parts of our identities and cannot be artificially cordoned off. Our reluctance to apply our learning to ourselves turns us into modern sophists. When we brush aside our public credo that pursuit of knowledge for its own sake liberates, we diminish ourselves as well as our claims to advance truth. Likewise, our professional lives remain spare apart from our personal compassion or our commitment to a shared humanity. Our experiences of growth and development as human beings influence what, why, and how we study and teach—and the accomplishments we achieve.

If separating the personal and the professional doesn't serve integrated selves, neither does collapsing the one into the other. Denying one's selfhood by stripping oneself of everything distinctively personal doesn't advance professionalism. The gifts and talents of distinctive experience and personhood languish, much as forbidding one's native tongue in work or school reduces the contributions one can make. This stripping creates an arid one-dimensionality, devoid of the intellectual and emotional complexity that pursuit of knowledge promises. Whatever objectivity one may be promoting becomes deceptive and thin. The values of the examined life for which Socrates argued disappear for lack of a life to examine.

Alternatively, collapsing the professional into the personal generates another kind of insistent individualism—perhaps even a dilettantism—in conflict with the discipline that pursuit of knowledge requires. There can be no Socratic examination worth the name in this kind of self-indulgent life. Developing hospitality requires that one balance and integrate the personal and professional. The point is not that one should bring all of one's work home—nor, of course, that one should bring all of home to work. The point, rather, is that these two aspects of our lives need to be in regular conversation. We are different personally because of what we know. And personal openness to who we are allows our professionalism to flourish.

Hospitality to Self

Hospitable educators are thoughtful—in two senses. First, they are considerate, showing sensitivity and discretion about others' circumstances. They are also thoughtful because they are full of thoughts. They are reflective about the world, about life, about who they are. Being thoughtful about oneself involves understanding who one has become—pursuing a kind of self-possession that should be a goal of educator and educated alike. Bruce Wilshire (1990) notes that education involves a simple but basic assumption: the self cannot be divorced from its evaluation of itself. "Where do I stand in the world?" "What has my life amounted to?" "What might I become?" (p. xviif.). Part of our quest for fuller selfhood involves answering these questions by recovering and understanding our past.

It is human to forget who we have been and to deny who we have become. Practicing hospitality toward ourselves means reclaiming, not hiding from, earlier identities. Age dims memories. We forget the large role that sheer good luck played in our careers just as we block out some of the dreadful experiences of graduate school,[1] the exhausting rituals of job interviews, or the grueling battle for tenure. When this happens, younger faculty understandably view us as unsympathetic and jaded.[2] But even younger faculty can forget the anxieties of student lives.

Daniel Kowalsky (2001) reminds us of the various "professorial sins and transgressions" that make the lives of students miserable (¶1). He asks, "Did you ever seek solace in the office of your adviser, perhaps to discuss a major dissertation crisis, only to have him open and read his mail (or his e-mail) while you poured out your heart?" (¶2). Perhaps more widespread are the cancelled classes, the papers still ungraded weeks later, the "commandeering of the lecture schedule by a scattered mind . . . and, most painfully, those endless hours spent waiting outside office doors . . . hoping in vain that a professor would show up for his office hours" (Kowalsky, 2001, ¶3). Yet even junior faculty, only a few years removed from this misery, can duplicate these very behaviors.

When we practice hospitality toward ourselves, we reclaim and reevaluate earlier moments of regret and anxiety as well as happiness. Some of what we recover Parker Palmer (2000) calls "wearing other people's faces" (p. 13). Those were the times we lived divided lives—when we hid our authentic selves because of what we felt we should be or do, when we allowed important others to impose their values and career expectations. Even our pursuit of self-knowledge may have been guided by others' images of who we were, rather than by the realities of our own experience and identity. Our spiritualities were not our own. The personae we adopted, the protective masks and self-serving stories we created, allowed us to continue. But there was a price. Living inauthentically creates a divided life, with inadequate congruence between inner and outer. Remembering these moments with openness allows us to learn from them, to see more fulfilling alternatives—behaviors more appropriate to our best selves.

Practicing hospitality toward ourselves also means recovering happier moments. We can be recalled to experiences marked by joy and clarity about our professional callings and desires—experiences obscured over the years by battles with insistent individualists. We can reclaim earlier moments of exhilarating discovery and deep contentment with teaching and research. We can return even to childhood—reexperiencing both its loneliness as well as our sense of the sanctity of the world and the abandon and openness with which we embraced it. Like Jerome Miller (1994), we may jump back over the years and recall how simple acts like running were sacraments, sources of joy and oneness with reality.

We may then be led to reflect on our current sacraments in the academy. What are they? Do we remain in a calculating mode, grasping the tools and rituals of academe rather than abandoning ourselves to them? Do we control academic inquiry, making its results our private acquisitions—parceling them out to a few colleagues or the rare worthy student?

Or do we let go and lose ourselves in sharing? Do we regard our publications and awards as personal ornaments, symbols of our industry and intelligence, or as contributions to broader communal efforts on which we are dependent? The exercises to which we commit ourselves form us in different spiritualities.

SPIRITUAL PRACTICES[3]

It is easy to forget that inquiry can be a way of life and not simply a system of methods and concepts. For instance, Pierre Hadot (1995) reminds us that discourse about philosophy—about the meaning of life—should be secondary to living philosophy. Interpreting ancient Greek philosophers, Hadot argues that historically, philosophy was not primarily a theoretical, abstract activity, but a commitment to a mode of being. He traces this theme through the history of Western thought and concludes that practicing philosophy as a way of life means using abstract theories to justify and explicate a way of life, not to substitute for it. Our theories are in service of the examined life. They rationally justify our stance, reinforce it, and communicate it to others. They are secondary, not the main thing.

Hadot argues that philosophy as a way of life consists in the practices, activities, and conduct that he refers to as spiritual exercises. They can be communal. A Socratic dialogue can be a spiritual exercise when performed in common—pointing toward the need to change self-understandings and convictions, to alter ways of being. Spiritual exercises can also be individual, involving "inner discourse and . . . spiritual activity: meditation, dialogue with oneself, examination of conscience, exercises of the imagination" (Hadot, 1995, p. 31). The aim is to challenge—perhaps to change—one's point of view and choice of life. These exercises have both moral and existential value. However, from antiquity to the present, it has been easier and more common to dwell in philosophical discourse without "putting into question [one's] own life" (Hadot, 1995, p. 31). It is easier to think of philosophy—and education more generally—as *informing* people rather than helping to *form* them as human beings.

A healthy academic spirituality has recognizable features. They may be differently displayed, but they reflect common dimensions and struggles. We can use Hadot's concept of spiritual exercises to consider three practices for every educator: attending to the other, seeking self-knowledge, and practicing appropriate academic asceticism.

Attending to the Other

Perhaps the foundational spiritual exercise is attending to the other. As learners, we aim to uncover ideas and experiences—to unveil and reveal them. In the process, we learn about both self and other, as well as how to define ourselves authentically in relation to the world. We learn how not to impose an unexamined, prefabricated definition of the world, or engage an arbitrary definition of the individual. We are called to attend to what *is* there—not to what we wish. Hospitable attending requires a kind of knowing that moves us toward, not away from, others. It draws on a fuller concept of reason, one that includes intuition and emotion as well as analysis. This kind of knowing sees not only individuals in their particularity, but also a oneness that binds us together as a community of learners.

These "others" express the plurality of worlds—the many cultural and intellectual traditions—around us. But whether familiar or strange, attending to the other requires the detachment of which Simone Weil wrote. Iris Murdoch names what blocks us from offering this kind of attention. In both the moral and the spiritual life, "the fat relentless ego" is the problem (Murdoch, 1970, p. 52). In recognizing claims that others can place on me, I have to let go the urgent, persistent attachment to my own needs that marks insistent individualism. Murdoch invites us to recognize that "personal fantasy" can be a major obstacle to this surrender. In attending to the other, one must overcome "the tissue of self-aggrandizing and consoling wishes and dreams which prevents one from seeing what is there outside one" (Murdoch, 1970, p. 59).

Once it becomes a way of life, attending to others relieves us of anxious choices about protecting self. Murdoch (1970) elucidates the cumulative values embedded in the practice:

> If we consider what the work of attention is like, how continuously it goes on, and how imperceptibly it builds up structures of value around us, we shall not be surprised that at crucial moments of choice most of the business of choosing is already over. (p. 37)

We attend from habit—neither thoughtless nor self-preoccupied. We do not focus on abstract and impersonal rules; attending is a way of being we have cultivated. "The exercise of our freedom is a small piecemeal business which goes on all the time and not a grandiose leaping about unimpeded at important moments" (Murdoch, 1970, p. 37).

The object of attention is both self and other. The self is an object, not in some kind of strained and awkward self-consciousness, but in the sense of self-awareness and self-acceptance. It is this awareness and acceptance of who one is and to what one is attentive that enable acute awareness and openness to the other. Paying attention to one's psychological needs and wholeness, one has attended to self in order to transcend self. This presence to oneself allows honesty with the other. The other is allowed to be itself even as the self is drawn into the particularity of the other.

Seeking Self-Knowledge

Presence to the other points up the importance of self-knowledge. As a spiritual practice, self-knowledge involves how to make sense of one's life—how to connect the complex and often disparate facts of professional and personal experience. Rather than anxiously chasing the status of "expert" that academic culture so often celebrates, practicing self-knowledge can lead to recognizing one's own shortcomings as well as one's gifts, acknowledging the role of good fortune, and crediting the contributions of others. Self-knowledge involves discernment and points toward humility. Parker Palmer (2000) reminds us how often "there is a great gulf between the way my ego wants to identify me, with its protective masks and self-serving fictions, and my true self" (p. 5). There is a great gulf between the promptings of insistent individualism and the deeply natural openness of our own inner wisdom.

However, it is not always easy to distinguish the false from the true self. I noted above that uncovering one's deeper selfhood is part of what is involved. Authentic self-appropriation also requires courage and perseverance. It includes naming, celebrating, and using one's talents and gifts; accepting oneself and relinquishing habits of self-denigration or self-hate, as well as those of perpetual self-congratulation; attending to one's testimony, confronting illusions, and examining motivations. It involves living out of our academic knowledge, as well as bringing our true selves to our profession—not separating person and work. It means combating our culturally invasive consumerism as well as identifying and attending to those questions most worthy of pursuit. It requires practicing discernment about the truth of our lives and our individual and corporate situations.

The point of taking time to reflect on one's inner life and values is not to promote self-preoccupation, but just the opposite. Practicing this reflection reins in the need to preen, to be center stage, to exaggerate one's importance and accomplishments, or to minimize the gifts of others in order to feel more important. It diminishes the lure and snare of *schadenfreude*. Through self-reflection we may discover what others already know about us: we resist novelty because it might bring loss of control. We cling to a past that's gone, or never was, and are held captive by our will to mastery. We reduce the deeper mystery of our lives to the confineable and controllable. Indeed, we may find that control has become the central organizing principle of our lives—and our spiritualities.

Finally, practicing self-knowledge involves openness to criticism. We cannot shape a true picture of ourselves unless we risk talking with colleagues about our teaching and research. Students are also part of this process. Although they are rarely in position to comment on a professor's subject-matter competence, they *are* equipped to comment on professorial openness and fidelity. Indeed, this spiritual practice of openness to criticism may require initiating procedures that facilitate more forthright student communication about professorial behaviors. With practice, one gradually acquires the skill to recognize pseudo accolades from students who play games to protect their own academic interests.

Fidelity in seeking self-knowledge also involves the broader sense of faith as trust. Three kinds can be identified. On the one hand, there is trust that openness to the other and the novel is worth potential disruption of comfortable routines and conceits. Taking this risk is seen as trust that larger goods will be revealed, discovered, or created. Since one does not know in advance what fruits might be born, practicing hospitality involves a second sense of trust.

This is the trust that the ends in which we place our confidence and to which we are loyal are *worthy* of that confidence and loyalty as ultimate centers of meaning and value. Our spiritualities are the stories of these commitments. They are never completely private. Those who know us well know our spiritualities. Some of us seek reputation or a thickened resume. Others are drawn into consumerism. I argue that different ends are more worthy of our loyalty, particularly openness to the other—including students and colleagues—as well as covenants of sharing and receiving without prejudice or condition.

Both forms of trust point to a third. This is the natural confidence that our daily lives illustrate and presuppose—the native trust or animal faith that reality will not deceive. It is trust in the constancy and hospitality of a larger structure of reality—one that transcends individuals and communities. For many, this larger structure is a permanent background to all activity, displaying the ultimate hospitality to which theistic world views attest. From this perspective, academic hospitality is best understood as embedded and rooted in this wider trust. It is this ultimate horizon of meaning that both frees us to attend to others without fear or dread—and also requires us to do so. Whether thematized in theistic or secular terms, commitment to the spiritual practice of self-knowledge points to hospitality as essential, neither an ornament nor a luxury.

Practicing Asceticism

Asceticism is a foundational element of self-knowledge. Through systematic self-discipline one works toward excellence in virtue and spiritual health, turning away from forms of self-indulgence. To limit asceticism to denial of sensual pleasure is to miss this broader context. Committing to academic asceticism is a way of dismantling the addiction of insistent individualism in favor of greater liberation and fullness of life.

The ascetic life demands a range of discipline. It requires us to break with familiar, comfortable routines and the masks we fashion to cope with vulnerability—forgoing the controlling power we employ and the weapons we create for agonistic rivalries. Relinquishing anxieties that we do not measure up to false or unobtainable ideals is another form of asceticism. When we practice the ascetic life, we accept honest feedback from colleagues and students. We submit our research to the scrutiny of others who hold conflicting positions. We continue in the classroom even in the face of an "I dare you to interest me" attitude from students.

The use and misuse of language is a particularly important arena for academic asceticism. It is our job to hone linguistic skills, but whether we use them to communicate or to harm is a spiritual concern. Concretely, an asceticism of language translates into a refusal to use language to posture, polarize, or abuse. It can also be a stripping exercise to challenge colleagues who use language in ways that violate or diminish others. Practicing an asceticism of language pushes us to offer the kind word rather than the cynical quip—or to remain silent when appropriate. It leads us to welcome new as well as old faculty members, administrators, and staff, learning who they are, marveling at their gifts, and expressing gratitude for their presence—rather than treating them as interruptions or inconveniences, barriers or obstacles.

A healthy spirituality involves living without craving acclaim or recognition—practicing hospitality without the need to be noticed as hospitable. It is practicing hospitality willingly, not willfully. The latter is simply another expression of insistent individualism, a form of spiritual narcissism. To be willful is to be prideful, seeking to control and master. To be willing, though, is to be mindful of ourselves as tempted by insistent individualism; to acknowledge its penalties, expense, and inability to sustain; and to seek alternatives. Recognizing and owning the truth about oneself leads to the kind of self-forgetfulness necessary for truly attending to the other.

Academic asceticism also sheds new light on the drudgery associated with college and university life. Papers are to be marked, committee meetings attended, research conducted, students recruited, speeches made, and funds raised whether or not one feels like it. Ascetics distinguish complaining that seeks mutual recognition of burdens in order to return to work refreshed, from complaining that evades responsibility (Bennett & Dreyer, 1994). For many, practicing asceticism points to the need to become better academic citizens—to attend more faithfully to our own institutions as they face the extraordinary challenges of new technologies, aggressive proprietary institutions, and rapid socioeconomic changes on a global scale.

In sum, recognizing and owning who we are is an essential spiritual task. Parker Palmer (1990) is correct:

> Our challenge is to overcome the common notion that a person is, or ought to be, a singular, monolithic, homogeneous self, and to acknowledge the fact that each of us is a congeries of many forces, a home for many selves. (p. 150)

This is not talk about multiple personalities, but about our multiple dimensionality. However, "most of us live by selecting one self from among the many—often the best and brightest self—and pretending to ourselves and others that this is the whole of who we are" (Palmer, 1990, p. 150). Instead of recognizing that we are a "home for many selves," we overlook our capacities for evil as well as for good, and gloss over how we are "cowards as well as heroes, gluttons as well as ascetics, sinners as well as saints" (Palmer, 1990, p. 150). And we fail to be open to our future— to practice hospitality as new forms of ourselves emerge and as we search for ways to understand and enliven them.

If we do not examine our own lives, how can we ask students to do so? Dwelling too exclusively in our own lives is a route toward insistent individualism, but openness to self need not mean absorption in self. The difference lies in why we attend to the self. Practicing hospitality toward ourselves means working toward the common good. Philosophy reminds us that reality is social, that each self is constituted by relationships with others. Authentic individual good involves the good of others. Implications for both ethics and spirituality follow. As Whitehead (1978) notes,

The antithesis between the general good and the individual interest can be abolished only when the individual is such that its interest is the general good, thus exemplifying the loss of the minor intensities in order to find them again with finer composition in a wider sweep of interest. (p. 15)

EGOISM, ALTRUISM, AND THE COMMON GOOD

On the surface, it makes sense to set philosophies of egoism and altruism over against each other. Egoists justify taking themselves as essentially self-centered and self-regarding. Altruists sacrifice themselves for the interests of the other person or the community. But this dualism of egoism/altruism ignores the inseparability of self and other, distinguishing what are in fact often entangled and inappropriately separated. Such dualism belies the truth that individual well-being is deeply connected and intertwined with the well-being of others.

Insistent individualists are so accustomed to their familiar self-oriented frames of reference that they diminish claims others make. Even a commendable desire to behave according to the expectations of our professional associations can be simply a plan to promote our purposes. To call self-preoccupation into question may require the sudden, unanticipated decentering of self-understanding that only the other can effect. Emmanuel Levinas suggests that it is the face of the other that presents the prior element in moral experience—leading one to recognize that as a center of meaning and worth the other presents legitimate claims.

We all have experiences that enflesh such claims. Casual, but candid, remarks from students or their critical comments on evaluation instruments may interrupt my customary self-appraisal and allow a more accurate picture of our mutual entanglement to surface. A colleague may summon courage to confront me directly with discrepancies between my behavior and my calling. The deep relational character of our existence may dawn on me gradually as I leave behind the competitions of insistent individualism and grow into maturity.

Eventually we claim as our own good the outcomes of contributions we make to the good of others. The more our actions enhance this common good, the greater the good we experience individually. The more responsive we are to the many communities to which we belong, the more fulfilled we become. Insistent individualists, by contrast, are oblivious to the interests of others until the point of collision. Whitehead reminds us that the self is constituted in relationship and finds fulfillment in relationship. His analysis of experience shows that every moment of actuality is by nature self-transcending in its impact on the future. Even selfish acts may include some larger good beyond and beside one's future experience.

Hospitality reflects this relationality as an ultimate fact of reality, blurring the sharp ontological opposition between self and other. To ignore or abuse the other is to diminish the matrix of which one is a part and from which one draws benefit. Hospitality as gift to the other is also a gain to the self. Indeed, being hospitable is a means to becoming who in fact we most truly are. Openness to others increases overall value for both self and other. We can speak without contradiction of loving and honoring both self and neighbor. This is the true rational goal—the philosophical expression of the ethical and spiritual maxim that we are to love the other *as* ourselves, not instead of ourselves.

Charles Hartshorne (1976) underlines this human responsibility for the future:

> The rational aim is the future good that we can help to bring about and take an interest in now, whether or not it will do us good in the future and whether or not we shall be there to share in the good. We share in it now, and that is all that present motivation requires. It is a luxury, not a necessity, if we can hope to have a future share in the good we make possible for others. Moses did not need to enter into the promised land. (p. 308)

Grounds for Hope

If we see this common good as only a goal, it forever escapes realization. But if we see that the good resides in the process, the story is different. For the process includes the inherited past—the realized as well as unrealized possibilities it bequeaths to the present.[4] Realized possibilities define those structures of value and accomplishments that need not have occurred but did, and to whose continuance we must attend. The ideals of the "more" and the "better" implicit in the past are also always before us. Inherited as unrealized possibilities, these ideals for the future reside in our present together with the realized facts that demand reenactment. The realized facts of our identity are the source of our continuity; unrealized ideals are the source of our morality.

These unfulfilled promises are at work in the background, haunting the present in ever new guises. Sometimes they do become instruments for enlarging our horizons of understanding. Resistance to them can be entrenched, but the hope is that eventually someone in the student body, the department, the faculty senate, or the administration will hear and begin to embrace these ideas—be they for greater recognition of the intellectual contributions of women and non-Western peoples, more environmental sensitivity, a more balanced pedagogy, or institutions of greater integrity. We do have grounds for hoping that fragmentation can be reduced and meaning salvaged from blandness and ennui, or even despair.

It seems odd to say that hospitality can develop out of insistent individualism. But even acts of selfishness can generate broader and finer possibilities that beckon for future realization. George Allan (1993) reflects that "by parochial ideals we can transcend our parochialism" (p. 279). Simple replication of a selfish past promises only staleness and boredom. That is the curse of insistent individualism—it promises more satisfaction than it can ever produce. In addition to repetition, novelty is required for a good life, and among the novel is inclusion of the interests of others. Bequeathing the practice of hospitality to the future provides hope for improvement. As our aims enlarge, chances for greater depth and intensity increase. As Allan notes, individuals "seek both their own good and a common good, or more accurately they seek their own good through a common good" (p. 277). True, conflict between possible futures and the necessary selection of some over others is inevitable. Yet that which is excluded makes the future possible and so has not perished completely.

The philosophies of Whitehead and Hartshorne help us to see that hospitality is not an abstract principle to be imposed upon our academic lives. It is an imperative that derives from the structure of reality itself. That is why educational philosophy is so important. How we act reflects how we have come to think and to value. Failing to appreciate the centrality of relationality to the nature of reality and to the constitution of the self disposes us to view reality as fragmented, the self as isolated and the other as threat. Spiritualities become insistently individualistic. But when the communities to which we belong are healthy, when there is mutual interaction and support, when there is hospitality in sharing and receiving of resources, insights, and criticism—then each self is enlarged, for elements of its good and the common good overlap and merge.

ACADEMIC CITIZENSHIP

The stability of an academic community depends upon a balance among the rights, responsibilities, and privileges of academic citizenship (Cross, 1994). Today the emphasis is clearly upon rights, and there is less emphasis on academic responsibilities—evident in the more sensational forms of irresponsibility we hear about. Conflicts of interest by trustees or faculty, presidential abuse of power, and falsification of data by researchers or public affairs officers violate the trust of others. But academic irresponsibility occurs in less sensational ways as well. Faculty meetings fail for lack of a quorum, committees suffer from lack of leadership, classes are cancelled for reasons of professorial convenience.

Elsewhere I examine other deficiencies of academic citizenship—including what I term "calling in sick," "looking the other way," and dwelling in rhetorical excesses such as unchecked complaining and polarizing discourse (Bennett, 1998, pp. 52-72). Such acts diminish not only individual citizenship, but also community attention to broader citizenship issues. As Clark Kerr (1994) observed, "the new academic culture places more emphasis on individual and group advantages and concerns and less on the overall welfare of the college and university as a self-governing community concentrated on advancing knowledge" (p. 9). These new communities are no longer defined by spatial proximity. Email, list serves, and the Internet are their infrastructure. The challenge of hospitality is to enrich our local communities with the fruits of these expanded societies of interest and expertise. The point is to contribute new value to our campuses, not to replace them.

Academic Standards

The common good we seek in the academy is associated with broad academic standards and developments. The collegial ethic of hospitality requires review of these standards as well—considering their fidelity to the past, to changing intellectual developments, and to anticipated societal needs and values. Disciplines can become insulated, self-absorbed, and internally fragmented. In search of status they can inappropriately imitate other disciplines and inquiries. What is essential for the common good is free, reciprocal flow of conversation and interaction, not ideological purity or organizational fragmentation.

Indeed, fidelity to standards means benefiting the wider public. This occurs through colloquia and popular presentations as well as publications written to facilitate wider understanding. This kind of writing is not encouraged when intellectual inquiry becomes overly professionalized—narrowing research and excluding wider participation (Wilshire, 1990). Protecting the purity of learning promotes the self-absorbed university—one that fails to address the broad social problems about which John Cobb and others complain. Academic writing is a good example. Instead of viewing it as a form of teaching, academics come to see it in terms of its benefits for achieving tenure and promotion.

William May (2001) observes that "much academic writing is filial rather than collegial; academics aim their prose *upward* to gatekeepers rather than *outward* to inquirers and peers and thus vitiate it as teaching" (p. 258).

It is not news that higher education has neglected these ethical matters. Edward Shils (1984) noted two decades ago that "the sure moral touch has weakened and the self-confidence of the academic profession in its devotion to its calling has faltered" (p. 6) His lament is as timely today as it was then:

> aside from a few fragmentary starts, which have been responses to particular abuses and grievances, the academic profession has done very little to promulgate a set of guiding principles which should govern its custodianship of knowledge in teaching and research, its role in the internal conduct of universities and its participation in the public sphere. (Shils, 1984, p. 6)

Indeed, there is no national body charged with formulating and overseeing these "guiding principles." The only national body that might set up and enforce ethical norms across higher education is the American Association of University Professors (AAUP). Unfortunately, it does not represent all the professoriate and it has no exacting membership requirements. It has no tests to assure that individual candidates for membership possess the knowledge and intellectual skills that might identify them as bona fide members of a profession. And the AAUP shows little willingness to rebuke or censure unprofessional professors—those who commit academic fraud, trample on the rights of the probationary faculty or of students, or in other ways violate the ethic of hospitality. It has chosen to scrutinize institutional treatment of professors; it has not censured individual professorial behavior that subverts educational objectives or principles.

The bulwark of academic integrity is peer review. The privilege of academic freedom rests on widespread active membership in the broader community of academic, not disciplinary, peers. It is in this broader community—not in narrow, self-interested and often exclusionary disciplinary enclaves—that mutual responsibility rests for evaluating the appropriateness of academic standards and behaviors as well as the accuracy of truth claims. Failing to attend to such academic citizenship jeopardizes the whole enterprise.

INSTITUTIONAL INSISTENT INDIVIDUALISM AND HOSPITALITY

An institution is more than the sum of its parts—more than an amalgam of the characteristics of its individual members. Its agency is greater, and other than, the aggregate agencies of its members as individuals. Further, its responsibilities are not exhausted by the separate, individual responsibilities of its members, even though exercised only through them. In short, the institution has its own identity and its own moral character. It too can be hospitable—or not. When hospitable, institutional structures extend the capacity of students, faculty, and staff to grow in relationship to each other and to the increase of knowledge. Disciplinary and organizational boundaries are porous. Honest and candid conversations and relationships are valued. But governance patterns can stand in the way of institutional integrity and efficiency.

Academic Capitalism

Rapid changes in information technology and in socioeconomic conditions have led many institutions to focus on efficiency at the expense of academic traditions and integrity. Substantial threats to institutional health, in some cases even of survival, seem at hand. Faculty and academic affairs units are perceived as poor team players—interested more in disciplinary developments than in institutional challenges. In fact, many institutions understand and honor traditional shared governance in name only. Top administrators and boards of trustees or regents, even state agencies in the case of public institutions, make and implement strategic decisions on their own—neglecting the most significant human resource they possess, their faculty.

Thoughtful educators have begun to argue that separating institution and faculty in this way leads to disaster. Accelerating since the 1980s, the globalization of economics and politics has been

> destabilizing patterns of university professorial work developed over the past hundred years . . . creating new structures, incentives, and rewards for some aspects of academic careers and . . . simultaneously instituting constraints and disincentives for other aspects of careers. (Slaughter & Leslie, 1997, p. 1)

Grounds for treating universities differently from other social organizations are undermined as the profit motive encroaches upon the academy—substantially increasing the role of market forces in faculty behaviors and institutional decisions. Faculty are devoting more energies to entrepreneurial activities that may have only marginal connection with their institutions and students. Institutions increasingly favor programs and faculty that attract external support, leaving traditional units and undergraduate education at substantial disadvantage. Slaughter and Leslie are not sanguine about the future.

Others have specific recommendations. The Associated New American Colleges argue for a new academic compact of reciprocity between faculty and their institutions (McMillin & Berberet, 2002). Their surveys show that faculty are happy with their work, not sure about their colleagues, but decidedly unhappy with the lack of institutional recognition and support—a situation mirrored in the larger world of American higher education. If institutions are to meet rapid economic and social change successfully, a new compact is required. On the one hand, faculty need to attend to issues of institutional citizenship, aligning their priorities more closely with institutional needs. On the other hand, institutions must attend to career-long faculty professional development precisely so instructors can respond to institutional concerns. The one-size-fits-all concept is unresponsive to faculty needs at different stages of their careers. In a rapidly changing world, institutions need to develop their "human capital" and then engage their faculty's knowledge and skill in search of creative institutional solutions.

Former university president George O'Brien (1998) agrees, arguing that "the future will require new structures of faculty responsibility *for the institution*" (p. 212). Economics and technology may easily combine to make the university as we know it culturally obsolete. "Come the present and future financial crunch, and expensive faculty professionalization is bound to be assaulted by adjuncts, franchising, detenuring, distance learning, and so down the hill" (O'Brien, 1998, p. 212). The future requires that faculty everywhere become accountable for institutional management as a whole, not just academic management. This is no small matter. "It involves changing many of the fundamentals of current faculty self-understanding, status, and the present governance structure" (O'Brien, 1998, p. xviii).

Forms of Institutional Hospitality
Institutional hospitality requires that colleges and universities leave their ivory towers to speak and listen to the broader global society. Because of their distinctive mission, land-grant institutions have led the way. Their agricultural extension centers and their schools of engineering and forestry have applied new knowledge for the good of the larger commu-

nity. But apart from them, John Cobb's rebuke to the university as a collection of self-centered specialties seems justified. Educators and their institutions have responsibilities to the broader public. These obligations cannot be met by hierarchical notions of intellectual excellence—by academic customs that frown upon the application of theory to societal problems such as poverty, violence, addiction, and pollution. Institutions can assist society without neglecting their mission to advance knowledge. Indeed, there is no advance in knowledge without sharing—and the sharing can be done without compromising long-term research or institutional integrity.

In other ways as well, institutions can attend to how committed they are to practicing hospitality. Consider the following four examples. On most campuses, the individuals with the greatest daily impact on students are often office, secretarial, and custodial staff. Those in security services are close behind. The broader public too is usually introduced to the institution through these same people. Yet almost everywhere they are at the margins of the institutional organizational chart and power structure. Rarely are their suggestions sought about hospitality, or even about physical barriers to it.

For instance, few institutions of higher education have been proactive in attending to special constituent needs. Most have let the broader culture lead the way. Access for the physically challenged became a standard feature on campuses only recently, and only as they struggled to meet new building code requirements. Rare is the institution, however well-endowed, that took the initiative. Nor have many institutions led the way in providing child-care facilities, even though most campuses are recruiting young faculty and more nontraditional students—the very ones who need such facilities. And only now is there a national push to develop equitable tenure-track policies for caregivers of the newborn and newly adopted—even though childbearing and child rearing years frequently coincide with traditional, and inflexibly defined, probationary periods.

Secondly, campuses are not skilled in aligning awards with overall individual contributions. Research university values continue to exercise a large influence. Accordingly, James Fairweather proposes adjusting rewards more closely to the character of the individual institution and its regional connections. For instance, greater value may be associated with faculty contributions to regionally relevant knowledge and technology transfer than to publication in nationally prestigious journals. Fairweather (1996) argues for the importance of

> an alternative concept of institutional prestige for teaching-oriented institutions and for schools serving local and regional

needs. Giving pay raises and recognition to faculty for promoting student internships with industry, for example, seems more in keeping with a regional comprehensive institution than giving faculty extra credit for obtaining grants from the National Science Foundation. (p. 70)

Thirdly, institutions could capitalize on their differences rather than accentuate their sameness. Not many institutions are in the business of discovering knowledge. Rather than attempting to mirror the research universities that *are* in that business, the majority of institutions should attend to the business of knowledge recovery and application. They should promote an ethos of learning nourished by the interaction of faculty and students with their institutional tradition—drawing out its distinctive values and revising or recreating them to address the present. Some historically black institutions have done this with great success.

Most institutions have specific traditions out of which they have developed—traditions they often fail to retain or acknowledge in any significant way. There may be an annual founder's day or similar celebration, or various buildings may be named in honor of earlier presidents or other worthies, but rarely does the institution's history inform its current activities. Church-related institutions are classic examples. Many trace their origins to special spiritual or religious traditions. Yet these same institutions often fail to incorporate their charisms in the activities of their institutional life. Outside of a special course or the office of campus ministry, faculty and students don't know their institutional traditions. Quaker schools forget to turn to George Fox or John Woolman. Jesuit schools don't turn to Ignatian rules for discernment. Paradoxically, these institutions fail their potentially distinctive individualities, electing instead the individuality of the herd.

Fourthly, institutions can be more hospitable to external publics. They can reach out to neighboring communities and share their facilities and special areas of competence. They can exhibit openness and responsiveness to changes in societal needs. They can provide intellectual resources for addressing developments in demography, the environment, technology, and the economy. Or they can remain cloistered institutions, indifferent to surrounding needs. These accountability issues are treated by many higher education institutions as public affairs rather than moral issues. That is, they are regarded as managerial or political, rather than moral, matters. Controversial obligations of a university to students, faculty, or neighbors, are treated as challenges for creative denials and spinning. In these and other ways, institutions neglect the common good.

CONCLUSION

Hospitality is not a counsel of perfection—only an invitation to be and do better. We all fall short of the standard suggested here—both individuals and institutions. Yet we cannot wait for leadership from the few great souls with clear vision. We cannot tread water until our institutions are more welcoming and guided by more central purposes. We must work with who we are and what we have. The cultivation of hospitality requires individual acts of openness which over time become habits and steady dispositions—and ultimately ways of life that nourish spiritually and satisfy ethically.

Along the way we help others, and they us, to transform our institutions into becoming more open, welcoming, and inclusive. We must involve both traditionalists and skeptics about tradition, both conservatives and liberals. We must honor those who seek knowledge for its own sake *and* those who want to apply it. We must aim for both intellectual mastery and puzzlement, both good control and wonder, confidence and curiosity. Cultivating and then practicing hospitality responds to a deep human need. It reflects the interdependence of things. It enriches relationships and makes possible new ones. It undergirds the very reason for the academy.

REFERENCES

Allan, G. (1993). Process ideology and the common good. *The Journal of Speculative Philosophy, VII* (4), 266–285.

Bellah, R. N. (1998). Courageous or indifferent individualism. *Ethical Perspectives, 5* (2), 92–102.

Bennett, J. B. (1998). *Collegial professionalism: The academy, individualism, and the common good.* Phoenix, AZ: American Council on Education/Oryx Press.

Bennett, J. B., & Dreyer, E. (1994, April). On complaining about students. *AAHE Bulletin, 46* (8), 7–8.

Carlson, E., & Kimball, B. (1994, Fall). Introduction by Ralph Lundgren. Two views of the academic life. *Liberal Education, 80* (4), 4–15.

Cross, P. K. (1994, October). Academic citizenship. *AAHE Bulletin, 47* (2), 3–5, 10.

Elkins, J. (2001, November 9). The ivory tower of tearlessness. *The Chronicle of Higher Education,* pp. B7–B10.

Fairweather, J. S. (1996). *Faculty work and public trust: Restoring the value of teaching and public service in American academic life.* Boston, MA: Allyn and Bacon.

Hadot, P. (1995). *Philosophy as a way of life* (A. I. Davidson, Ed. & Trans.). Cambridge, MA: Blackwell.

Hartshorne, C. (1976). Beyond enlightened self-interest. In H. J. Cargas & B. Lee (Eds.), *Religious experience and process theology: The pastoral implications of a major modern movement* (pp. 301–322). New York, NY: Paulist Press.

Jeavons, T. (1993, Spring). Humanizing doctoral education: Honoring student aspirations. *Liberal Education, 79* (2), 50–52.

Kerr, C. (1994, January/February). Knowledge ethics and the new academic culture. *Change, 26* (1), 8–15.

Kowalsky, D. (2001, December 18). Do I have junior faculty syndrome? *The Chronicle of Higher Education.* Available: http://chronicle.com/jobs/2001/12/2001121801c.htm

May, W. F. (2001). *Beleaguered rulers: The public obligation of the professional.* Louisville, KY: Westminster John Knox Press.

McMillin, L. A., & Berberet. W. G. (2002). *A new academic compact: Revisioning the relationship between faculty and their institutions.* Bolton, MA: Anker.

Miller, J. (1994, July). Joy and gravity: A meditation on the will to live. *Second Opinion, 20* (1), 57–69.

Murdoch, I. (1970). *The sovereignty of good.* New York, NY: Routledge.

O'Brien, G. D. (1998). *All the essential half-truths about higher education.* Chicago, IL: University of Chicago Press.

Palmer, P. J. (1990). 'All the way down': A spirituality of public life. In P. J. Parker, B. G. Wheeler, & J. W. Fowler (Eds.), *Caring for the commonweal: Education for religious and public life* (pp. 147–163). Macon, GA: Mercer University Press.

Palmer, P. J. (2000). *Let your life speak: Listening for the voice of vocation.* San Francisco, CA: Jossey-Bass.

Ruddick, L. (2001, November 23). The near enemy of the humanities is professionalism. *The Chronicle of Higher Education,* pp. B7–B9.

Shils, E. (1984). *The academic ethic.* Chicago, IL: University of Chicago Press.

Slaughter, S., & Leslie, L. (1997). *Academic capitalism: Politics, policies, and the entrepreneurial university.* Baltimore, MD: Johns Hopkins University Press.

Whitehead, A. N. (1978). *Process and reality* (corrected ed.) (D. W. Sherburne & D. R. Griffin, Eds.). New York, NY: The Free Press.

Wilshire, B. (1990). *The moral collapse of the university: Professionalism, purity, and alienation.* Albany, NY: State University of New York Press.

ENDNOTES

1. "Almost everyone who has gone through a Ph.D. program has horror stories to tell. . . . These stories may be about incredible work loads and stress; arbitrary, trivial, or simply inappropriate demands by their committees; or bureaucratic institutional hurdles and demands that seem to have nothing to do with ensuring or providing quality doctoral education" (Jeavons, 1993, p. 50).

2. See the interesting and informative exchange between an older and a younger professor as they discuss respective hardships in their careers (Carlson & Kimball, 1994).

3. Portions of what follows in this section also appeared in "Spiritualities of, Not At, the University," *Theoforum, 33* (1), January, 2002, 123–139.

4. I follow here Allan's interpretation of Whitehead's *Adventures of Ideas* (Allan, 1993).

An Essential Metaphor: Conversation

5

I have argued that hospitality is essential to the work of the academy. How should we envision that work? What do teaching, research, and service properly include? Definitions change from institution to institution, but a number of metaphors are at hand. Metaphors express and embody our underlying conceptual schemes or world views. Most traditional metaphors for the work of the academy are atomistic, and we have explored how atomism is unsatisfactory. The metaphor of conversation, however, points us in the right direction by suggesting the essential activity of the academy and its connectedness.

In this chapter I review some unfortunate metaphors we have inherited. Then I consider the metaphor of conversation and philosopher Michael Oakeshott's comments on it. Next I identify some of the specific merits of the metaphor. Finally, I consider various implications of conversation for our understanding of learning and teaching. In the next chapter I look at other implications of conversation for education and argue that the metaphor applies to all of higher education, not just the liberal learning to which Oakeshott restricts it.

FINDING THE "RIGHT" METAPHOR

Academics possess a rich range of metaphors for teaching and learning as well as for our life together. Most are inherited, but a few are new. Unfortunately, many are mischievous for student and instructor alike. They distort the character of teaching and learning. They misrepresent what most of us would recognize as central to our calling as educators. They distort our philosophies, our ethics, and our spiritualities.

Transmission and Storage

Two unfortunate metaphors are education as transmission and storage of information (as in stocking and filling student minds) and production of credit hours or graduates (as in the output of a factory). Students are portrayed as passive recipients of material transmitted. They have no active role in assessing and integrating what they receive. Information is packed in, not evaluated. There is no sense of student and instructor on a journey of discovery—of constructing and exploring meaning. These metaphors do not suggest cultivating individual judgment, competency, and sensitivity—or pursuing insight into self and identity. They do not contemplate any larger active role in which students themselves initiate learning. Nor is there place for a spirituality we would recognize as healthy.

As a result, the concept of authority is skewed. It becomes lodged in the instructor rather than in relationships among students, instructor, and subject matters or skills. However, it is not the instructor's interpretation of standards we want students to master. This throws autonomy into replicating someone else's authority. We want students to achieve authority for themselves—to be able to support their own interpretation of the truth of a matter, of how things are.

The transmission and storage metaphors seem decidedly mechanical, even mechanistic. They suggest that relationships among learners are properly superficial, as are those between instructor and learner, and both of them with the subject at hand. Student and instructor are self-enclosed, related only externally to one another. Further, roles are fixed. Words or images bearing ideas and meanings are loaded by sender and unloaded by receiver. Even the material to be transmitted seems prepackaged—in uniform quantities for ease and efficiency of delivery.

Under the influence of these metaphors, college and university faculty see teaching tasks primarily as dissemination. As Anderson (1993) observes, "this conception of educational purpose, and only this, can explain such otherwise incomprehensible rituals as the large lecture method of instruction, the standardized textbooks and the objective examination" (p. 25). Technique, not reflection—diligence, not curiosity—are the virtues to be cultivated. The metaphors carry additional poignancies. Students spend time and energy obsessing whether they are storing the right items. Will they be on the test? What is their shelf life? Others wonder whether this is information they will need later in life. What, if anything, does it mean for one's humanity?

Production

Scarcely better than transmission or storage is the notion that education is a kind of production—that campuses are factories making knowledge and knowledgeable students. The production model pictures education as developing finished products from raw materials. Students are objects on an assembly line awaiting shaping and stamping. At the end, they are packaged for marketing and then dumped, presumably ready for employers. In this metaphor, entering students are the basic commodities, whereas graduates reflect the various grinding, reshaping, polishing, and other applications of education. General education, to the degree it is considered, provides some quality control—some adjustment for snarls and defects in the production line.

Even obvious facts of education are at variance with this account. Students are different from each other in talents and needs. Often there is not a stable, uniform body of significant skills or knowledge that lends itself to transmission. Much knowledge becomes available only in the process of educational activity. Student learning is always in the making, not an external and prefixed commodity. Rather than standing outside the production line, the "product" becomes concretely present only in and through mutual inquiry. The production metaphor also ignores longstanding, difficult issues respecting the relevant dimensions of a body of knowledge as well as debates about protocols for selecting from it.

Nonetheless, this metaphor plays a key role in the growing perception that higher education is less a social institution than an industry that trains the workforce and advances economic development. The metaphor contributes to the commercialization of higher education—to the institutional sense that its main purpose is working with products, markets, and customers. It casts education as a consumable rather than also and primarily an inherently valuable human activity and a treasure of human intellectual and creative achievements.

As a key metaphor, production suggests the logic of the marketplace—educational goods and services are private, not public, and their purchase and accumulation by one party is at the expense of others. Institutions are primarily vendors in competition with other vendors, rather than social entities charged with advancing and sharing knowledge and understanding as public goods. Guided by the metaphor of production, institutions seek to stamp students with skills and data rather than induct them into conversation with great thinkers, past and present, for whom exploration, criticism, and personal appropriation of ideas matter.

Battle and Territory

These metaphors also suggest that instructors are competitors rather than collaborators for a common good. The associated metaphors of battle and territory (protecting and defending turf) authorize this unfortunate concept of academic life and generate the deformed ethics and spiritualities of insistent individualism. It is worth recalling Deborah Tannen's (2000) description of the agonistic character of the academy: "The way we train our students, conduct our classes and our research, and exchange ideas at meetings and in print are all driven by our ideological assumption that intellectual inquiry is a metaphorical battle" (p. B7).

Despite their purchase in our academic discourse and behavior, these metaphors are unfaithful to our lives. Learning does not occur in these ways. Stacking or pouring, transferring or producing, simply does not reflect the relational activity of learning.[1] Teachers learn from students, students learn from other students, and learning itself is a profoundly interactive process. Producing elevates market imperatives, emphasizes higher education as an economic sector, and ignores the legacy of learning as self-reflexive and of academic areas as indispensable regardless of narrowly defined cost-effectiveness. Properly expressed, learning means experience is interrogated and the fruits (theories, facts, skills, values, and self-understandings) become personal possessions and competencies. Further, these possessions and competencies are shared. Indeed, they emerge only in the process of sharing. And in being shared, the competencies are seen as having a bearing on personal identity—on who one understands himself or herself to be.

Likewise, despite its influence, a metaphor of territory is unfaithful to faculty as a community of scholars working to advance a common good. Unfortunately, academe has developed a deep commitment to territory (and market share) as a root metaphor. It is grounded in insistent individualism and generates the military images and language that Deborah Tannen and others deplore. Thus we hear (and say) our territories must be defended. Other departments or institutions are invading our property, our market share. We speak of border skirmishes or of being besieged by aggressive faculty or administrative opponents. We refer to power vacuums and undefended turf. Throughout, "territory" works against community and common good. What is mine is by definition not yours. Some ideological groups may enshrine private property in this way, but academic communities cannot and remain either academic or communities. They become aggregations of individualists.

Metaphors and a Culture of Anti-Intellectualism

Ironically, these metaphors contribute to the culture of anti-intellectualism against which the academy rightly protests. This culture justifies pursuit of knowledge by emphasizing its utilitarian value—how much it is worth on the market and what it contributes to social standing and prestige. It suggests that might makes right. The metaphor of production is inherently utilitarian and that of stacking or pouring is closely connected. These metaphors work against seeing learning as having significant internal effect. They work against understanding higher education as a place for self-exploration, personal creativity, and the life of the mind—for critical thought, for exploration and dissent, for developing citizens and souls. The time for discarding them is long past.

The metaphors we use *are* important. Our speech influences our behavior and the values we absorb and express. Language not only reflects our thinking, but contributes to how we construct reality. As Bellah, Madsen, Sullivan, Swidler, and Tipton (1991) observed, "institutions are very much dependent upon language: what we cannot imagine and express in language has little chance of becoming a . . . reality" (p. 15). We can couple that observation with their additional reflection that we often neglect "the power of institutions as well as their great possibilities for good and evil. The process of creating our institutions is never neutral, but always ethical" (Bellah et al., 1991, p. 11). Often we are unaware of the ethical influence our concepts and metaphors have. They may be so deeply ingrained and so widely prevalent they are opaque to us. As a result, unrecognized pedagogical metaphors prevent us from promoting the learning we seek. And even when consciously employed, metaphors continue to have significant power if unexamined.

Thinking of liberal education, but making a broader point, Marshall Gregory (1987) observes that we have internalized a number of utilitarian metaphors. They are part of the world views we take for granted.

> We are disheartened to see large and powerful forces working against us, forces that would replace intellectual play with the search for physical jolts, critical thinking with sloganeering, community with competition, tolerance with bigotry, persuasion with coercion, and compassion with selfishness. (Gregory, 1987, p. 105)

Instead of challenging these forces, though, we let them "undermine our hope of success and as our hopes of success diminish, confusions, resentments, and cynicism often grow" (Gregory, 1987, p. 105).

If we come to see the influence of the metaphors we use, we can secure greater clarity about problems they create and gain new insight into better practices. We can judge the appropriateness of our metaphors to the ends we pursue. Metaphors point to our underlying world views. Like transmission, production, and territory, many metaphors are atomistic and unfaithful to the ultimate connectivity of our existence. Of all people, educators need to examine their world views and the metaphors that constitute and illustrate them.[2]

Conversation

I propose "conversation" as a more suitable metaphor for education because it reflects much of what we do at our best. It is not an esoteric concept, nor are we external to the activity it pictures. Conversation is an ordinary activity, something in which we all participate. It is not a special technique available only to the few nor is it the latest pedagogy, the fad of the moment. There is no great magic at stake—no technological wizardry is required. The only issue for educators is whether we will employ it to engage our students, colleagues, and ourselves in review of the familiar and the promise of the new.

The metaphor of conversation suggests that people with different intellectual interests and histories have important things to say to each other. The process is back and forth—comment or question, followed by response, which in turn generates a rejoinder, and so on. One immediate advantage of this metaphor is that learners are seen to be active participants. Another advantage is that conversation identifies the other as a necessary participant in our own learning. Rather than defending turf, faculty learn from each other and their students. Instead of presenting students as obstacles or other faculty as competitors and threats, conversation reveals them as genuine colleagues with whom we are linked in pursuit of greater understanding. Indeed, the metaphor of conversation extends across the complex work of academe. Good research and scholarship, as with good teaching, are like good conversations—with students, colleagues, traditions, texts, and oneself. And conversation extends across the campus of integrity, across boundaries between arts and sciences and professional schools.

OAKESHOTT AND CONVERSATION

Let us examine further the metaphor of conversation. It is a wonderful, powerful, and provocative metaphor.[3] It speaks to much of our work and identity, and is a key element in healthier spiritualities, ethics, and philosophies of higher education. Some of these dimensions have been analyzed by the late English philosopher Michael Oakeshott. We would do well to consider Oakeshott's suggestions—critically, because they need a bit of repair—and to incorporate the metaphor within a collegial ethic of hospitality.

Oakeshott suggests that acts of scholarship and service as well as teaching and learning are best understood through the model of conversation. In conversation, he contends, "different universes of discourse meet, acknowledge each other and enjoy an oblique relationship which neither requires nor forecasts their being assimilated to each other" (Oakeshott, 1991, p. 490). These "universes of discourse" include the voices of literature, science, history, the arts, politics, economics, philosophy, the more applied skills, and so forth—representatives of the wide range of human achievement. There is no fixed number, for the conversation is forever unconcluded. New voices are always possible, as are new modulations within established ones.

Voices, Idioms, and Modes of Understanding

What Oakeshott calls voices are the various idioms or modes of understanding that constitute our human inheritance. They are not simply collections of beliefs or perceptions. They are languages of understanding. Together, they present "a manifold of invitations to look, to listen, and to reflect" (Oakeshott, 1989, p. 17). Each voice has its own complex logic and value, something we understand best when we explore its relationships with other voices—none can be fully understood apart from others. Our very humanity consists in learning how to claim, possess, and then dwell in this rich inheritance. It constitutes a mirror in which we can recognize and acknowledge who we are.

It is through conversation that we learn of our past (the always already existing and ongoing world of ideas and interpretations of ideas), interpret for ourselves its variety of understandings, accept what we judge appropriate, and in expressing ourselves contribute to the experience of others. It is through our conversation that we both enact and disclose ourselves. In Oakeshott's view, educational conversations may include, but are considerably more than, disputes and quarrels, assertions and denials—the conflicts and disagreements of the academy. When employed, arguments are used constructively to clarify issues, not vanquish opponents. The key point is respectful engagement with the other. The objective is what Oakeshott calls acknowledgment and accommodation, not indifference or conquest. It is to take account of the other respectfully and mutually—not to ignore or to oppress.

The act of educating is always local and particular, but draws us into the larger, more historical and comprehensive conversation that is our heritage. There is no limit to the voices in this ongoing conversation. Perhaps the most common is that of practical activity. Each voice has its own character and manner of speaking. With their privilege of leisure and unfettered discussion, colleges and universities are places set aside by society especially for this work of becoming human. "A university is not a machine for achieving a particular purpose or producing a particular result; it is a manner of human activity" (Oakeshott, 1989, p. 96). The special task of the campus is not just to host and display conversation. It must also prepare and invite students to participate.

This kind of learning is not natural in the sense of automatic or instinctive. It is not something done to or for us—it is a self-conscious and self-imposed engagement with ideas, something we must do for ourselves, though with the help of others. Some seem never to pursue learning. Others tire easily and early. What we seek to understand "is concerned with perceptions, ideas, beliefs, emotions, sensibilities, recognitions, discriminations, theorems and with all that goes to constitute a human condition" (Oakeshott, 1989, p. 8). For those who do pursue it, higher education helps them claim, appropriate, and dwell in the world of meanings that is our culture and constitutes our humanity. Participating in the human conversation in this way is a form of *paideia*—of forming our character—as well as of developing knowledge.

As we form meaning in interaction with others, we form ourselves. We build upon patterns of connectedness already present, interpreting and extending them, and creating more meaning. Conversation points to a common ground always already present that enables voices to interact, regulates their power, and cultivates our sensibilities. The result, as Oakeshott (1991) notes, is that

> education, properly speaking is an initiation into the skill and partnership of this conversation in which we learn to recognize the voices, to distinguish the proper occasions of utterance, and in which we acquire the intellectual and moral habits appropriate to conversation. (p. 491f.)

Privileged Voices

The conversation must be carefully conducted. Not all voices are equal. Some are thoughtlessly privileged. Feminists call attention to the prominence of the male timbre. Others note the absence of non-Western voices. Oakeshott (1991) himself deplores the common disposition "to impose a single character upon significant human speech . . . the voice of argumentative discourse, the voice of 'science', [while] all others are acknowledged merely in respect of their aptitude to imitate this voice" (p. 489).

The academy has seen some humanities imitate—indeed, almost replicate—the sciences. Earlier in the century logical positivism took this road in philosophy. More recently, Ruddick, Tompkins, and other students of literature lament the expense in literary theory—as Elkins does in art history.

Oakeshott also adds that the voice of practical activity is likely to dominate. In the United States our vaunted pragmatism, our problem-solving dispositions, and our reported disinterest in intellectual matters often elevate facts over values. Sometimes this transmutes into an elevation of power and privilege as well. But philosophical positivism and social privileging are problems in other countries also. Wherever they appear, they challenge the full conversation in which our human heritage consists. Without the involvement of other voices, the conversation becomes problematic, even boring.

There are other ways in which conversations go astray. Some become enslaved by the language of appetite or consumerism, rendering them unable to converse with other voices. Even muted voices can be problematic. The fragmentation and competitions of the academy tempt each voice toward self-promotion. "Each voice is prone to *superbia*, that is, an exclusive concern with its own utterance, which may result in its identifying the conversation with itself and its speaking as if it were speaking only to itself. And when this happens, barbarism may be observed to have supervened" (Oakeshott, 1991, p. 492). What Oakeshott calls barbarism is a kind of insistent individualism, an excessive—indeed exclusive—preoccupation with one voice. Then, faculty and curricula alike become inhospitable.

Although Oakeshott's distress at the collapse of conversation into barbarism is transparent, he does not delineate clearly an ethic to govern the conduct of conversation. It is not enough to celebrate civility. Conversation is not simply enculturation, simply induction into a particular, comfortable way of life. It is induction into a way of questioning, as well as appreciating, other ways of life. Conversation introduces us into reasons as well as procedures that colleges and universities consider worthy. It appraises current practice against the standard of a greater hospitality. So let us look more closely at various features of the metaphor of education as conversation and their contribution to an ethic of hospitality.

The Merits of Conversation

Several features of "conversation" recommend it as the key metaphor for higher education. Consider six: the pluralism of our times, the importance of discernment and empathy, the constitution of our humanity, the incorporation of activity and imagination, experiential and civic learning, and the absence of hierarchy.

Pluralism

First is the obvious, important point that a conversation requires an other. In an interior dialogue I may review important issues with myself, looking at them from different points of view. Internal dialogues can be stimulating and help me decide upon a course of action. But at some point, interior and private conversations must be informed by more public ones that directly engage others, those different from myself.[4] It is a poor kind of conversation in which only I talk—making my learning so public that I drown out the voices of others and remain uninformed by their perspectives.

A conversation is more than a soliloquy. The other cannot be simply another myself. Indeed, that the other is in many ways different from myself points to the inability of the self to find completion by and in itself. There must be a multitude of important others—bearing substantial gifts of different perspective and experience. At the least, they bring confirmation and validation. But they bring novelty and enlargement as well.

We live in a time of increasing pluralism respecting almost everything—culture, religion, gender roles, etc. The voices of our times are more varied and numerous than in earlier times. This pluralism presents both challenges and opportunities. It challenges familiar ways of looking at the world and ourselves. Through conversation with quite different others we are drawn out of ourselves. The opportunities pluralism provides are invitations to understand ourselves within larger frames of reference as world citizens. Through conversations with the other our purchase on the human condition and the variety of human achievement can be extended; we can be mutually enriched, and our spiritualities deepened.

We have seen how selves are fundamentally social in nature, despite what our individualist behaviors suggest. Hospitable conversation provides protection against self-delusion. We need others to whom we must listen carefully to learn more about ourselves—what we really think and who we are. Self-understanding is something already achieved *and* a task accomplished only by moving outside ourselves and attending to others. We must pass over and come back. Indeed, we can be said to truly possess our learning and identity only when able critically to evaluate them from external points of view.

To understand education as conversation is to appreciate the different kinds of liberation learning promises—from ignorance, parochialism, lack of self-insight, and obsession with power. Education as conversation decenters and deconstructs positions that privilege—while reminding us of the importance and value of our collective past as the foundation of the present. Educational conversations present opportunities to reflect collectively on what may be shared in common, but experienced differently, perhaps even discordantly. Attending to others provides us grounds that what they experience is not totally unlike our experience. Yet hospitable conversations avoid the impossible requirement that we all experience the same things. Precisely because of conversation with others we can generalize without making unsupportable universalistic claims.

Discernment and Empathy

Second, practicing hospitable conversation requires exercising discernment and empathy. It involves attending carefully to what the other is sharing and how one is responding. The metaphor challenges the self-centeredness that can characterize the new college student as well as the experienced college professor. It invites everyone to put earlier, limited habits of thought and interaction behind them. It challenges every voice that seeks to become privileged. It invites everyone to ask new and better questions, to listen more closely, and to practice the hospitality that characterizes confident, humble members of the broader human community.

For both moments of hospitable conversation—sharing and receiving—cultivating habits of empathy is necessary. Sharing requires relating in ways intended to facilitate understanding—in ways neither aggressive nor apologetic, intending neither to establish superiority nor shore up defenses. The objective is to offer myself in relationship to others, so that they may understand what I am sharing and why it is important to me. Truly hospitable conversations require searching for ways to convey clearly thoughts and experiences. They require that we attend to the testimony we provide.

Likewise, receiving involves relating to the other in ways that promote understanding what he or she is sharing, not in preparing a quick rebuttal. It involves empathetic listening, disciplining oneself to provide a sympathetic ear. The point is not to acknowledge a new external authority but to begin to think in ways that include the other. Openness to the learning of the other involves cultivating the ability to consider what things look like from his or her perspective—what intentions as well as desires might be at work, given his or her history and culture.

Like sharing, receiving requires effort and imagination—holding in abeyance one's own truths while divining those of the other through careful attention and question. In a word, it requires the humility to pass over. Room for the other must be prepared by putting one's own preoccupations to the side. This other can be distant in time as well as space. The conversation can be with one's reclaimed earlier self as we saw, with someone else from another time and place altogether, with ideas and texts of all kinds—including those that convey our inheritance and teach us how to claim and practice it.

Critically evaluating what is received is part of hospitable conversation, but it comes later and focuses on what can be improved. Prior to judging the other's position, we must first understand it—from the point of view and intentionality of the other. Only then is it appropriate and fruitful to ask hard questions, criticize, and challenge assumptions. Only then, if at all, are polemics in order. Hospitable conversation calls for an array of views rather than tests of ideological purity, and certainly not annihilation of opposing positions. Difference is an asset, not a liability. Consensus or closure is rarely possible, or even desirable. New insights can always be uncovered and hospitality reflects a shared concern for flourishing and well-being—not just some equilibrium among competing positions.

Constituting Humanity

Third, education plays an enormously important role in honoring, conserving and extending what makes us human. By participating in conversation we lay claim to the human inheritance. Unlike passive metaphors for learning, "conversation" makes clear the active role that the learner must play. It will not do simply to overhear conversation. That is like education as transmission or production. We must participate. There are no generic voices. We must find and use our own—bringing our talents, perspective, and experience to the greater conversation. Without a voice, we are diminished, and have not earned or honored our humanity.

But using our voice involves understanding and then engaging the "inside" of other voices—using the grammar or logic, the mode of thinking, that governs their idioms. Edward Farley (1988) notes the seriousness of what this means:

> One studies ancient Buddhism for the same reason one studies Freud, James Joyce, or Whitehead. Something is being laid claim to in these texts which may have to do with reality and truth, with the way things are, could be, or should be. Utter existential indifference to the truths posed by or laid claim to in the subject matter is a deadly virus, a virtual AIDS of education, any education. (p. 180)

"Conversation" is a pragmatic metaphor. Oakeshott clarifies this point by distinguishing between the language and the literature of a voice or mode of understanding. A literature is a body of knowledge—the creation of those who master its language, its manner of thinking. Oakeshott (1991) has in mind the distinction "between the 'language' of poetic imagination and a poem or a novel" (p. 192)—or that between a scientist's manner of thinking and a textbook expressing that thinking. A literature is a product generated by a language. We study a literature for itself and for the language it enshrines and reveals. Learning a language enables us to create imaginative worlds and dwell in our own creations— rather than to take flight solely on the wings of another's imagination.

Learning in higher education involves self-understanding. There is a self-involving element in conversation that other metaphors obscure. Actively using languages and participating in broad conversations consti- tute a statement about oneself that is quite different from simply having studied a literature or body of knowledge. The latter is rarely self-referen- tial. By itself, it has less power to transform, to make an inner impact. Working in the language does. One's own experience and talents lend new dimensions to what one contributes to, as well as what one takes from, conversation.

Acts, Imagination, and Direction
Fourth, we can extend "conversation" to include acts—not only perfor- mative utterances, but also gestures and deeds. Employing our various senses, we use our embodiedness to shape and express intellectual and spiritual traditions. We enrich teaching and the scholarship we share through developing and expressing human interiority—revealing inhab- ited rather than pure (or empty) space.

We are captivated by expressive individuals and disappointed by lack- luster and impassive ones. Sound has a certain priority. It enhances a broader sense of conversation. The voice reveals human presence and bears story and temporality. Deeds carry a similar weight in enabling and conveying attention to the other. Actions often do speak louder than words. In particular, institutions convey through their acts the degree of their interest in conversations with students, faculty, staff, and neighbors.

Conversations cannot continue long at high levels of abstraction. Successful conversations are both imaginative and concrete. Elements of narrative help invite empathetic, informative, and reciprocal engagement with others. "Thoughts of different species take wing and play round one another, responding to each other's movements and provoking one another to fresh exertions" (Oakeshott, 1991, p. 489). Unlike highly abstract conversations, concrete conversations yield deeper cultivation of the self and greater understanding of the other. Participants return to specific, concrete situations of fact in order to bring personal illumination out of their questions. There is a back and forth process. Oakeshott (1991) speaks of participation in conversation as "an unrehearsed intellectual adventure" (p. 489). At its best, conversation is exhilarating.

Finally, conversations build on one another. There is directionality to them. Things generally move forward, even though it is always possible— and sometimes necessary—to retrace steps. At the same time, good conversations avoid repetitiveness. Conversations that continually circle back upon themselves are judged boring. Those that have become dull, leached of vitality, must be freshened. New things must be introduced. Neglected or forgotten elements from voices in the past can be recalled. As Oakeshott (1991) notes, a university

> is concerned not merely to keep an intellectual inheritance intact, but to be continuously recovering what has been lost, restoring what has been neglected, collecting together what has been dissipated, repairing what has been corrupted, reconsidering, reshaping, reorganizing, making more intelligible, reissuing and reinvesting" (p. 194).

New interpretations of older utterances, new applications of received insights, and new discoveries or achievements become parts of vigorous conversation.

Civic Learning

Fifth, "conversation" points us toward civic learning. What and how we learn are informed by a range of experiences. How we apprehend and understand the broader world reflects who we are as well as that to which we attend. We learn outside the traditional classroom—through applying or extending classroom-derived concepts, developing insights about ourselves not previously possessed, and discovering new things about the world.

Civic learning is not just active learning—it is not simply participating in our own learning, important though that is. Civic learning occurs in and through our interaction and conversation in settings outside the classroom—in encounters such as practica, internships, and service learning in partnership with community agencies and activities. These are all forms of reflective engagement with the broader communities that in subtle ways form us. They provide opportunities to exercise our voices in thoughtful conversation with the voluntary and public associations that constitute our heritage and environment. Civic learning evokes Whitehead's famous observation about learning that becomes inert knowledge when unapplied and unused. Civic learning also illustrates Whitehead's point that theory is derived from experience even as it also illuminates experience. It is in their interaction that conversation in the larger sense takes place, enriching students and faculty.

Some of these conversations engage the intertwined moral and civic issues facing us today—issues such as access to housing and medical care as well as effective primary and secondary education, sound employment and environmental policies, and assessing the conflicting claims of pluralistic decision-making from the local and regional through the global levels. Adequate conversations evaluate potential actions for addressing these issues and recognize that civic engagement is essential for sustaining democracy. Educators have both opportunities and obligations to promote public conversation about social issues—conversation best effected across curricular and extracurricular lines. The spiritual exercises considered in the previous chapter provide important reasons for engaging in this conversation and transforming it from well-reasoned judgments into actions.

Likewise, institutions need to be civically engaged—to be in serious conversation on neighborhood, regional, national, and global issues. Without these genuine, sustained conversations, institutions rightly incur the condemnation that John Cobb leveled and they demonstrate the arrogance the public seems increasingly to associate with higher education. Institutions teach students about moral and civic responsibility by their own behaviors as well as the opportunities they provide for civic engagement and action. Through what they do institutions teach how important it is to act competently and responsibly in the world.

Authenticity and the Absence of Hierarchy

Authentic academic conversations require that participants pull their weight. Pursuing truth is a collective effort. The university's strong proscription of plagiarism reflects this point. Instead of contributing their own effort and insight to the community search, plagiarists live off the work and insights of others, claiming them as their own (O'Brien, 1998). This is a form of identity theft. Fraud is even more offensive for it falsifies the collective effort. Colleagues cannot learn from the "discoveries" of the fraudulent.

In this context, the institutional behaviors we examined earlier are problematic indeed. Providing fabricated data or other misrepresentations attempts to control the broader conversation and subverts the values without which there is neither conversation nor education. Likewise, excessive use of adjunct instructors reduces the number of core stewards of the academic enterprise. It constrains conversation about the integrity of the education offered. And intentionally introducing conflicts of interest by developing for-profit subsidiaries reestablishes atomism and insistent individualism.

At the individual level, hospitable conversations lack established hierarchies. There is no prior order of standing among the voices. There is no master of ceremonies, no keeper of the gate or bouncer who examines credentials. All are permitted who can get themselves accepted.

> A conversation does not need a chairman, it has no predetermined course, we do not ask what it is 'for'. . . . Its integration is not superimposed but springs from the quality of the voices which speak, and its value lies in the relics it leaves behind in the minds of those who participate. (Oakeshott, 1989, p. 98)

Of course, Oakeshott is talking about a "real" conversation. In the academy, the only credentials required for initial participation are interest and competence—and manners. How evenly the conversants are matched or how substantial their staying power is disclosed later.

However vigorous, conversations are usually inconclusive. Unlike arguments, conversations wax and wane, but are rarely decisively concluded. Like learning, conversations can always be resumed and developed further. So too with the work of the academy. Arguments are important, but a conversation is more than an argument and any conclusions one might draw at one moment could be overturned in the next.

SOME PHILOSOPICAL HABITS

Without an implicit relational framework within which reciprocity and mutual appropriation are conceptually appropriate, genuine conversational sharing and receiving appear impossible or as betrayal and theft. Claims of incommensurability arise and tribalism supervenes. Yet, conversations *do* occur, bypassing both incomprehension and imperialism. We can explicate this fact only through a prior and underlying relational framework. Indeed, it is precisely in contrast to this mutuality of relationality that we judge exploitation and dominance to be oppressive realities.

Yet, philosophies such as atomism have not served us well. In many ways our age is defined by the contrasting positions of scientism and various forms of postmodernism. In either position, education lacks enduring and compelling reasons for its own activity. Norms by which we might judge inherent excellence seem weak and relativistic. When we insist upon the primacy of the so-called value neutrality of scientific objectivity or when we deconstruct all formal frameworks of understanding, we abandon the grounds from which we can argue for our educational concerns and values. Why should the public, or academics themselves, support an enterprise whose fundamental purposes and values cannot be defended in scientific terms or are to be judged relative to each person and his or her economic and social class? As a method requiring careful replication of results by others, science is indeed hospitable. But as a larger, exclusive world view, science cannot in its own terms account for its value; and if, as some postmodernists claim, reality is no more than what each individual or community holds it to be, then educators are poorly positioned to claim special authority or support from the public.

Without an encompassing framework or procedure within which issues of social order are recognized and discussed, ethical analysis in academe is reduced to utilitarian management and adjudication of differences.[5] When academics authoritatively declare the universal lack of authority of encompassing frameworks or procedures, contests of power become the alternative. Issues must be constantly readjusted to shifting alignments of interests. For at least these reasons, the academy needs the larger framework and procedure that the concepts of hospitality and conversation provide. It is through them that different perspectives and standpoints can be openly discussed, evaluated, and balanced. Difference becomes a source of new awareness and interaction rather than a problem, even though enlargements are partial, never complete.

In his discourse ethics, philosopher Jurgen Habermas reminds us that the objective of communicative discourse is always to bring about understanding. The underlying premises and procedures of communication provide this larger framework. Even in times of pronounced pluralism, with their conflicting cultural *ethoi*, there are common moral dimensions of discourse. Each party has an obligation to defer to the other, to give at least as much attention and consideration to the other as to oneself—to take with as much importance what the other is saying as one insists upon for oneself. The exchange must on both sides be free of fear of coercion or deceit. Both sides must be willing to follow where reason and the better argument, not self-interest, directs. And both sides must have equal opportunities to speak, assert, offer support, and challenge.

Thus, the conditions of communication everywhere involve consensual or cooperative interactions rather than coerced ones. Competent speakers of a language know the difference between the original communicative intent of language used to seek agreement, and the derivative strategic use of deceit or manipulation to secure compliance. Actions intended to reach understanding are primary and original. They enable us to criticize parasitic communication disorders such as controlling or manipulating others (Habermas, 1984). Indeed, linguistic deceit can occur only because the hearer assumes that the speaker is intending to secure mutual understanding or agreement. The listener presupposes that the speaker is prepared to redeem his or her implicit claims if questioned—to present and defend data employed, to reconsider motivations, and to try again to communicate clearly.

Central to discourse ethics, and to hospitable conversations, is the joint expectation that each party readily accept the responsibility of redeeming validity claims. There are three: the claims to truth, to right action, or to the reliability and sincerity of a speaker or writer. Often only implicit, a validity claim is something that holds transsubjectively—it is not simply internal to the speaker or writer. Our ability to understand the meaning communicated by the other requires that we assess it as presenting validity claims about which we can, and perhaps should, properly inquire. In presenting validity claims, the speaker is referring the hearer to a social world of shared expectations—the relational community of which I spoke earlier.

This is the community already at hand but also always in process of being constructed anew. The speaker considers that what he or she has to say *deserves* recognition by the other. The process of accepting and redeeming claims is one of acknowledging that the claims are *worthy*. Throughout the conversation the speaker also acknowledges (again, often implicitly) that the other is authorized to ask that the speaker present support for his or her claims. Of course this means that hospitable conversations require that speakers open themselves to external evaluation and potential criticism.

Expanding upon the discourse ethics of Habermas, Seyla Benhabib (1992) observes that the necessary conditions of communicative speech include "the principle of universal moral respect" and "the principle of egalitarian reciprocity" (p. 29). By the first principle all who are able to participate should be invited to do so. The second principle extends to everyone the opportunity to engage in the full range of speech acts, including raising new issues and asking about presuppositions. Benhabib focuses on the process of discourse where all can participate equally, even though agreement on further specific universal norms and values may escape us.

The underlying mechanism is the reversal of perspectives for which hospitality calls. The other is always concrete and specific, reflecting the plurality of modes of being human. We are to attend imaginatively to the point of the view and reasoning of this other. This kind of attending is an imaginative act, not necessarily one of acceptance or identification. And the goal need not be consensus, much less unanimity. It is to acquire understanding, and on the basis of understanding also to "seek some reasonable agreement in an open-ended discussion" (Benhabib, 1992, p. 9). In short,

> in conversation I must know how to listen, I must know how to understand your point of view, I must learn to represent to myself the world and the other as you see them. If I cannot listen, if I cannot understand, and if I cannot represent, the conversation stops, develops into an argument, or maybe never gets started. (Benhabib, 1992, p. 52)

There are broad institutional implications to conversation and discourse ethics. Academic communities must free themselves from systematically distorted communications. They must keep their commitment to the authority of reason and to the better argument, as well as promote the conditions through which the better argument can be recognized and honored. I have already noted some institutional distortions—encouraged by the competitive drives of the market economy and desires to prosper in relationship to the other and to put the best face on bad institutional news.

Conversation as Play

George Allan (1997) argues that the internal meaning of a college resides not in its mission or purposes but in its conversation. Purposes and mission can change without a college ceasing to exist. They are external to the college's essential identity. What cannot change, though, is the commitment of the college to conversation. Opportunities genuinely to engage others are essential for the health of the ongoing collegium. Some engagements are small, but others are potentially transformative—and all can generate new concepts and personal insights. Without an unqualified commitment to conversation at its heart, no institution is a college or university—regardless of its other purposes, activities, or accomplishments.

With both Allan and Oakeshott we can understand education as a form of "play"—an activity in which we construct possible worlds, but not with any immediate necessity to employ them as means to some end. "The characteristic gift of a university is the gift of an interval . . . a moment in which to taste the mystery without the necessity of at once seeking a solution" (Allan, 1997, p. 113f.). The learner is released from suffering the consequences of his or her contribution to the conversation. Ideas are "tried on," not immediately implemented. The point is to consider and evaluate new concepts for making sense of things and envisioning new ways forward. We may consider brand-new perspectives; we may simply take stock of ourselves and the resources of our traditions.

But if we choose to call education play, we understand that it is "serious play"—an activity in which the moral practices that give us our brand of humanity are learned and reviewed. We confront the world we inhabit and consider anew how to enact and disclose ourselves. Playing a new game is not riskless. Serious engagement in the conversation means we suspend prior commitments and patterns or habits—and the very process of imaginatively entertaining alternatives may render it impossible to return to earlier mindsets and habits.

The habits we form become consistent patterns of behavior (Allan, 1996). They are how we develop our character and economize. We cannot constantly attend to the details of life. We develop frameworks or rituals—scripts or patterns—to use in similar cases. The focus of our attention is not on the details of our movements, but the context in which we move in our accustomed ways. We can see this movement in terms of play and work, or of withdrawal and return—withdrawal from a present engaged life to consider novelties at our own speed, and then return to the engaged and practical life, not only refreshed but now enriched and empowered with these new experiences. Upon return, some of our experiences can be shifted from the simple imaginative consideration of ideas to their employment in working hypotheses designed to solve problems. Withdrawal and return are parallel to what we termed passing over and returning—to considering the other and then returning with new insights. In both cases there is a shift between 1) continuing the conversation, recognizing that any conclusions are always tentative in order to keep different perspectives from becoming hardened positions, and 2) using the fruits of the conversation to solve problems and develop habits.

Conversation, Community, and Spirituality

Traditional colleges and universities have the power to promote conversation and the community it reflects and extends. Rather than imitating for-profit institutions, they can make their particular traditions a strength. Their central campuses, their balanced core curricula, their academic freedom, the intellectual lives they cherish are precious assets that proprietary institutions lack. Using the University of Phoenix as a synecdoche for the proprietary sector, Alan Wolfe (1998) suggests that Phoenix should remind traditional academics of what they do best:

> Those of us who believe in libraries and laboratories, seminars and intense discussion . . . the compelling truths of the humanities, the unexpected discoveries of science, and the sheer spontaneity and excitement of minds trying to figure out ideas for themselves ought to welcome the University of Phoenix. (p. B4)

It can return us to what we do best.

These traditional academic conversations are multiple and have multiple parties. The mutual teaching and learning that occurs through faculty reading and commenting on colleagues' drafts of syllabi, essays, and books is a common form of academic conversation. The interaction that is part of team teaching is another, as is the conversation that follows classroom observations, or the general discussion of curriculum and program review or recruitment and hiring initiatives. Hospitable conversations are marked by openness to new ideas, as well as by disciplined efforts to appreciate them as appropriate challenges to familiar presuppositions and frameworks. They seek balanced evaluations constructed to be helpful in the development of the new rather than defensively to apologize for the old.

Sabbaticals, promotions, the receipt of major awards or other forms of collegiate recognition, even the rare intimate conversation with colleagues or students, and certainly the event of changing jobs—all can stimulate reflections on more significant, perduring purposes and issues in the academy. In our times of appetitive preoccupation and instrumental pursuits, the metaphor of conversation reminds us that communication is a sacred trust. Our goal must be to listen and speak with great care—putting routines and biases to the side while seeking understanding at the deepest level.

Our spiritual exercises can help us leave behind shallow reflections on personal injuries, ongoing quarrels and competitions, preoccupations with the comparative size and heft of our curriculum vitae, even our lamentations about the decline of student abilities. Genuine, valuable conversations evoke reflection on the twists and turns and overall success of our original sense of calling—what originally led us into the professoriate. And they may evoke as well a sense of regret for lost opportunities for genuine enrichment.

Most of us need to rediscover and reclaim our sense of intellectual identity and purpose—the broader and deeper purposes that we brought to the academy. Academic conferences may be more important in provoking this process than in disseminating the latest disciplinary developments or newest pedagogical gospel. This need for reflection is heightened by time on task, but also by the increased commodification and profit-orientation of contemporary higher education. We need to remove ourselves for a time from the push to remain competitive, to accommodate the extra students, or to tutor the unprepared. We need resources to cope with the life-draining effect of continued struggles, the prosaic preoccupations versus the properly animating spirit and ethos of the whole. Conversation can provide these resources.

CONCLUSION

There are good reasons for considering conversation our key metaphor in expressing the nature of effective learning, reflecting on the character of academic community, and understanding our work as teacher/scholars. Unlike many received images, conversation points toward the objective and subjective integrity of voices and idioms; the importance of the active engagement of those participating—faculty and students alike; the social and self-referential character of education; the need for hospitable openness to the other—near and far; the roles of spirituality, narrative, and adventure.

Education invites us into the multitude of voices, idioms, and other representations of the human achievements and self-understandings that constitute our inheritance. It is by learning to engage in this conversation that we succeed to our inheritance, constitute our own humanity, and contribute to that of others. Through their conversations, colleges and universities offer opportunities for the systematic, deliberate, and constructive practice of hospitality. They provide the occasion and the context for exploring, examining, evaluating, and reconstructing individual and collective goods. Theirs is a precious trust that is jeopardized by compromising behaviors.

Finally, conversation invites us to consider the importance of hospitality and covenant as allied concepts in a collegial ethic. The truth is always pluralistic and provisional. Differences that emerge in conversation present opportunities for reconciliation and mutual transformation through deeper and more subtle concepts than mere oppositional ones. As we see in the next chapter, conversation has multiple implications for our work as teacher/scholars and for the educational community we create and nourish. It is a rich and capacious metaphor that extends to many forms of education, professional as well as liberal learning.

REFERENCES

Allan, G. (1996, Fall/Winter). Playing with worlds: John Dewey, the habit of experiment, and the goods of democracy. *Soundings, 79* (3–4), 447–468.

Allan, G. (1997). *Rethinking college education.* Lawrence, KS: University Press of Kansas.

Anderson, C. W. (1993). *Prescribing the life of the mind: An essay on the purpose of the university, the aims of liberal education, the competence of citizens, and the cultivation of practical reason.* Madison, WI: University of Wisconsin Press.

Bellah, R. N., Madsen, R., Sullivan, W. M., Swidler, A., & Tipton, S. M. (1991). *The good society.* New York, NY: Random House.

Benhabib, S. (1992). *Situating the self: Gender, community, and postmodernism in contemporary ethics.* New York, NY: Routledge.

Bennett, J. B. (1998). *Collegial professionalism: The academy, individualism, and the common good.* Phoenix, AZ: American Council on Education/Oryx Press.

Farley, E. (1988). *The fragility of knowledge: Theological education in the church and the university.* Philadelphia, PA: Fortress Press.

Gregory, M. (1987, Summer). If education is a feast, why do we restrict the menu? A critique of pedagogical metaphors. *College Teaching, 35* (3), 101–106.

Habermas, J. (1984). *Theory of communicative action* (I. T. McCarthy, Trans.). Boston, MA: Beacon Press.

Oakeshott, M. (1989). *The voice of liberal learning* (T. Fuller, Ed.). New Haven, CT: Yale University Press.

Oakeshott, M. (1991). *Rationalism in politics and other essays.* Indianapolis, IN: Liberty Press.

O'Brien, G. D. (1998). *All the essential half-truths about higher education.* Chicago, IL: University of Chicago Press.

Tannen, D. (2000, March 31). Agonism in the academy: Surviving higher learning's argument culture. *The Chronicle of Higher Education*, p. B7.

Wolfe, A. (1998, December 4). How a for-profit university can be invaluable to the traditional liberal arts. *The Chronicle of Higher Education*, p. B4.

ENDNOTES

1. Of course, there are other common metaphors, equally unfortunate. Among them are the banking metaphor in which teachers create lines of credit which students draw down as they need and the newer "conduit" image of teaching as downloading files of information into student minds. The cooking metaphor describes teachers who distill or boil things down for their students. Other metaphors portray student minds as clay and wax awaiting impressions, or as empty rooms to be furnished. Organic metaphors—such as instructors planting seeds, clearing brush, fertilizing soil, cultivating or strengthening flabby muscles, etc.—come closer to the relationality for which I am arguing, though they still neglect student activity.

2. In an earlier publication (Bennett, 1998, pp. 109–115), I introduced two other metaphors for teaching and learning—conceptual construction and dance. The first emphasizes the theories, facts, values, and sensibilities we carry within us and that give us identity, perspective, and tools for engaging each other and the world. The metaphor of the dance emphasizes the social, risky, and self-implicating interactions among faculty and students characteristic of good teaching and learning. Both metaphors have considerable merit, but they presuppose the metaphor of conversation I develop here.

3. In this section, with the permission of the Association of American Colleges and Universities, I incorporate parts of "Liberal Learning as Conversation" which appeared in *Liberal Education, 87* (2) (Spring 2001), 32–39.

4. The philosophical point is that there can be no truly private language. The conditions of language are themselves public, and must be invoked even in a private one.

5. I draw here on language I used in "The Academy and Hospitality," originally published in *CrossCurrents: The Journal of the Association for Religion and Intellectual Life,* Spring/Summer, 2000, Vol. 50, Nos. 1 & 2, 23–35.

The Uses of
 Conversation 6

As a metaphor for education, "conversation" applies not just to the classroom, nor is it just for students. It applies throughout the institution and characterizes the diversity of faculty work. As conversation, teaching, scholarship and service are interactive and self-referential. Each is self-involving and requires others. Each highlights both reason and imagination. Each is both disciplined and open to unanticipated developments. This chapter explores in greater depth some of the implications of the collegial ethic of hospitality and conversation for teaching, scholarship, and service.

TEACHING AND LEARNING

If education is throughout a kind of conversation, what can we say about hospitable teachers and teaching? I offer four observations: instructor authority is complex—both already, and not yet. Successful teaching involves inviting as well as structuring inquiry. Teaching points to a collegium it helps create. And it requires individual and collective self-regulation.

The Complexity of Authority

The authority of the instructor is both given and something to establish. Faculty members have an initial home-turf advantage. They work in settings that highlight their authority. However challenging the specific setting—crowded classrooms, required courses, students in courses well beyond their preparation or abilities—a structure of authority is already in place. The instructor is at the head of the class, chooses the pedagogy, and constructs syllabi, assignments, and course objectives. Whether the class is located down the hall or over the Internet, he or she selects evaluation mechanisms and timetables, establishes conditions under which those enrolled can continue, and usually assesses overall student performance. Students as well as faculty take this for granted.

On the other hand, instructor authority must be individually established. Even in favorable settings, faculty members must create conditions for continued learning. Usually there is little time, and success is uncertain. Techniques are important. Involving students in active learning, using learning communities and other forms of collaborative processes, attending consistently to individual learning styles, engaging judicious assessment measures—all these help students find and develop their own voices. But techniques are never sufficient. Beyond them is the person and character of the individual instructor. Students easily discriminate between hospitable instructors interested in *their* learning and those who are rote and distant, simply going through "educationally correct" paces.

Good teachers know that learning is not a possession to be acquired, defended, and sequestered. It is to be used, shared, and extended. No learning occurs in a vacuum and good teachers are sensitive to the particularity of the other. They select with care the examples they use, case studies they assign, and topics of discussions they promote. They support student creativity and encourage individual talents. They are committed to uphold student self-respect—not to provide pity or therapy or even necessarily to enhance self-esteem. They help students distinguish between educational wants and needs. They thread between the extremes of parentalism and relativism—between imposing their own positions, and letting anything go. Successful instructors also continue to learn. They add to their knowledge, investing in new learning rather than simply drawing down past capital. They exercise their own voices. They teach out of firsthand engagement, not simply the engagements of others.

When they do these things and live this way, instructors create and extend their authority. When they don't, they establish conditions for failure—for themselves and their students. Faculty relinquish authority when they forget about relationality, cease trusting others, and abandon education as conversation. Their ethics lose tensiveness, becoming flabby or rigid, and their spiritualities shrink. Teaching is a vocation, not just a job—it is a calling that makes more of us. It stands in contrast to behaviors that make less of us—through our insistent individualism or the corrupting practices of others and our own institutions.

Issuing Invitations

Hospitable instructors know they can only invite students into conversation—not force or compel them. Forced conversants learn little more than that forced conversation is agonizing. Whitehead (1967b) noted that "education must essentially be a setting in order of a ferment already stirring in the mind" (p. 18). Instructors cannot *create* student motivation. But they *can* set in order what is "already stirring" so as to avoid dead ends. They can connect academic inquiry and everyday experience. Some teachers start with the inquiry and ask students to bring their experience to it. Hospitable teachers are more likely to start with student experiences and then bring questions and interpretations from academic disciplines. They nurture the conversation by observing what Whitehead (1967b) called the natural rhythm of learning with its three pedagogical moments: learning starts with romance, moves into precision, and culminates in generalization which then precipitates more romance—and so forth. The moments are interwoven, but a specific moment predominates at each stage of the rhythm.

The stage of romance holds out a new idea or experience, something tantalizing but still unfocused. It highlights "the excitement consequent on the transition from the bare facts to the first realisations of the import of their unexplored relationships" (Whitehead, 1967b, p. 18). Hospitable teachers introduce the detail of precision at the right time—*after* romance has evoked student interest in the conversation. Probably much of the anger Jane Tompkins (1996) reports at the boredom of her elementary school experience— "the repetitiousness, the formulaic quality" (p. 32)—stems from pedagogical practices that dwelt on discipline and precision at the expense of romance. She was forced to stay with "Dick and Jane" and other tedious exercises when she was yearning for avenues into the wider world.

By contrast, hospitable instructors start with the novel and the arresting. They acknowledge where their students are, and they throw the light of wonderment upon the ordinary. These instructors realize the importance of imagination. They know that learning must hold "within itself unexplored connexions with possibilities half-disclosed by glimpses and half-concealed by the wealth of material" (Whitehead, 1967b, p. 17). It is the lure of discovery, of exploring the unknown, that draws learners forward. Students learn to place themselves imaginatively within the viewpoint or stance of the new and the strange—to experience the other directly, not just "objectively" as a distant object. Simone Weil's "attention" and Parker Palmer's "displacement of self" are invoked and practiced.

It is only in the second stage of precision that hospitable instructors introduce abundant detail and bring self-conscious critical thinking into play. Detail is studied for the abstractions it exhibits. Coherence rather than breadth is emphasized. Assumptions that were imaginatively considered earlier are now analyzed and challenged. Discipline is rigorous and conspicuous. Principles are discerned, skills are developed, and techniques are mastered. Even so, classroom precision has limits. Gabriel Moran (1997) also sees education as conversation: "The classroom . . . is a place for a peculiar kind of conversation—ultimately a conversation about the nature of conversation" (p. 213).

Finality is not the point. The skillful teacher "turns the words of the conversation back on themselves. Every question asked, every problem raised has ambiguity built into the formulation" (Moran, 1997, p. 213). Clarity is forever a goal, not an achievement. Conversations may be unconcluded, but they do have a direction. "We can hope to narrow misunderstandings even if we cannot reach complete agreement" (Moran, 1997, p. 213). The job of the instructor is both to invite and to channel—"to be certain that there are enough voices in the discussion and that the terms of the dispute are carefully reflected upon" (Moran, 1997, p. 213).

The third moment in the rhythm, the stage of generalization, occurs when learners own and engage in new ways the principles, skills, and techniques they have discussed. The point is to catch on and to carry on. As Wittgenstein (1963) says of the moment when knowing occurs—"Now I can do it" (p. 59). Now students have the understanding and insight to continue without the instructor. They use their knowledge to add value to experience—to discover and apply patterns and relationships in new areas. Practice is liberated and freedom is increased. Indeed, now the student can instruct others—helping to shape self and others into persons of humane sensibilities and sound judgment.

In this process, hospitable instructors tailor conversation to the circumstances of the learner, remembering that learning is to be used. Otherwise it becomes inert and burdensome knowledge. The stage of generalization is really an initiation into new forms of life, themselves always self-transcending—always issuing into new moments of romance that call for ever new adjustments in precision. New questions emerge as fresh phases of romance unfold and initiate new cycles of the rhythm of learning.

Hospitable conversations emphasize the learning paradigm. Teaching is but one means of producing learning. This paradigm contrasts with metaphors that highlight activities, like lecturing, that emphasize faculty control. Under the influence of images like storage and production, what passes for conversation is rarely hospitable. It is engaged with an eye toward instructor power and security—reducing faculty vulnerability by limiting risk and exposure. Controlling conversations promote hierarchies and heighten individual status—creating the competitions and separatism of insistent individualism.

Paths to Failure

The paths to instructional failure are broad. One route to killing student excitement is to squelch the ferment of novel possibilities by insisting prematurely upon theory and precision. Another is to downplay or omit generalization—to neglect interpreting novel experience through expanding, engaging, and testing new forms of life. Students remind us of our pedagogical failures when they ask, "What does this course have to do with *my* life?" Academic excellence is not opposed to human relevance, to the application of learning to self, society, and world.

Both romance and generalization are ways of honoring patterns of connectedness that undergird our lives. Attending to these patterns sustains us in our efforts to move beyond our narrow selves. Precision by itself does not. When higher education loses sight of vibrant connections with individual lives, it works against itself and moves toward a deadening, rather than enlivening, spirituality. All students are to be welcomed to the community of scholars and encouraged to develop their intellectual skills. Honoring the rhythm of learning is a welcome way to make this happen.

Instructors also follow a route to failure when they dwell *only* on their own experiences—reading solely from their own scripts, drowning out or distorting other voices. In authentic educational conversation, instructors present these other voices *and* add their own tonality and nuance. They reveal why the selected voice is personally important and where it is inadequate, thereby contributing to the conversation and inviting their students to respond. If higher learning does not affect our inner selves, it violates our credo that only the examined life is worth living and that truth is liberating. Faculty show by their own example the difference learning makes.

They seek a middle path between bland disengagement from what they teach and intemperate advocacy and proselytizing. They have firsthand knowledge of the subject matter and can articulate the standards immanent in it. Instructors, Victor Worsfold (2000) reminds us, cease being authoritative and become authoritarian when they lose the capacity to explain *why* their way of teaching is "a right way to go about the business of education" (p. 119). This "right" way mediates the relationship among instructors, subject matter, and students. Familiar alternatives to this triadic relationship are forms of education such as transmission or production that impede the development of student autonomy.

Creating a Collegium

Like students, instructors are empowered when they dwell in the metaphor of conversation. They too must find and use their own voices, engaging in and contributing to conversation. They cannot be neutral transmitters of others' voices—tape decks that present recordings, devoid of their own imaginative renderings and reflections. "First-hand knowledge is the ultimate basis of intellectual life. The second-handedness of the learned world is the secret of its mediocrity. It is tame because it has never been scared by facts" (Whitehead, 1967b, p. 51). Truly to teach is to abandon timidity, to court vulnerability, to risk failure.

Honest teaching requires being accessible to students as well as justifying assignments and evaluations. It includes careful comment on students' work. It means persisting in conversation in the face of student indifference or hostility—especially when one must acknowledge "I don't know." The hospitable instructor is a subject-matter resource without being an "authority" in the way Jane Tompkins rightly condemns—one whose position others are to treat as authoritative, demanding imitation, and thus fostering dependency. But Tompkins (1996) overstates the point in claiming that "you have to be willing to give up your authority, and the sense of identity and prestige that come with it, for the students to be able to feel their own authority" (p. 147). The best learning calls for authority for *both* instructor and student. As facilitator of learning, the teacher is indeed host. But teachers require students; it is students who create teachers; so teachers are also guests. Further, teacher and learner, host and guest, are constantly interchanging roles and activities.

Faculty practice these things as a matter of course in a healthy academic community. They recognize students as well as other faculty as colleagues in the etymological sense, as linked together. Taking this linkage seriously, they create the collegium—the heart or core of the educational enterprise, the center that holds things together. Without hospitable conversation and other forms of mutual engagement, the collegium falters and eventually disintegrates. Concerns for self-promotion and self-protection drown out other voices. Instead of a conversation there are soliloquies. The *superbia* of which Oakeshott wrote occurs when faculty fail to attend to students and to each other, to be open to each other's interests and work, and to model genuine conversation.

To be sure, simply calling for more conversation cannot alone produce it. Exhorting turns into haranguing and hectoring. But faculty knowledge ought to have large personal effect. It should make a difference in one's voice and teaching. It should push one toward creating the collegium—and inviting the sharing and receiving of hospitable conversation. Hospitable instructors in the educational conversation are accessible models of self-regulated learners. Harry Payne (1996) reminds us of our critical role in modeling the virtues we recommend:

> The strengths and weaknesses we faculty and staff members display . . . are sharply watched and constitute part of our teaching. Our students study us, as well as their academic courses and each other. We teach the academic and character virtues insofar as we *display* and *enact* those virtues. (p. 25)

This is a heady and somber fact. Who we are, what we do, as well as what we say and how we say it, are elements of our teaching. Efforts to disguise ourselves or to present politically correct faces are more easily detected by students and colleagues than we may recognize or want to accept.

Hospitable instructors are exemplary, not elite, educators. Elite educators remain at a distance from others. The exemplary are in the midst of others. They are within, not outside, the learning community. It is exemplary educators, not elite ones, in whom authentic educational authority inheres. Through their own behavior they illustrate why more than acquiring a credential is at stake. Their own personal and professional lives attest to the value of participating in the conversation. Oakeshott (1989) presents the faculty role in modeling education as conversation by using another metaphor—"Not the cry, but the rising of the wild duck impels the flock to follow him in flight" (p. 62).

We know that much teaching in higher education is highly privatized. Unlike other professions where practitioners observe and talk with one another about the nature of their practice, most faculty teach behind closed doors. After emerging, they rarely talk with others about what they did. Parker Palmer (1993) suggests that this custom may have origins "in some misguided concept of academic freedom, but it persists . . . because faculty choose it as a mode of self-protection against scrutiny and evaluation" (p. 8). It is sad and ironic, Palmer observes, that precisely "this choice of isolation leads to some of the deepest dissatisfactions in academic life" (p. 8).

And the consequences are not only individual in nature. Institutions can scarcely improve their teaching mission in the absence of honest, continuing conversations about teaching and learning. Instead, "the most likely outcome . . . is that people will perform the function conservatively, refusing to stray far from the silent consensus on what 'works'—even when it clearly does not" (Palmer, 1993, p. 8). At the very least, we should talk with instructors about whose teaching students complain year after year—and from whom we shelter our better students. We avoid them because they are colleagues, we want to be nice, and they are tenured. However, in working around them—listing their courses as taught by "staff" is a favorite tactic—we short change students and ourselves.

SCHOLARSHIP

Authority Again

The authority of the scholar is also complex. On the one hand, there are structures into which every new scholar is inducted. There are protocols for validation of learning, for peer review, and for presentation of find-ings. These protocols, together with the cachet of funded research and participation in learned societies, represent a preexisting structure of authority. The hierarchy of presses, journals, and conferences provides an additional element of standing. Within one's discipline, these are widely known and accepted.

On the other hand, behind the structures of scholarship stands the person and character of the individual. The hospitable scholar is genuinely open to conversation about the insights and criticisms of others, however threatening or painful, and allows them purchase upon his or her thinking. Openness improves the quality of scholarship, provid-ing on balance more careful and better argued positions as well as more fruitful connections with other inquiries. Likewise, the hospitable scholar is one who presents his or her findings to others in accessible terms, rather than in recondite discourse. Hospitable scholars consider how their work contributes to the broader culture within which it occurs. What is its wider human significance? How might it interest and help others? What are the background public questions, concerns, and issues that it addresses?

The successful teacher/scholar attends to these matters consistently. This is a matter more of fundamental character and disposition than highly self-conscious rule-directed behavior. Faculty who rigorously remind themselves of the importance of hospitable conversations are likely to become successful teacher/scholars. But the most successful are those already disposed toward openness to the other and for whom rules and principles are only guides. They know firsthand the vulnerability of the teacher/scholar—the anxious and debilitating fear of others as threats to intellectual safety, the risk one takes in accepting the responsibility of facilitating learning, and the possibility of ridicule from colleagues when presenting scholarly findings. But for them, the best defense is not aggressive offense, but persistent openness. They practice courage and persevere.

In conducting scholarship hospitably, we accord the objects of our inquiry appropriate respect, fight biased preconceptions, and welcome new disclosures. Hospitable scholars refuse the temptation to domesticate their object of study—to render it private property subject to their own rules and control. In forgoing control, in resisting the temptation to stake out property claims, they put present standards and preunderstandings in perspective. Many are unwilling to do this.

Others, though, see scholarship and writing as spiritual practices. They protest the commodifying of writing, reducing it to a currency minted for career advancement—and then trading the necessary units for tenure and promotion. Instead, they understand writing as a way of practicing how to attend and to receive the world through the work of others, dwelling in this work and conversing with it in order to discover what one thinks, and then inviting others to respond. We can write about our scholarship so that we invite others into conversation, or we can write to exclude them.

As a spiritual practice, writing is a sacrament of the academy. It is a form of testimony with the good of others at its heart. It draws on the virtues of humility, perseverance, and courage. Humility is necessary because our writing is never good enough. We must persevere, constantly revising in order to find just the right word and phrase. And we must be courageous, precisely because we believe that what we write should matter to others. This "requires that each writing project begin and end with others, both those near at hand, and those we may never know, but to whom and for whom we write" (Paulsell, 2002, p. 29).

Common Responsibilities

Every scholarly and creative project exists in a larger context. Scholarship is not opposed to teaching and service. It need not separate us from each other or from the broader public. Often, though, academic publications are inaccessible to anyone beyond a small group of initiates and we fail to convey why our scholarship matters. Privatizing the excitement and value of discovery and learning is a form of inhospitality. Broader conversations about why discovery and learning are important contribute to the public good. As Frank Rhodes (1998) observes, "most of us regard our scholarship as completed when it is published, exhibited, or performed. But we need to move beyond mere publication to explanation and advocacy for research as such" (p. 9).

When we fail to explain research findings and passions, we desert our colleagues and abandon a public that in the long run will support us only when we make understandable what we do and why it deserves support. Rather than a private affair, hospitable scholarship is a conversation that relates us *to* others, rather than separates us *from* them. Progress in this kind of scholarship may involve conflict, but consistent advance is marked by constructive conflict, not the competitions of insistent individualism. Parker Palmer (1998) reminds us that "competition is a secretive, zero-sum game played by individuals for private gain; conflict is open and sometimes raucous but always communal, a public encounter in which it is possible for everyone to win by learning and growing" (p. 103).

Scholarly competitions marked by drawn-out and aggressively individualistic battles over status, territoriality, or possession are inevitably unproductive. The cost of protecting oneself is simply too high. Anxiety and fatigue win out. However, false peace is also damaging. Passivity, inattention to one another, and disinterest in either challenging or confirming truth claims are no better than aggressive competition. In the long run, truth and learning are advanced only by mutual interest in sharing and receiving perspectives and ideas. Jointly interrogating concepts and evidence is essential.

But traditional competitions continue to stand in the way of hospitable conversations. A classic example is the chasm between the sciences and humanities delineated in C. P. Snow's analysis of the two cultures. Now, though, differences between humanists and scientists can include not just subject matter and method, but issues of morality. For instance, some humanists claim that scientists hide under a mask of value neutrality, presenting a pure and disinterested inquiry into reality while concealing their own personal and group ideologies. By contrast, these humanists present themselves as working to reveal elements of social construction in all inquiry. Theirs, they suggest, is the more honest way because ideology is everywhere. From their perspective, "humanists tell each other where they are coming from. Scientists act as if they come from nowhere" (Bauerlein, 2001, p. B14).

In truth, though, the commitment of scientists to rigorous peer review makes theirs the more defensible way. As Mark Bauerlein reminds us, the real difference between scientists and humanists is that the former rely on a community of diverse peer review in order to filter out unwarranted individual bias. Most humanists do not. Scientists must be able to replicate the studies they review. The individual scientist may be loaded

with ideologies, self-preoccupations, ruthless ambitions, and other characteristics of insistent individualism. But scientific claims to objectivity emerge
only when a community of sufficiently diverse reviewers warrants them.
Indeed, the scientific community tacitly assumes "that individuals act on
vested interests, career demands, and political pressures. Peer review doesn't
overlook these things. It determines whether they have corrupted the
inquiry. That is how individual bias and collective objectivity coexist"
(Bauerlein, 2001, p. B14). The objectivity of science is a relational, not an
individual, accomplishment. It is an achievement of the collegium.

Other academic competitions also obscure common values and
commitments. For instance, our squabbling suggests that teaching and
research are opposed, if not incompatible, pursuits. Time spent on one is
deemed unavailable for the other. Yet our traditions remind us that effective,
energetic teaching requires thoughtful, disciplined attention to scholarship.
And any scholarship of value must be presented to others in understandable
and provocative ways that facilitate further research and learning—elements
characteristic of good teaching as well. Hospitable educators honor connections between teaching and research rather than defining them opposition-
ally. They know that conversation enriches both activities. They also know
the academy enjoys its many privileges on condition that it exercises ongoing and collective self-regulation.

Hospitable Conversations and Critical Inquiry

Failures in hospitable conversation constrain critical inquiry as well as
connections with others. Critical inquiry requires open, respectful, and disciplined conversations among those with different perspectives. But these can
be difficult to initiate. Distinguishing between scholarship and speculation,
Whitehead (1933) observes that the

> thorough-going scholar resents the airy speculation which
> connects his own patch of knowledge with that of his neighbor.
> He finds his fundamental concepts interpreted, twisted, modi-
> fied. He has ceased to be king of his own castle, by reason of
> speculations of uncomfortable generality, violating the very
> grammar of his thoughts. (p. 138)

The temptation of the scholar is to stay in his or her own castle, to resist
connections with neighbor scholars. They work in different patches of
knowledge, and learning their concepts and methods is time-consuming and
difficult.

However, we need both scholarship and speculation. We need the carefully defined analysis of limited dimensions *and* the development of more general concepts that connect and correct various domains of knowledge. We need reliable, traditional canons of interpretation and practice that have served us well. We need careful attention to stubborn fact and the selective orderings of established practice. Problems must be manageable. But we need as well to test the limits of these canons, to analyze the presuppositions of specific positions, and to consider newer and broader schemes that extend our understanding and serve us better in the changed circumstances of a global community. Otherwise, the manageable becomes the trivial.

Even though we need both scholarship and speculation, we seem to have an excess of scholarship—of practical reason, and of things studied apart—and a deficiency of critical speculation. We neglect the construction and use of general concepts to establish connections between domains of knowledge. Precisely because things are lived together, they must be studied together. Without general concepts that serve as conversational bridges, we remain trapped in our castles and territories. We become individualists even though we depend upon the work of others and are recipients of vast traditions of prior scholarship.

Engaging in scholarly conversation involves respecting evidence and upholding the standards of critical temper. Consider, for instance, scholarship about the past. Practicing conversational hospitality means dealing with our historical inheritance in neither an antiquarian (as objects of curiosity) nor absolutizing manner. The one way trivializes the past; the other sacralizes it. On the one hand, honoring our inheritance requires more than dwelling on dates, battles, formulas, and creeds. These data abstract from human activity. They omit the interiority of the practices— their implicit claims about reality and the self. Treating the past in an antiquarian way makes it an inert object, rather than the living heritage in which we dwell—a heritage that viewed with sensitivity, and combined with the challenges of the present, can evoke transforming possibilities for the future.

On the other hand, sacralizing the past refuses the critical speculation for which Whitehead is calling. The strength and vigor of conversation rest not in defending the old against the new, but rather in the renewal and creativity that conversation with the past can provoke. Openness to new ways of understanding the past is essential to being confirmed or contradicted, to having ideas expanded or disturbed. Hospitable scholars attend to the past to address new challenges and accommodate intriguing new possibilities. This can be difficult work. Considerable effort may be required to recognize new, revised standards and insights as possibilities for the self, analogous to what has born fruit in past experience.

What is required is reflection on the past as a carrier of values for the present. This is education as conversation with traditions. Indeed, this is what O'Brien (1998) suggests we recognize as the "tradition *of* tradition-ing" (p. 191)—learning how traditions have developed their own inner rationales, their shared languages of critique and appraisal, their standards of discourse and assessment. And learning that it is critical openness to traditions and to future revisings of those traditions that ensures the vitality of any tradition.

SERVICE

Teaching and scholarship are often distanced from service. But the three are ultimately inseparable, their borders fluid and porous. They are short-hand ways of speaking about one complex activity, not three discrete ones. Teaching must be energized and fortified by scholarship even as it raises questions that require scholarship; the "making public" that is the completion of scholarship is teaching; both teaching and scholarship are forms of educational service, and without them there is no academy.

In its broader sense, "service" points to ensuring that the conditions for hospitality and conversational integrity in teaching and scholarship are in place. It calls for faculty to attend collectively to the health of the collegium, both internally and externally. Even though their main interests and primary covenants are often disciplinary—rather than rooted in the institution where they work and draw paychecks—faculty must attend to institutional academic integrity. Although situated in dispassionate critical reason and universal principle, they are also entangled in, and must attend to, the history and destiny of their institutions.

Institutions can help. Thus, the institutions of the Associated New American Colleges call for a new academic compact between faculty and institutions—a covenant marked by greater reciprocity of attention and accommodation, a deeper recognition that faculty work and institutional purpose shape and require each other (McMillin & Berberet, 2002).

On the one hand, institutions need to share more information with faculty, invite greater participation, and provide incentives to contribute to overall institutional governance. Institutions need to attend to their faculty as their key capital resource. On most campuses this involves greater institutional openness to the needs of faculty at different stages in their careers. It suggests providing more personalized faculty development support, for instance, than a uniform approach. With better support, faculty can contribute to institutional vitality at a time when institutions need to become more responsive and resilient in the face of rapid change and fierce competition.

On the other hand, faculty need to attend more energetically to their institutional citizenship—especially where cultures of institutional fragmentation and faculty preoccupation discourage it. "Who am I?" is related to "Where am I?" One way of increasing faculty interest in contributing to institutional vitality is to change reward structures, increasing unit accountability by evaluating and rewarding the performance of programs and departments, not just individual faculty accomplishments. The goal should be to promote institutional as well as broader academic citizenship (McMillin & Berberet, 2002).

I am speaking of an enlarged, more fundamental sense of service— one that includes responsibility for the care and nourishment of the local common good. In this primary sense, service underlies teaching and scholarship or research—becoming the most inclusive and most important of the traditional triad. Service is the most encompassing category because it elevates our professional obligation to make hospitality, conversation, and covenant constitutive elements of all teaching and research. However, it has been customary to treat teaching as the inclusive category. After all, to teach well is to foster learning and any work of scholarship or research must prove its worth by contributing to learning. But service also contributes to the learning of others, and in a more inclusive way. Teaching informed by scholarship is basic, but service is working to assure that this concept of teaching prevails. As an inclusive category, service means commitment to teaching informed by scholarship as well as concern for the integrity of one's discipline *and* institution.

Teaching and learning give colleges and universities their distinctive reasons for being. Otherwise they could be replaced by think tanks and research institutes. Indeed, at various times, countries *have* located research elsewhere in order to emphasize the centrality of teaching. But without ongoing research, teachers go flat in living off past capital. Scholarship and research are important in their own right, but it is institutional teaching to which they can contribute and in which they find their college and university home. It is the fundamental service responsibility of educators to ensure that this conversation occurs—that the insight, imagination, and understanding of learning are generated by teaching informed by scholarship. Teaching and learning are central to the university. Service is fundamental to securing this centrality.

Societal expectations may violate these conditions. Legislators and other public figures often pressure institutions for services that distort true educational priorities. These public figures may say they want good teaching, but what they really mean is contribution to regional economic development. Others want *their* values celebrated and advanced, not criticized, by the academy. Nonetheless, the proper service of colleges and universities is to promote learning marked by critical reflection, not economics, politics or personal preferences. No other institution has this distinctive social role. Only the academy is chartered to conduct critical reflection as a service to society. It is in support of this service that the familiar claims for institutional autonomy and professional academic freedom are grounded.

Unfortunately, faculty and administrators often regard service as the least important of the triad. They speak as though the key issue were whether service for which one is paid is as meritorious as that which is voluntary, and they debate the best way of measuring an individual's participation in committees which he or she lists as service activities. Debates about measuring contributions can be valuable. And the ordinary understandings of service are essential—attention must be paid to academic advising, committee work, hiring and promoting, and curricular revision. But underneath these activities is the bedrock requirement that the conditions that make for hospitality in the academy are in place. Attending to this requirement is the fundamental service each educator owes. This responsibility, I suggest, is at the heart of what being tenured entails, not merely protection of academic freedom—much less, job security.

Promoting Diversity

Understanding service as promoting conditions that advance learning requires honoring and promoting diversity. It means bridging boundaries that exclude. Too often, the collegium is narrowly defined in terms of disciplinary purity, department control, or other forms of exclusion. Fear of contamination or even absorption by the other reinforces this view. But we do not promote diversity by assimilating the other into our frames of reference or by projecting our experience on the other. Diversity corrects and supplements the inevitable partiality of the individual. To promote and appreciate diversity is to acknowledge that the other can make a difference, perhaps creating new knowledge and significant changes in self-understanding.

When this happens, barriers between the self and other can be crossed. The gaps that separate are bridged, altering the boundaries that define selves. There is greater appreciation of commonality between host and guest—appreciation of shared need and insight. The challenge of diversity extends beyond welcoming women and minorities, providing appropriate support and fair opportunities—much as this needs to be done. On many campuses adjunct or part-time faculty are treated as strangers or as deficient in academic credentials and thus excluded from serious participation in the collegium. Sometimes the collegium is closed to administrators with faculty credentials. In these and other cases, individuals are subsumed under some limited defining principle or category and restricted from full participation in, and contribution to, the collegium.

Openness to ourselves and to reclaiming our past is also important. When we are uncomfortable with ourselves, our fear and anxiety prevent us from being hospitable not only to strangers but even to colleagues. For coworkers often present the greatest threat to intellectual or professional standing. The result is mutual suspicion and defensiveness, and sometimes hostile rivalries—not the conversation we need. The hospitality that undergirds and fuels conversation is about relationships, not possessions or territory. It involves creation of shared space. It means enlargement of personal identity. It requires elimination of unnecessary boundaries, while preserving and protecting those necessary to remain individuals. Hospitable conversations involve a sense of self and self-confidence, of appreciation for our own traditions, value, and identity, that provide the strength and self-respect required to be genuinely open to the other.

Conversation About Education

Education as conversation requires conversation about education. Among the most rewarding topics are those in which participants return to the expectations that brought them into education and compare them with current realities. For instance, a common lament is the deficiencies of today's students. Palmer (1993) describes this faculty penchant: "nothing is easier than to slip into a low opinion of students, and that opinion creates teaching practices guaranteed to induce vegetative states even in students who arrive for class alive and well" (p. 11). Palmer's diagnosis is that the apparent indifference, even hostility, of many students reflects another aspect of the culture of fear noted earlier. Here it is the students' own fear that is at issue. "The young have been thoroughly marginalized by the elders of this society, and their deepest response is not an angry rejection of us but a fearful internalization of our rejection of them" (Palmer, 1993, p. 11). Palmer contends that even nontraditional students can be fearful of the teacher's judgment, however skillfully they mask it.

A community of conversation with colleagues about teaching is the best way to move ahead. Perhaps, Palmer suggests, in such conversations we can see more deeply into ourselves. It may be that "we cannot see the fears that haunt our students because we ourselves are haunted by the fear that our students have rejected us" (Palmer, 1993, p. 11). In addressing this fear, some of us opt for a preemptive strike. "We defend ourselves against the implicit judgment on our lives by declaring our judges intellectually and morally bankrupt" (Palmer, 1993, p. 11). Clearly, conversation about our teaching and students needs to consider the broader issues Palmer raises.

Some institutions have found that cross-departmental groups provide the best environment for conversation. Too often departments contain residue and crosscurrents from prior disagreements about policies or practices. Faculty may be unable to separate colleagues from positions they defended. Department meetings may also be too large to provide the comfort and security necessary for sharing oneself. Accordingly, some institutions encourage the formation of special interest groups composed of five to eight faculty from different disciplinary areas who meet at times and on topics of their own choosing (McMillin & Berberet, 2002). Other institutions have established central units where faculty conversation about personal goals as well as teaching and research can occur.

Another locus of conversation about education is the space between academic and student affairs. Faculty often overlook the resources of student affairs staff in gaining keener insight into the cultures within which their students dwell. Peers exert powerful influence upon students as well as faculty—creating different kinds of collective insistent individualism. Counselors, residence hall directors, student union staff, and others can provide helpful clues on issues of student values and behaviors. And they, in turn, can profit from faculty conversation about instructional experiences.

After the September 11, 2001, attacks, a number of faculty report that incorporating into their classes discussion of the definition and import of terrorism has evoked an engagement otherwise lacking in encounters with their students. For many, the need to attend with intellectual interest and openness to cultures long ignored suddenly became clear. Shared human concern provides a bridge between the syllabus and the world we inhabit. Discussions among faculty about how to strengthen and cross this bridge provide opportunities for reviewing issues their course objectives should pursue.

From time to time educational conversation should focus on the broader meaning of peer review. Self-congratulatory talk about peer review is justified only when we are prepared to make it work—when we actually engage colleagues in serious, sustained conversation about educational goals, values, and standards. These conversations remind us of the expense of insistent individualism. Are the brief pleasures of upstaging opponents worth the damage created or the loneliness of isolation that results? It is only in regular, disciplined, and hospitable conversation that we exercise our calling and earn the privileges society has bestowed upon us as educators. We must provide peer review to others and insist they provide it to us.

Such conversations could help us become better models of humanizing knowledge. To our students and the broader public, we may appear not to believe ourselves when we declaim that higher education is intrinsically, rather than merely instrumentally, valuable—at the same time that we also complain about being underpaid and undervalued by society. Educators should not live in poverty. But we argue against ourselves when we appear to give greater voice to our own well-being than to the importance of student learning or to criticism of materialism and acquisitiveness. We witness best to academic integrity and a wholesome spirituality in articulating and modeling the meaning of higher learning, presenting a compelling and coherent picture—a contagious personal demonstration of valuing the life of the mind.

Engaging in, rather than avoiding, courageous conversation about the raveled edges of contemporary higher education can rejuvenate initial enthusiasm and provide hope for the future. We might find answers to some of our questions: How did education become a series of impersonal transactions between fragmented purveyors and consumers of learning? Why have we allowed fear of failure and lack of hospitality to reinforce each other? Why have we failed to deal with the chronic malcontents among us—those whose negative spirituality drains vitality and energy from the academy? Why do so many faculty profess their right and their desire to be involved in governance issues only to disappear when it is necessary to commit time and energy? Why do so many administrators become inaccessible and secretive?

CONVERSATION AND CURRICULUM

The metaphor of education as conversation relates to institutional structures as well. Conversation rather than territory should characterize departments and disciplines. Indeed, the institution itself should facilitate conversation. Its educational mission should itself *be* a conversation. This has clear implications for curricula. In examining the

importance of conversation for liberal learning and professional curricula alike, we must expand Oakeshott's position.

Liberal Education

At various points, Oakeshott expressly identifies the conversation of the
academy with liberal learning. For instance, he notes that as an education
in the importance of imagination, liberal learning initiates us

> into the art of this conversation in which we learn to recognize
> the voices; to distinguish their different models of utterance,
> to acquire the intellectual and moral habits appropriate to this
> conversational relationship and thus to make our *début dans
> la vie humaine.* (Oakeshott, 1989, p. 39)

Oakeshott's identification of conversation with liberal learning is
eminently appropriate, but unnecessarily restrictive. Attention to larger,
humane values and habits does indeed define liberal learning, but should
occur in professional education as well. It is here that we need to repair
and extend Oakeshott's thought.

Can we find grounds within conversation itself for a more extended
and hospitable concept of liberal learning? I think so. The understandings
we seek in conversation are often sought simply for themselves and as
such are ends in themselves. But even these understandings call out for
use in further conversation and in doing, making, and in yet more understanding—not for being sequestered or packed away. Conversation *is* an
apt metaphor for education, but liberal education needs to be dispersed
throughout the curriculum and the institution. In fact, we can use the
distinction Oakeshott draws between information and judgment to
expand the reach of liberal learning.

Information includes the facts, intellectual artifacts, and definitions
that are explicit ingredients in knowledge. Information provides rules, or
rule-like propositions, with which we are able to do, make, or understand
things. But facts and rules of information are never sufficient. Information never tells us how it should be used. Rules set limits, but conflicts
between rules are not resolved by more rules. Nor do rules direct one's
deepest understandings and expressions. "Art and conduct, science,
philosophy and history, these are not modes of thought *defined by* rules;
they exist only in personal explorations of territories" (Oakeshott, 1989,
p. 59). These "territories" are the "wide open spaces where no rule runs"
(Oakeshott, 1989, p. 50).

Therefore, in addition to knowing "that," there must be knowing "how"—there must be what Oakeshott calls judgment. Knowing how to engage information and rules, judgment is tacit or implicit, not propositional in the way of information. Judgment "is not merely unspecified in propositions but is unspecifiable in propositions" (Oakeshott, 1989, p. 54). At an elementary level, it is evident in skills like speaking a language. But judgment is more evident and far more important in addressing the larger challenges of how to live. "The further we go from manual and sensual skills the larger becomes the place occupied by this component of knowledge. . . . its place in art and literature, in historical, philosophical or scientific understanding is almost immeasurably greater" (Oakeshott, 1989, p. 55).

This knowing "how" is not something taught. There is no course on judgment any more than there is on hospitality. Judgment is rather something imparted in and through the information that is taught and learned. Judgment is not a different kind of information. It is, I suggest, akin to the insight into humanity and the human condition that for Oakeshott is achieved only through participation in conversation. But acquiring judgment is part of *all* education—including professional education.

We can also look to Whitehead's philosophy of education for help. In education we seek to possess our cultural inheritance as well as to revitalize our experience. We claim and then employ our inheritance for our renewal and recreation. Learning must be applied; unapplied learning is inert knowledge, a deadweight and a curse. Of course, understanding is an end in itself when sought simply as such. It is good in itself, as we say, and may be sought with no further, ulterior purpose or use in mind. Nonetheless, as Whitehead suggests, the nature of learning implies that it be used. If, for instance, the value of poetry includes delight in its presence, then precisely the experiencing of that delight is its use. Inert knowledge has no value, no application to self, no delight.

"Pedants," he observes, "sneer at an education which is useful. But if education is not useful, what is it? Is it a talent, to be hidden away in a napkin? [Education] is useful, because understanding is useful" (Whitehead, 1967b, p. 2). Harry Payne (1996) makes a similar point, reminding us of the oddity of some familiar declamations about the value of learning:

> We do sometimes talk about liberal learning as 'learning for its own sake,' presumably opposed to learning for specific technical and professional purposes—and seem to imply that this posture makes liberal learning superior. I have always found

such a position to be puzzling. Learning is hard work, and I am not at all sure it makes sense to learn for 'its' sake. Somehow I think we can show that all learning is for the sake of *something* beyond the act of learning itself. (p. 18)

To argue that one ought to study something completely independent of any potential usefulness suggests that it has no application to self, no practicality in this basic sense. This seems perverse because liberal learning is liberating, not useless; profoundly practical, not impractical. One pursues liberal education because it is its own reason—not because there is no reason. And its own reason is to add "control to the flux of experience" (Whitehead, 1936, p. 264). Life is as vague as it is orderly. Clear ideas with fixed meanings often fail before the court of experience. Far from applied liberal arts being oxymoronic, they seem essential in making our way through the unchartered waters, the open seas, of our lives.

Liberal learning involves the passing over and coming back we examined in Chapter Three. It facilitates stepping outside one's experience in order to examine it critically, to become aware of its limitations, and—thereby—to become liberated from its constraints without sacrificing its benefits. This is especially important in sharing texts and experiences we cherish, examining them from the standpoint of the other, while also critically absorbing the other's cherished texts and experiences. These moments of passing over and coming back raise questions that can be a tonic rather than a toxic substance and are part of the quest for a fuller selfhood, for imagined and desirable ways of being.

The notion that our spiritualities and ethics are largely fixed *before* college discounts the freedom of the present. It undervalues the agency of hospitality and presupposes a substantialist concept of the self, with personal identity established early and continuing largely unchanged. It is a philosophical and pedagogical mistake. Our identities continue to arise out of our relationships with others and the opportunities these relationships create.

Professional Schools
Conversation requires that every opportunity be seized to overcome the structural fragmentation of the modern university. Rather than standing apart from them, universities need to include professional schools for the elements of connectedness and suggestiveness about the world they represent. Schools of medicine, law, and business should not stand at the periphery. The business of the university is precisely to promote conversation among its schools, not to block it.

Universities have largely forsaken the certainty that Descartes and subsequent generations sought. In the present intellectual context, knowledge is related to and conditioned by one's particular perspective. It is a view from here, not from nowhere. Knowledge is relational to the concrete world. "True rationalism must always transcend itself by recurrence to the concrete in search of inspiration. A self-satisfied rationalism is in effect a form of anti-rationalism. It means an arbitrary halt at a particular set of abstractions" (Whitehead, 1967a, p. 201). The concrete, the world of our practice, is always more than our concepts capture. We can always learn more.

Hence the university needs close association with applied inquiries, especially those in which systematized understanding is prominent. Whitehead urges that we recover the concrete: "our traditional educational methods . . . are far too much occupied with intellectual analysis, and the acquirement of formularised information. . . . we neglect to strengthen habits of concrete appreciation of the individual facts in their full interplay" (Whitehead, 1967a, p. 198). I have argued that connectivity and relationality are metaphysically basic, that is, fundamental in reality. Our tendency to select, abstract, and isolate obscures these elements of connectedness. But if a university is to be a place for comprehensive study and conversation, it must be connected in its approaches and structures. Issues of societal management and improvement cannot be separated from those of meaning and truth. Professional schools belong within the university, not at the margins.

CONCLUSION

Conversation is a rich and capacious metaphor that extends to many forms of education. It involves both privilege and vulnerability. Educators have positions of authority and are entrusted with important service to students and to society. Generally they enjoy status and the benefit of the doubt. Yet their very status and privilege make them vulnerable. The risk of failure is high, often magnified by anxious uncertainty even about the definition of failure itself. Hospitable conversations are one way to reduce the risks. They decenter and deconstruct positions that privilege some at the expense of others—while reminding us of the importance and value of our past as the foundation of the present and the future.

Responsible educators know that teaching and learning occur in the context of hospitable conversations. Students and faculty interchange roles as they share and receive learning. Informed by the contributions others have made, scholars offer their own insights to the ongoing conversation. And through their attention to service, all educators support the conditions that undergird the practice of hospitality. Conversation provides coherence among these varied activities of teaching and learning, research and scholarship, service and engagement. And it should extend across the campus. The voices that constitute our human inheritance are heard in business as well as law, in the health sciences as well as technology. No matter what school or faculty one has in mind, to understand education as conversation highlights the liberation that higher learning promises.

REFERENCES

Bauerlein, M. (2001, November 16). The two cultures again: Tilting against objectivity. *The Chronicle of Higher Education*, p. B14.

McMillin, L. A., & Berberet, W. G. (2002). *A new academic compact: Revisioning the relationship between faculty and their institutions.* Bolton, MA: Anker.

Moran, G. (1997). *Showing how: The act of teaching.* Valley Forge, PA: Trinity Press.

Oakeshott, M. (1989). *The voice of liberal learning* (T. Fuller, Ed.). New Haven, CT: Yale University Press.

Oakeshott, M. (1991). *Rationalism in politics and other essays.* Indianapolis, IN: Liberty Press.

O'Brien, G. D. (1998). *All the essential half-truths about higher education.* Chicago, IL: University of Chicago Press.

Palmer, P. J. (1993, November/December). Good talk about good teaching: Improving teaching through conversation and community. *Change, 25* (6) 8–13.

Palmer, P. J. (1998). *The courage to teach: Exploring the inner landscape of a teacher's life.* San Francisco, CA: Jossey-Bass.

Paulsell, S. (2002). Writing as a spiritual discipline. In L. G. Jones & S. Paulsell (Eds.), *The scope of our art: The vocation of the theological teacher* (pp. 17–31). Grand Rapids, MI: William B. Eerdmans Publishing Company.

Payne, H. C. (1996, Fall). Can or should a college teach virtue? *Liberal Education, 82* (4), 18–25.

Rhodes, F. H. T. (1998) The university and its critics. In W. G. Bowen & H. T. Shapiro (Eds.), *Universities and their leadership* (pp. 3–14). Princeton, NJ: Princeton University Press.

Tompkins, J. (1996). *A life in school: What the teacher learned.* Reading, MA: Addison Wesley.

Whitehead, A. N. (1933). *Adventures of ideas.* New York, NY: Macmillan.

Whitehead, A. N. (1936). Harvard: The future. *The Atlantic Monthly, 138* (3), 260–270.

Whitehead, A. N. (1967a). *Science and the modern world.* New York, NY: The Free Press.

Whitehead, A. N. (1967b). *The aims of education and other essays.* New York, NY: The Free Press.

Wittgenstein, L. (1963). *Philosophical investigations* (G. E. M. Anscombe, Trans.). New York, NY: Macmillan.

Worsfold, V. L. (2000, Fall). Faculty excellence. *Perspectives, 30* (2), 113–127.

Community and Covenant

7

I have argued that the virtue of hospitality and the metaphor of conversation are essential ingredients in a healthy spirituality of higher education. I have explored their role in a philosophy that aims at holistic, organic, and integrated higher education. And I have considered their contribution to a more generous, authentic concept of academic ethics. Throughout, the major contrast has been the paradigm of insistent individualism, the all-too-prevalent ethos that glorifies a spirituality of self-preoccupation, a philosophy that advances fragmentation, and an ethics that risks the well-being of the very ones whose good educators are charged to promote.

Most of us are neither as self-preoccupied as insistent individualism suggests, nor as open to others as hospitality invites us. But we cannot simply sit in the middle, deciding who we are by failing to decide. How we relate to each another reflects which paradigm we endorse and what spiritual exercises we practice. Our choices steer us toward quite different concepts of community. I argue for the academic community as collegium, rather than as an aggregation of individualists. I also argue for the priority of covenant over social contract.

COMMUNITY AS COLLEGIUM—
NEITHER COLLECTIVE NOR AGGREGATION

How should we evaluate forms of academic community—the patterns of relationship among individual faculty members, students, colleagues, and institutions? The concept of the collective offers the prospect of harmony, but violates the integrity and creativity of members. Its uniformness bleaches out distinctiveness and dissipates energies. Individuals are submerged, their distinctiveness dwarfed and smothered. Collectivism represents a failure to achieve either individuality or community.

But understanding academic community as an aggregation of individualists is also unsatisfactory. In pursuing their private agendas, insistent individualists often work at cross purposes—thwarting each other rather than promoting mutually enhancing activities. There is little concept of a common good to promote. Self-preoccupation with career and comfort, pursuits elsewhere, or competitions with colleagues and students takes its place. Leibnitz's monads come to mind—beings without windows or doors to each other. But insistent individualists have few grounds for assuming Leibnitz's pre-established harmony or Adam Smith's invisible hand that guarantees a greater good.

Neither collectivism nor aggregation is satisfactory. Denying genuine individuality, collectivists reduce plurality to mere appearances that cloak an underlying unity. For their part, insistent individualists make community a matter of appearance. Both understandings discourage efforts to attend to and support one another, to connect and correct.

The Healthy Collegium

In contrast to collectives and aggregations, the healthy collegium is a community of real individuals linked through mutual relationships. It is the locus for the joint transformation of possible educational goods into actual ones. Members are bound together by a love of learning and by the conviction that *how* they foster learning is important. They appreciate one another as diverse individuals in common commitments. Independence of mind is celebrated, but exercised in community rather than in isolation. I prefer the name "collegium" for this form of academe. It connects us with the past and evokes elements of a closer-knit academy. But others may prefer different names such as "learning communities."

The collegium is more than a set of arrangements among individuals. Individuals *are* primary—only individuals exercise agency and experience value. But who they are and how they experience value is profoundly influenced by the social relationships they construct and within which their lives are constituted. Individuals do not first exist and then enter into relationships with others. Individuals are constituted by the societies within which they dwell even as together they constitute society for each other. To change one is in some way to change the other.

Understood in this way, community involves relationships grounded in multiple commitments and goals. There are individual and communal poles. We know some individuals are better teachers, others better researchers—and they may change these interests and skills with time. But through their various pursuits, members acknowledge a common endeavor to which they dedicate their distinct contributions. Community is both one and many. It is a many of distinct individuals and yet a one in terms of their common commitment; it is a multiple unity and a unified multiplicity. Mutual commitment is the decisive unifying factor—not location, space, or class name. A faculty "community" can be unified in occupying all of the third floor of Old Main, yet be sadly inattentive in their interactions and not at all unified in their common commitments—as we saw with the Yale philosophy and the Columbia English departments.

Purpose-defined institutions. How do the patterns of commitment that constitute a collegium function? Two understandings present themselves: the first is that these patterns define the purposes, objectives or goals of the collegium. The second considers them as laying out its internal character (Allan, 1997). The first understanding focuses on the ends a collegium serves. Today we may speak of them as the educational outcomes that members seek together, although sometimes the "end" is simply an agreed-upon means or process. A collegium is unified to the degree its members agree on the purposes (the goals or processes) they pursue in teaching and research as well as in service.

Thinking of academic institutions in this way, we can distinguish among them in terms of three different types of purposes to which their members commit. None seems to provide viable grounds for a compelling sense of unity or community. The first kind, what George Allan calls the "faithful community," is deeply rooted in its past. A faithful community is a traditional institution, inculcating the tradition and piety of its sponsoring community. Its unified moral mission determines its curriculum. The sponsoring community sanctions both the educational ends and the means for achieving those ends. These means and ends are related to an underlying world view that claims its values and purposes are universal in scope.

Church-related colleges, as well as aspects of the university proposed by John Henry Newman and Robert Hutchins, are classic examples of the institution as faithful community. The culture-oriented educational institution of which Bill Readings (1996) writes is another example, oriented toward preserving and extending the treasures of the nation—its literature and frameworks of beliefs, values, and practices. The purpose of what Readings calls the "university of culture" is to inculcate in the young the best of history and tradition. We are reminded of the university about which Oakeshott writes. Almost all versions of the faithful community are under attack by our growing pluralism and its rival versions of history.

A second type of purpose-defined institution is the "guild of inquirers." Members commit themselves to rational argument and careful empirical observation. This is the familiar secular institution, perhaps one we attended in graduate school. Its purposes center around the Enlightenment ideal of self-critical inquiry. Institutional emphases are less upon the ends than the means of education, and the scientific method is the model for inquiry. Facts, not values, are usually key. Some call this the positivist university, holding that it is devoid of values susceptible to cognitive or rational analysis (May, 2001). In the positivist university, values are emotive and arbitrary, reflecting only subjective preferences. Today's pluralism takes a toll here as well, for the increasing variety of inquiries requires increasingly narrow specialists. Distinctive methodologies, separate journals and conferences, and esoteric terminologies divide us. Communication suffers and the lie is put to a unified community.

The third type of purpose-defined institution is what Allan calls the "Resource Center." These familiar colleges and universities focus on providing students with job-related credentials. Both educational means and ends are up for grabs. Students are seen as customers seeking to become successful in the workplace. Postmodern institutions, these campuses authoritatively declare the universal lack of authority and celebrate freedom and individuality at the expense of a coherent curriculum. Readings terms this type of institution the "University of Excellence." However, the term "excellence" has been emptied of meaning and external reference. Only exchange value remains—what people are prepared to pay. Worth has been reduced to market value. There are no other criteria of excellence.

None of these three offers broad grounds for a compelling commitment to the collegium. The institution of the faithful is on the wane; the institution of the guild of inquirers is deeply fragmented; and the postmodern institution lacks a core agreement on either the means or ends of education. If we look to institutional mission, goals, or structure by themselves for providing higher education with compelling integrity and strength, we will be disappointed. We should look rather at the second set of forms of togetherness as fundamental for colleges and universities. These point to the *internal* being and identity of the collegium—the hospitable environment it provides for its members as they, in conversation with each other, create and constitute that environment as well as its purposes, objectives, and goals. As Oakeshott (1989) observes, "a university is not a machine for achieving a particular purpose or producing a particular result; it is a manner of human activity" (p. 96). Indeed, he adds, to make an educational institution's purposes, functions, or mission primary "is an unfortunate way of talking" (Oakeshott, 1989, p. 96).

Conversationally defined institutions. It is conversation—conducted within the community as well as directed outward to other communities—that both creates and expresses the collegium. As we saw, conversation is true dialogue, not sequential or seriatim monologues. It involves the open sharing and receiving (the speaking and listening) characteristic of genuine hospitality. Marked by respect toward participants as well as subject matter, it is neither controlled nor controlling. Indeed, conversation requires that participants put at risk the routine and other familiar presumptions and suppositions in which they dwell. Then something new can happen. For conversation is not talk without consequences. It can revive purpose-defined institutions.

The hospitable openness of conversationally committed communities requires appreciative, but not uncritical, evaluation of the other. The common good of the collegium stands in potential judgment upon all particular interests even as this common good is the outcome of individual interests in interaction. The task of each member is to elicit and sustain the marks of community that empower others without expense to genuine individuality. Perhaps it is commitment to an outcomes-oriented curriculum that unifies the collegium. Or it may be service learning or an emphasis upon study abroad that constitutes the internal environment of the institution. In any case, it is respectful discourse and joint projects as a key means of mutual recognition, enrichment, and common activity that create and sustain the collegium.

Members cultivate the patience to identify and acknowledge the suppositions and implications of their different positions—matters often brought to light only through interactions, through the back and forth of question and answer. Letters, memoranda, email communications, and telephone conversations are important parts of this process. But the rich potential of face-to-face interaction and dialogue characteristic of a healthy collegium do the most to strengthen both individual and community.

As David Ford observes of face-to-face meetings, it is in such concrete encounters that personal interactions occur. Reflecting the emphasis that philosopher Emmanuel Levinas places on the face, Ford (1999) observes that "all accounts are abstractions from the intimate particularity, the layers of meaning, the look in the eyes" (p. 18). It is in the contingencies of such meetings that significance occurs. "A word, a glance, an instantaneous interpretation, a confrontation, a dissimulation, a misconstrual, an indirectly conveyed attitude—these can be turning points, moments of insight, decision or shame" (Ford, 1999, p. 18). Not all such face-to-face meetings are hospitable; those that are create and nurture the collegium.

It is in hospitable meetings that the individual becomes more completely and distinctively himself or herself, the faces of others light up, and the group as a whole is animated. Thinking of the individual through the metaphor of the face, we can say that each face is distinctive at the same time it is a locus for connections with others. Conversations require voices, as we saw, but voices must be embodied—in texts and in persons who create, engage, and interpret texts. The effect of insistent individualism is to render others faceless, ironically depriving them of their individuality.

Conversationally defined institutions value independence, but do not consider it sufficient. Emancipation from uncritically appropriating the past or unthinkingly accepting the influence of others is a fruit of practicing openness. But understanding autonomy as emancipation alone is problematic and leads to thinking we are self-contained. It promotes insufficient voices, inadequate plurality, and paltry dialogue. In addition to emancipation, we must attend to the inescapable interdependencies of our lives—to connectivities that we explore, cultivate, and cherish. We need the reshaping of the self that comes from engagement with the other—not imposed by the other, but made available so that each self is newly constituted through its relations. Autonomy and connections are both/ands, not either/ors. Without the achievements of the past we are without foundation for engaging the new. But past achievements are often fragile and easily lost, and their continuation requires engagement with the other and the new.

The lesson of community is that both individual and collegium identities are nurtured and extended by relationships with others. The interaction and reciprocity of conversation make ethical and spiritual differences. They illustrate how hospitableness is cultivated, as well as why it is important. Otherwise there is no effective, reliable common good, only transitory and shifting goods. The collegium with its traditions of interpretation and expression provides the context within which members can initially formulate and test their experience and insights—seeking to capture what is of genuine moment rather than passing fad or fancy.

Common Decision-Making and Celebration

The healthy collegium is marked by enduring convictions and steady involvement rather than grudging and unreliable compliance. Members do not simply find themselves in a collegium. They participate and create it, not just conform to it. They share decision-making as well as common tasks and intellectual resources.

Members pull their weight in attending to community responsibilities and chores. They appreciate the power and fragility of the collegium. They recognize that colleagues are not generic, interchangeable parts but individuals who bring special values and distinctiveness to the relation-ship. Each is fundamentally, but not reductively, relational. Each is shaped by personal experience, gender, geography, religion, and race. Each inherits the collective condition, perspectivally appropriated and reflecting his or her own unique experience. Each responds internally to this shared inheritance—and in sharing responses makes possible new experiences and values for others.

Some educators prefer to describe the academic community in terms of family. But as I noted earlier, most of us are uncomfortable when we hear our presidents and deans speak of the faculty as one great family. We came together voluntarily as professionals and we think our community should be one of mutual academic purposes and commitment to reason, not necessarily one of shared personal intimacy—or acrimony. It is acad-emic commitments, not marriage vows or blood ties, that bind us. We want to belong, not to be lost in some extended family or smothered in some nuclear one.

Other educators may observe that there is a form of unity in the disci-plinary organizations into which academic professionals are incorporated. But it is hardly the unity of a collegium, for disciplines are defined by exclusion—of those outside the profession, those within who do not fit, the inadequately credentialed or the adjunct faculty, or other parts of the self beyond the intellectualistic element (Wilshire, 1990). Instead of the collegium, the disciplinary corporation appears as both a collective and an aggregation, yielding both an excess and deficiency of unity.

Faculty collective bargaining. Similar issues surround faculty collec-tive bargaining. By now established in many college and university facul-ties, collective bargaining has proved itself a workable way of securing agreements on important personnel and financial issues. Accordingly, some may argue that commitment to collective bargaining and the reci-procities it displays constitutes a form of unity parallel to that of the collegium. After all, union members check some of their insistent indi-vidualism in committing to representation for common bargaining purposes.

However, this commitment is insufficient to establish a collegium. Once certified, a faculty unit falls outside the collegia that constitute an academic institution. The forms that give a union identity and continu-ity are not those internal to the collegium that mark its educational and intellectual dimensions. Forms defining the faculty collective bargaining unit point to purposes external to the collegium, purposes involving salary and working conditions—not educational or intellectual commitments. No faculty labor union establishes a curriculum or awards degrees. Its members do so, but as the faculty of the collegium. The membership of the unit and the collegium overlap, but their commitments are different. Only confusion comes from identifying them.

A more productive understanding of the collegium realizes that academic selves are what they are because of connections and relationships with colleagues—established and expanded through conversations in the agora, the forum, the faculty meeting, or through the Internet. A healthy collegium is itself a center of value, established and maintained by its members, all of whom are in various ways different because they are members. The liabilities of insistent individualism and the war of "all against all" are recognized and hospitable alternatives are held up and embraced.

The Collegium as Ideal

The special internal order of a collegium reflects the interests of its members, its institutional context, and the broader educational values and loyalties it embraces. Through their mutual covenantal commitments and contributions, the members' autonomy and distinctiveness become embedded in their collegium. It is precisely in this work and conversation of the collegium that its further development occurs. Rarely is this growth without some friction. However, productive argument and dissent can best occur in the collegium—as covenantal community it provides a context of mutual respect, not domination or indifference.

To practice mutual respect is not to be a hospitable dupe. Rather, it is the best way to keep from being duped. For hospitality points toward an open-ended commitment to the well-being of the other. The working assumption in a healthy collegium is that there are no utterly irreconcilable conflicts. The tools for addressing conflicts are those of conversation, not raw political pressure. Members presume that differences can be negotiated, compromised, or—at least—lived with. Some issues may need to be put to the side until times are more favorable, but commitments may be made to return to the discussion at a specific future date.

Through the practices of their faculty and institutions, students develop the moral sensibilities with which they recognize a common humanity amidst multicultural differences. Indeed, it is within contexts of relationality that student and faculty rights and responsibilities as positive and constructive claims have purchase. The common good of the collegium stands in potential judgment upon any particular individual interest even as this common good is the outcome of these individual interests. Robert Paul Wolff (1969) identifies much of the collegium when he defines academic community as

> a community of persons united by collective understanding, by common and communal goals, by bonds of reciprocal obligation, and by a flow of sentiment which makes the preservation of the community an object of desire, not merely a matter of prudence or a command of duty. (p. 127)

Of course the collegium I have described is an ideal, something to which we aspire. We never achieve its full reality though we know it to be the necessary locus for nurturing hospitality. Collegium leaders cultivate openness by creating room for the distinctiveness of members. They discourage modes of individuality that generate selfish preoccupations—practiced by those skilled at rationalizing narrow and self-regarding pursuits. Some are masters of false hospitality, using it to manipulate or to neutralize threats. Some control by placating, seeking to maintain authority by appearing to yield it, thereby keeping students and colleagues alike in confusion. Others exult in extensive rehearsals of their positions—charming, conquering and securing admiration, but showing little interest in listening, receiving stories from others, exchanging positions, or other forms of reciprocity.

By contrast, in the ideal collegium, colleagues challenge and supplement each other. The need to control is mitigated, if not surrendered. Testimony is given with care. Discernment and humility are practiced. As a consequence, the good of the collegium is pursued in ways that embrace and share the goods of the members in a quest for mutual fulfillment. Self-fulfillment is not inevitably arrayed against the fulfillment of the other, however much embracing another's position may initially appear to compromise one's own. Even in these circumstances, attending with greater energy to the position of the other generates benefit to the individual, given the social nature of the self and community. Indeed, in ideal collegia these acts of hospitality are critical ingredients of the hope that intellectual, personal, and political differences can actually unite rather than simply divide.

Gathering In and Sending Out

We can use the metaphor of being gathered in and sent out to say more about the character and work of the collegium (Cowan & Lee, 1997). Though often religious in usage, the metaphor describes other patterns of behavior and seems particularly appropriate in describing the work of academics. One need only consider the effect of faculty meetings, of national conferences, or of the academic calendar of semesters or quarters in bringing colleagues together and then dispersing them.

Being gathered. In the academy, gathering and being gathered suggest *how* members of the collegium come together. They describe the members' activity together, the nature and workings of their covenant with each other as they commit to a community that embraces their differences. Frequently the commitment is less to common things to be done, and more to a common *way* of doing things—a shared commitment to uphold the character and quality of engagement and adequate agreement on how this can be carried out.

For instance, how members are gathered involves the ways they jointly choose to use conflict constructively, how they honor quite different individual talents and use them to enhance the common good, how they undertake and practice mutual communication, and how they present themselves and the good of the collegium to students, colleagues in other areas, and to the broader public. As gathered, members of the collegium have the opportunity and obligation to be *gathering*—to bring colleagues into full participation in the work of the collegium. This may require repeated invitations to participate more deeply. It may necessitate confrontations when common tasks are neglected.

These common tasks and mutual relationships have potential for significant personal value. Each individual is a member of many groups and communities, often choosing how to be immersed in them. As we have seen, the collegia to which people belong *do* make differences in their personal as well as their professional lives. The rigid bifurcation and separation of these lives involves expense to both sides. There is also expense when personal and professional are sentimentally merged. Neither can be excluded; a balance of both should be sought. The objectivity which academics properly value is best attained when the unavoidable perspective of the personal is acknowledged and critical exchange and sharing with other professionals become habits.

Being sent. In distinction from being gathered in, being sent out refers to how members of the collegium relate to other individuals or groups and work externally as a collegium. Being sent involves witnessing publicly to the fundamental convictions and pledges that distinguish the collegium. Members remain individuals, of course, but they are also representatives and agents of the collegium. A collegium is deficient when its members do not cultivate relationships with other communities. In separation from others, collegia deprive themselves of the added value available only through interaction. The hospitable collegium is known as interested in contributing to other communities as well as receiving from them.

These moments of gathering and sending need to be developed as well as integrated. Each moment enriches the other and each is necessary to the other. When the collegium attends inadequately to its own internal work and to the growth of its members, it is deficient as a community. It lacks depth, we say, and is superficial. It has little to offer other communities and little capacity to receive from them. Inadequately gathered, unenriched by novelty of idea and diversity of persons, a collegium marked by repetition of old patterns is stale and in decline.

For instance, some disciplines tend to define themselves in deliberately monomodal and ahistorical terms. In this country, for example, the discipline of philosophy has only recently begun to engage its history as an integral part of its identity and practice. Theology is another example where systematic work is often conducted with little engagement with the historical traditions out of which it emerged. Many inquiries separate matters of culture from those of nature and are then unable to integrate them. Other disciplines seem stuck in the ideological difficulties they create for themselves. One wonders, for instance, whether the fragmentation of the once celebrated English department at Duke was related to its simultaneous emphasis upon intellectual rigor and the implication of some forms of postmodernism that there is no objective knowledge. Collegia that do not address the deficiencies of the disciplines they present wind up duplicating them. We can say that these collegia are inadequately gathered.

On the other hand, without interest in other groups or in attending with appropriate openness to them, the collegium is also inadequate. On the surface, it appears to serve its own members, but it does so deficiently when the broader context for their work is ignored. Connections with other collegia must be nurtured. The perception and conception of each can be challenged, corrected, and enlarged by those of other individuals and communities. Inadequately sent, in separation from others, the collegium slips into decline—reiterating rather than extending and enriching its existing competencies. Both gathering and sending, coming together and going out—both the inner and the public life—are necessary.

Institutions and Collegia: The Question of Size

Apart from the single-purpose institution or college, it is the rare institution of size that can now be called *a* collegium. Most institutions have become too big and too complex to host the conversations of a collegium. Some are gigantic—for instance, the roughly 100 mega-sized research universities that we have learned to call multiversities (Muller, 1994). At best, they are large aggregates of collegia. At some point, this kind of institution is as a whole much less than the sum of its parts.

Indeed, Clark Kerr (1995) has told us that the research institution incorporates "competing visions of true purpose, each relating to a different layer of history, a different web of forces" (p. 7). As a consequence, he concluded, this university "is so many things to so many different people that it must, of necessity, be partially at war with itself" (Kerr, 1995, p. 7). It is certainly not a center of value parallel to the centers of value it incorporates. Structural fragmentation is inevitable.

> A university anywhere can aim to be no higher than to be as British as possible for the sake of the undergraduates, as German as possible for the sake of the graduates and research personnel, as American as possible for the sake of the public at large—and as confused as possible for the sake of the preservation of the whole uneasy balance. (Kerr, 1995, p. 14)

Rather than being itself a collegium, it is the "confused" context for collegia—communities for which it serves as the infrastructure.

The challenges to leadership in these institutions are especially difficult. The forces that characterize instructional and faculty enterprises also apply to overall organizational and administrative structures. Individuals responsible for specific operations often have little understanding of, or communication with, others elsewhere in these large institutions. The channels though which conversation can be nurtured are limited. University-wide committees can help, but may not be numerous nor meet frequently. Faculty lounges or dining rooms are often inadequate, frequented only by a small group of regulars. Staff may have no place to congregate. The mega-sized research institution in particular has a large number of autonomous units, not unlike the rugged individuals and departments we looked at earlier. Often each tub is expected to sit on its own bottom—leaving the arts and humanities at a moral and fiscal disadvantage, and contributing to overall fragmentation, confusion, and vagueness.

Perhaps the ability to view these institutions as collegia declined with the diminishing emphasis upon undergraduate education and general or liberal education. The widespread decline of the core curriculum in the late 1960s and beyond reduced the need for faculty to talk and collaborate. In any case, the grounds for the authority of megaversities to prescribe expectations for their graduates is now conceptually problematic and infrequently debated. It is the school or more likely the department (whose status as a collegium may also be in doubt) that warrants the appropriateness of expectations for its graduates and assures the public that these expectations have been adequately met. Rather than an overarching collegium of inquiry, this kind of institution is more likely to be only a multiplicity of collegia, at best enjoying only a weak kind of family connection. Of course, smallness itself is no guarantee of community. Small colleges and universities can be seedbeds of insistent individualism. Their very size can exacerbate the ease and intensity of competition and self-preoccupation. But on the whole, practicing hospitality seems considerably more daunting in the larger organizations.

Chickering and Kytle (1999) summarize the relevant scholarly findings about the impact of institutional scale or size on students: "sixty years of research documents the superior educational value of small, residential colleges" (p. 109). They have in mind the educational fundamentals of institutions—what we have termed the character of their conversation about learning, indeed the conversation that *is* learning. It is conversation that transforms students into lifelong learners and engaged citizens. It occurs most readily and productively in the manageable residential setting, where academic studies and out-of-classroom activities can be in relationship—where active learning focused on self-understanding and commitments to values larger than self are as important as information transfer. It is the small, human-scale environment of the residential college, not the mega-campus, that provides the conditions and support for the collegium.

Of course not all institutions can create residential or cluster colleges. Other ways of securing comparable advantages involve the "downsizing" of larger institutions through creating multiple smaller group opportunities for students to interact and converse with others—some like-minded, others not. Scholars of higher education note that such opportunities include academic activities like honors and peer-tutoring programs as well as discipline and interest-based clubs (Pascarella & Terenzini, 1991). Broader activities are available through participation in team sports and intramural activities, theater and journalistic projects, social and volunteer clubs, religious organizations, etc. The objective, of course, is to reduce student isolation and anonymity—to increase opportunities to cope with significant challenges, to extend existing skills and knowledge, to vary experience and expand self-reflection and self-testing.

Regardless of the size of the collegium or the institution in which it is nested, membership should extend across divisions between faculty and staff. Of course, different functions are associated with these positions. Staff may rarely teach in a classroom, and faculty may attend to few of the details that support teaching and learning. However, each has regular opportunities to enrich the work and lives of the other by practicing hospitality and forgoing the secrecy rooted in controlling power. It is not just administrators or executives who violate Fish's rule about communication. One former faculty member who took a staff library position discovered that "staff members don't have careers—they have jobs" (Young, 2002, ¶5). Her point is that opportunities for mutual assistance and collaboration were never developed, or even valued. Exclusion was the rule. Collegiality and interaction among administrators, faculty, and staff were minimized by "separate lunch hours and breaktimes for each group" (Young, 2002, ¶7).

The concept of academic community proposed here is a rigorous one. A variety of factors stand in its way: too much conflict, decreasing financial support and increasing entrepreneurial competition, too few willing to practice community as worthwhile or valuable, reward structures that promote insistent individualism rather than relational or collaborative endeavors, the size and complexity of institutions, and so forth. Simple fatigue can set in. In its fullness, collegial academic community will ever elude us. But as a regulative idea of what we are at our best, it serves as both a standard against which to measure ourselves and a lure that can draw us out of ourselves. As an ideal, the collegium is intimately connected with the concept of covenant.

SOCIAL CONTRACT OR COVENANT SOCIETY?

The prevailing way of thinking about relationships among and between individual faculty members, students, colleagues, and institutions resembles a social contract. Relationships are voluntary associations in which rights often receive priority over obligations. Clear boundaries limiting responsibilities are identified. In addition, social contracts can be dissolved when parties deem it to their advantage.

A contrasting way to view the academic community draws on the idea of covenant. Covenantal relationships are formed by commitments to the intellectual well-being of the other that take precedence over the restricted boundaries of the social contract. Covenantal language emphasizes the intellectual and creative legacies to which we are heirs and for the care and extension of which we are now responsible. It reminds us of obligations we assume to each other in attending to this inheritance.

The Social Contract

In a social contract interactions are dominantly instrumental. Each individual is expected to protect his or her self-interest and does not feel particularly constrained to watch out for the other. Students and their institutions are often described in contractual terms, particularly at those institutions George Allan labeled Resource Centers. Tuition payments are swapped for credits and credentials. Faculty describe course expectations in contractual terms: a minimum amount of prescribed competency is required to pass the course; more is specified for a higher grade, etc.

Faculty also understand themselves as bound to colleagues and to their institutions through contracts of rights and responsibilities—often tacit, though sometimes recorded in extraordinary detail. These social contracts convert the self-protection of insistent individualism into mutual protections of separate interests. The common good is seen as an outcome and sum of these individual negotiations and contractual arrangements. Community is secondary—derivative rather than primary.

Lurking in the background is the myth that individuals agree to surrender some autonomy in order to secure intellectual and professional benefits otherwise unobtainable. Those who support social contract thinking understand these group arrangements as concessions that in an ideal world would not be needed. Our world is imperfect, however. Various group arrangements *are* needed. Then the articulation of rights becomes necessary to defend the individual against other individuals and the majority.

The academic community as rooted in social contract thinking reflects the influence of Hobbes and others in elevating individualism and undermining the basis for public discussion and pursuit of a substantive common good. As a consequence, the social contract concept of community implies that public life is primarily of instrumental worth—often tiresome, but presumably necessary for more satisfactory private lives. In effect, the collegium as social contract is a collective contrivance of individual convenience and encourages a kind of minimalism—do no more than what the contract requires.

Many academics fall into the social contract mentality. Some enter the academy that way. But for others, age, routine, fatigue, and fear of the other contribute to the insistent individualism that develops. Over time, institutions encourage, reflect and perpetuate this separation. Governance systems emerge that deflect extreme self-interest—they protect the institution from narrow conceptions of member interests—but they do so at the expense of promoting a coordinated pursuit of a common good. These systems rely on elaborate checks and balances to protect individual and institutional rights—balances that often paralyze rather than facilitate creative responses to rapidly changing socioeconomic challenges (Longin, 2002). Not only is this version of the academy not what we initially bargained for, but most of us are not sure how to negotiate safe passage in it. By itself, the social contract hardly provides sustaining motivation to collaborate with others since its ultimate logic is separateness, exclusion, and isolation.

However, it is a step in the right direction. The advantage of a social contract rests in the dignity tacitly ascribed to partners. The contract provides rights and requires accountability in the transactions undertaken. Nonetheless, contract thinking elevates a narrow concept of self-interest. It emphasizes boundaries and constraints and masks a fragile truce, easily broken when self-interest prompts. The contract is minimalistic, focused on specific activities and objectives, its duration usually short-term, and it requires few personal ties among members. The covenant promises broader value that entails commitment to the well-being of the whole in joint activities.

The Covenant and the Collegium

The collegium as covenant is rooted in members' commitment to each other in public pursuit of a common good. Covenants are public vows, declarations, or pledges to the other. They are created and maintained through the promises of each member to others—the promises of practicing hospitality, of being open in sharing and receiving, and of committing to mutuality and reciprocity. The covenantal community is both internal and external to its members, cherished privately and visible publicly. It exists because members of a covenant society relinquish privilege and independence vis-a-vis each other. As Robin Lovin (1986) describes the expectations of covenant relations,

> a covenant society is one in which the members . . . not only
> hold their neighbors to a higher standard of conduct than they
> might if they were just thrown together at random; they
> expect more of themselves and they acknowledge that others
> who share in the covenant have a right to examine and criti-
> cize their behavior. (p. 135)

And, we might add, that they have obligations to respond.

Basic to forming and sustaining the collegium as a covenantal society
is the faithful, reliable attention of members to each other. We learn how
to be scholars from others, and we draw our standards and values as well
as our knowledge and skills from the learning communities in which we
dwell. Our work is initiated, critiqued, and sustained in conversation with
colleagues. And it is in actions of mutual reciprocity that the community
achieves its covenantal identity. They provide the common ground that
supports a common good. The collegium is no more a natural phenomenon than it is a contractual one. It must be created and it requires more
than the easy, reversible promise of a contractual community. A covenant
suggests obligations and opportunities that cannot be fully specified in
advance. However, new members must be welcomed and mentored to
live convenantally, their gifts identified, and their presence celebrated.
Developments in society and in knowledge must be studied for the
opportunities they create.

As a covenantal community, the collegium forms and informs
members in the qualities of hospitality. For some, such formation is a
reinforcement of character traits already in place and practiced. For
others, formation in hospitality requires transformation—a change from
rules imposed from without to dispositions nurtured from within. In
both cases formation sustains bonds among members—forms of connectivity marked by mutual respect, interaction, and reciprocity. The chief
mechanism is conversation. At its most hospitable, sharing involves
disclosing inner parts of oneself—particularly aspects of the personal
meaning and value one attaches to the inquiry at issue. Such intimate
disclosures may be rare, but being hospitable means being prepared for
them.

The best educational sharing is ungrudging, free and spontaneous. It
does not calculate the extent of goods to be shared based on those
expected to be received. But neither is it unappreciative of gifts already
received. In fact, sharing is often prompted by gratitude for these gifts,
such as the wealth of scholarship we inherit as well as the labors of earlier

teachers who initiated us into this achieved learning. "No one," writes William May (1996), "can graduate from a modern university and professional school and think of himself [or herself] as a self-made man or woman" (p. 74). Education is communal in origin as well as destiny. Gifts already received include the ongoing support of education by society—corporations, foundations, government, voluntary associations, and parents and friends.

And one should not forget the many students at whose expense and forbearance early (and continuing) lessons in teaching were learned. Ongoing debts are owed them. Indeed, upholding the good of the student is a priority in the academic covenant. Students' relative lack of knowledge and their neediness often place them in a poor position to protect their interests. They depend upon the fiduciary role of their instructors and institutions—students trust that their professors and institutions honor the trust *they* have assumed.

In the covenantal community, members commit to values and actions such as mutual interaction, hospitable reciprocity, and shared standards of excellence and accountability. Covenantal communities have historical as well as contemporary thickness. The past functions as a reservoir of values and accomplishments that provides direction for the future. An adequate possession of tradition means awareness of the possibilities for the future bequeathed to the present by the past. Douglas Sturm (1998b) brings together these several points nicely: "the idea of a social covenant bespeaks a world in which we already belong together, but are called repeatedly to acknowledge that fact anew and to determine what the forms of our life together shall be" (p. 186).

The interaction of members in a healthy covenantal collegium creates capacities and forms of distinctiveness that exceed what individual members are in separation from the collegium. The concept of self as social and relational is fundamental to these mutual covenants and promises. Sturm (1998b) suggests the motivation involved when he observes that

> within a covenantal community, each member is acknowledged with deepest respect by all others and is nurtured and advanced by the relationship. In and through all other purposes served by this form of association, the common purpose pursued by all is to maintain and enrich the association itself, but precisely because the association is integral to their own self-development as social beings. (p. 43f.)

As we saw earlier, dualistic oppositions between self and other—leading to theories of egoism and altruism—are inadequate.

Parties to a social contract say, "So much and no more." The contract points to responsibilities and obligations, but it highlights boundaries to these responsibilities. Social contract thinking diminishes the elements of gift—of freely, even spontaneously, sharing. Covenants, by contrast, emphasize commitments to the well-being of the other. Parties in a covenantal relationship say, "What else can I do to help?" Contracts can be easily dissolved or even abandoned. Covenants cannot, though they can be neglected. The covenant has a broader duration and expression of personal identity—I am a teacher even when I am not at the moment teaching. As William May (1983) observes, "contracts are external; covenants are internal to the parties involved" (p. 119).

Covenants, Commitments, and Conversation

In a covenantal relationship members draw more deeply on each other. Internal to who they are, the covenant is not a transient and passing thing. Covenants are built up and nourished through giving. They create spaces where elements of the generous and the gratuitous—not the narrowly self-interested—can be exercised. Leaders of collegia encourage the mutual appreciation of members as different, with diverse gifts, even when engaged in common commitments and activity. Each is in some way significant to the whole—and little of this can be precisely predicted and contractually specified in advance. Particular duties give content to the future, but the covenant extends beyond them to unforeseen contingencies.

Individual members sustain the agency of the covenanted community. They must be genuinely engaged, for the covenantal community has no use for quid pro quo understandings or other arrangements that shield indifference under the guise of tolerance. The common good members pursue is not a collection of private individual goods, as in a social contract theory. Instead, it is the good of the members as they covenant to work *with* each other, a covenant effected through rich cognitive and affective symbol systems and shared standards of excellence.

We have examined the many ways in which conversation suggests the root character of educational activity. Together with covenant it points us toward relationships in which each is committed to the welfare of the other as a partner in the conversation. Given the greater knowledge of the faculty, the concept of the covenant requires active attention to promoting the learning of the lesser party—not a hands off (here it is) attitude. The hospitable teacher does not shield self from the ignorant other. Nor does the hospitable institution ignore its workers on the margins. Covenantal relationships go even further for they demand attending to the irresponsible in one's midst—to colleagues and leaders who have broken the covenant. Working responsibly means addressing, not overlooking, their failure and this can be difficult indeed.

The concept of covenant includes the mutuality to which hospitality directs our attention. In any relationship founded on a covenantal image, "a reciprocity of giving and receiving nourishes the professional relationship. The professional does not function as benefactor alone but also as beneficiary. In teaching . . . students need a teacher, but the teacher also needs students" (May, 1983, p. 115f.). In such an educational relationship learning flows in both directions. Students "provide the teacher with a regular occasion and forum in which to work out what he or she has to say and to rediscover the subject afresh through the discipline of sharing it with others" (May, 1983, 115f.).

Most institutions that embrace the covenant image recognize a need for rituals to remind, refresh, and recommit to the work of the covenantal society. Occasions involving academic garb—and these need not be limited to graduation—provide a public reminder of the long tradition in which academics stand. They offer as well an invitation for participants to recommit themselves in fidelity to the hospitable promotion of learning. Special retreats are another venue for individuals mutually to recommit to shared and expanded contributions to the common good. Similarly, even personnel procedures such as evaluation activities can become ritualized occasions for serious review and recommitment to the mutuality and reciprocity of the work of the collegium. The best evaluation processes include opportunities for peer suggestions, enlarging the life of the collegium.

Academic collegia don't simply happen. Even in the most fortuitous circumstances, they require individual and collective work in their inception and continuance. At their best, as we saw, these collegia are rooted in a deliberate, joint covenant and commitment of their members to a genuine mutuality that both disciplines and liberates. The covenant *disciplines* individual gifts and energies by directing them toward the common good. Members are enlarged and empowered by becoming part of something more than themselves, yet something in which their own individual talents and contributions are significant. At the same time, members are *liberated* from the narrowness and sterility of dwelling in isolated and uncoordinated activities. Academics are most free when practicing active, authentic hospitality—not when dwelling in narrowly focused efforts to shield self from others.

Institutions

Colleges and universities that embrace the idea of the covenant are known for committing to the advancement of student learning as an overriding institutional objective. Critics of higher education like Alexander Astin have drawn our attention to the expense involved when campuses aggressively pursue individual reputation and resources as the most effective way to pursue academic excellence. Unfortunately, being perceived as smart is commonly a far more important institutional value than developing student talent (Astin, 1997). Institutions must go beyond such pursuits and values to address the education and development of talent and learning. As Astin (1991) notes, "the truest measure of excellence is the institution's ability to affect its students favorably, to enhance their intellectual and scholarly development, and to make a positive difference in their lives" (p. 8).

Institutions that value covenant over social contract also know they exist to serve societal needs. They are truthful, rather than secretive, about themselves. They work with other colleges and universities to improve access to information, whether through more accessible accreditation reports or publicizing student engagement and outcome survey activities in which they participate. They seek to establish effective consortia rather than unnecessarily duplicating facilities and service. And they nurture their faculty, rewarding service and collaboration. They let proprietary institutions cultivate the competitive ethos.

The covenantal community offers more promise for developing rich and satisfying individual and institutional spiritualities. The affirmation of community replaces the isolation of atomism. The integration of the personal and the professional counteracts the rational instrumentalism of insistent individualism. The value of attending to the other offers opportunities to move issues of personal identity and authenticity from the periphery to the center of higher education.

Yet we know why social contract, not covenant, thinking is so prevalent. Burdens are already heavy at most institutions—many faculty feel a real need to cut back, rather than extend themselves. Those who embrace the covenant get taken advantage of. The same handful of faculty are called upon repeatedly for service. Gestures of openness are abused, rather than shared or returned. Generosity leads to burnout. Apprehensions in these arenas lead to more social contract thinking. Likewise, few boards of trustees or regents reward presidents or other administrators for covenant thinking—for advancing consortial interests or nurturing faculty needs even at the expense of institutional prestige or productivity.

Perhaps too few presidents suggest that boards should do more to nurture a covenantal environment. Here too the result is more social contract thinking and behavior.

In its heightened form, the concept of the collegium as covenant society stands against the reality of much of the academy. But I believe it presents an attractive, ongoing ideal. Yet, it is more than an ideal, for the very existence of the academy as a community of conversation characterized by discovering, sharing, and enlarging knowledge requires at base a covenantal rather than a social contract commitment. Nevertheless, the actual realization of this covenantal community is always partial. Sometimes the problem is simply lack of desire for its realization. Sometimes conflict within the collegium becomes destructive rather than constructive—and then chairs, deans, and other academic leaders must develop strategies of reconciliation. At other times, we sense the value of a collegium but consider the notion to be an unsolvable academic version of the one and the many. Then conversations and essays like this may be helpful in pointing toward resolutions.

CONCLUSION

Academic life is essentially a moral pursuit, not one for which morality is an option or an add-on. Value decisions are ubiquitous, and academic life and work affect students, colleagues, and others in quite complex ways. Only some educational relationships are instrumental in the way that a social contract suggests. Most of the work of the academy, especially teaching, requires the concern for the intrinsic welfare of others that is a mark of the highest form of moral behavior. At its best, the academic community is a kind of covenant society rather than a social contract community. Membership is not narrowly limited or constrained in the way of contracts.

Far from teaching, research, and learning being impersonal interactions or exchanges of information with no potential impact upon selves, the covenantal form of community makes clear how significant relational impact occurs. Within such a community, we are more able truly to be hospitable—to welcome the excluded, remain open to the unpopular, and transcend academic classes and disciplinary boundaries.

Even though insistent individualism will always be with us, covenantal hospitality is the better option. The collegium is itself testimony and recognition that problems are not fixed in isolation or learning promoted through fragmentation. Of course, there are degrees of covenantal hospitality. Leadership is necessary to evoke consistent and energetic passion for new ideas and for rethinking past positions—all in the context of open and mutual sharing.

REFERENCES

Allan, G. (1997). *Rethinking college education.* Lawrence, KS: University Press of Kansas.

Astin, A. (1991). *The unrealized potential of American higher education.* Athens, GA: The University of Georgia Institute of Higher Education.

Astin, A. (1997, September 26). Our obsession with being 'smart' is distorting intellectual life. *The Chronicle of Higher Education,* p. A60.

Chickering, A. W., & Kytle, J. (1999). The collegial ideal in the twenty-first century. In J. D. Toma & A. J. Kezar (Eds.), *Reconceptualizing the collegiate ideal* (pp. 109–120). San Francisco, CA: Jossey-Bass.

Cowan, M. A., & Lee, B J. (1997). *Conversation, risk, and conversion: The inner and public life of small Christian communities.* Maryknoll, NY: Orbis Books.

Ford, D. F. (1999). *Self and salvation: Being transformed.* New York, NY: Cambridge University Press.

Kerr, C. (1995). *The uses of the university* (4th ed.). Cambridge, MA: Harvard University Press.

Longin, T. (2002). Institutional governance: A call for collaborative decision-making in American higher education. In L. A. McMillin & W. G. Berberet (Eds.), *A new academic compact: Revisioning the relationship between faculty and their institutions* (pp. 211–221). Bolton, MA: Anker.

Lovin, R. (1986). Social contract or a public covenant? In R. Lovin (Ed.), *Religion and American public life* (pp. 132–145). Mahwah, NJ: Paulist Press.

May, W. F. (1983). *The physician's covenant: Images of the healer in medical ethics.* Philadelphia, PA: The Westminster Press.

May, W. F. (1996). *Testing the medical covenant: Active euthanasia and health-care reform.* Grand Rapids, MI: Eerdmans.

May, W. F. (2001). *Beleaguered rulers: The public obligation of the professional.* Louisville, KY: Westminster John Knox Press.

Muller, S. (1994). Presidential leadership. In J. R. Cole, E. G. Barber, & S. R. Graubard (Eds.), *The research university in a time of discontent* (pp. 115–130). Baltimore, MD: Johns Hopkins University Press.

Oakeshott, M. T. (1989). *The voice of liberal learning* (T. Fuller, Ed.). New Haven, CT: Yale University Press.

Pascarella, E. T., & Terenzini, P. T. (1991). *How college affects students: Findings and insights from twenty years of research*. San Francisco, CA: Jossey-Bass.

Readings, B. (1996). *The university in ruins*. Cambridge, MA: Harvard University Press.

Sturm, D. (1998b). *Solidarity and suffering: Toward a politics of relationality*. Albany, NY: State University of New York Press.

Wilshire, B. (1990). *The moral collapse of the university: Professionalism, purity, and alienation*. Albany, NY: State University of New York Press.

Wolff, R. P. (1969). *The ideal of the university*. Boston, MA: Beacon Press.

Young, L. (2002, January 29). Losing status: A former faculty member takes a staff job. *The Chronicle of Higher Education Career Network*. Available: http://chronicle.com/jobs

Engaged, but not Heroic, Leadership   8

This final chapter weaves together the concepts we have been examining—insistent individualism, hospitality, conversation, and covenant—in the context of reflecting on leadership and the differences that leaders can make. Like other faculty, staff, and students, leaders reflect the two modes of self-understanding and being we have discussed. Some leaders are insistent individualists and promote a social contract. Others model and facilitate hospitality, conversation, and covenant. Most reflect some combination of both.

Over the years, I have explored leadership challenges faced by department chairpersons and school deans. In this chapter I reflect on some of my findings, noting that they apply as well to other educational leaders such as faculty senate members and student affairs officers. Most midlevel leaders struggle with the academic tradition of defining leadership in terms of individualistic values and mythologies—of seeing the leader in terms of the Western images of the "hero" we explored earlier.

Then I examine the position of institutional president. Here too some leaders practice clear forms of insistent individualism. They are heroic figures, like the fabled cowboy. Almost inevitably, their behaviors foster campus suspicion, fragmentation, and isolation. Other presidents are closer to the relational individualism for which I have been arguing. They model the importance of conversation by practicing hospitality and honoring covenant.

One obvious difference between midlevel leaders and presidents is the larger platform the latter possess to set the philosophical, moral, and spiritual tone of the institution. If the tone is hospitable, midlevel leaders find their tasks easier and more fulfilling. If executive leadership is not hospitable, however, most chairpersons and deans report their positions to be both more difficult and more important.

MIDLEVEL LEADERS

In their essay about the failure of the academy to attend to its own professional conduct, Henry Rosovsky and Inge-Lise Ameer (1998) remark on the oddity of college and university teachers studying the norms of every profession except their own: "We can ruin a life just as easily as any doctor or lawyer. Do we assume that an understanding of professional conduct is a genetic trait among Ph.D. students?" (p. 120). The question is rhetorical, for the situation is serious. Rosovsky and Ameer lament that older professors no longer initiate younger faculty into appropriate standards of conduct. Increases in the size and diversity of institutions, together with more specialized research and consulting, have led to the neglect of "the professor's pastoral duties" and his or her "institutional citizenship" in the intramural community of students and teachers (Rosovsky & Ameer, 1998, p. 120). Individual and institutional competition have made things worse and academic leaders such as presidents and deans have often been unwilling "to set clear tasks and clear limits" (Rosovsky & Ameer, 1998, p. 120).

Pastoral Duties

Although they deplore this situation, Rosovsky's and Ameer's suggestions for addressing it are scarcely robust. Their remedy is limited to providing minicourses on professional conduct for graduate students contemplating faculty careers. Altogether absent is any reference to help for current members of the academy who may be ruining the lives of students or colleagues right now. Nor do the authors convey concern that it will be years, if not decades, before their proposals for reform could have any significant purchase on the academy. And even in proposing minicourses for graduate students, Rosovsky and Ameer assign no value to the behaviors that express the underlying and cardinal virtue of professional conduct in academe—hospitality. Both pastoral concern and institutional citizenship flow from practicing hospitality, not the other way around. The authors move directly to training programs, but they presuppose an unexamined social ontology of individualism.

Although both their analysis and their remedy are flawed, Rosovsky's and Ameer's concerns are surely on target. Individual and collective attention to pastoral duties and institutional citizenship *has* declined. But it is at the level of department chairpersons, senate members, and deans, not in graduate seminars, that more immediate reform is likely to occur. Chairpersons, for instance, are located precisely where faculty neglect of pastoral duties and institutional citizenship can occur. It is in academic departments and divisions that answers must be forged to current (not just prospective) questions of appropriate professional conduct. It is in terms of their departments that most faculty, old and new, understand themselves to be professionals working in settings governed by broad disciplinary standards and values. And, of course, it is with department instructors as well as department curricula and requirements that students must contend. Chairpersons, therefore, are ideally situated to know the many ways that academe can ruin lives. Together with faculty senate members, they enjoy a position and standing that provide special opportunities to advance conversation about the meaning of intellectual hospitality, of authentic ethics, and of appropriate and fulfilling spiritualities.

School deans are in the best institutional position to support faculty leaders and chairpersons in these efforts. Indeed, many of their responsibilities parallel those of chairpersons. They are natural and indispensable allies with similar objectives. Only the breadth of their responsibilities is different. Successful chairs and deans tap into unifying visions and exercise interpersonal skills necessary to effect those visions. They engage and support individuals and individual departments without appearing to favor one over another. Both chairs and deans work to elicit an appropriate unity out of an aggregate of individualists possessing competing interests. The dean works through chairpersons in pursuit of a broader vision just as chairs work through their faculty in furthering their version of that vision (Bennett, 1990).

What Rosovsky and Ameer call "pastoral duties" are both intellectual and moral. Faculty members cannot facilitate growth in learning apart from attending to both the particular individuals with whom they are associated (colleagues and students alike) *and* the character of interactions with them. People are different in their talents and gifts as well as in their learning objectives, values, and needs. Practicing a generic hospitality does not work. One size does not fit all. It is no part of moral or intellectual hospitality to treat people identically when equal treatment requires recognizing their different circumstances.

Being a hospitable leader means recognizing that colleagues and students have different contributions to make to each other and to the classes and groups of which they are members. Practicing this kind of leadership means modeling and enabling contributions that are thoughtful and sensitive to the humanity of the other—that are respectful of individual dignity, even though that respect may not be initially returned. Perseverance as well as integrity is required. Hospitality cannot be reduced to quid pro quo arrangements and remain hospitality. Such reductions empty hospitality of reciprocal openness to the new relationships for which it is calling. Truly practicing hospitality means working toward a mutuality of connections and conversations that advance the good of each individual involved as well as the common good of all—however distant that mutuality might at times appear.

In addition, senate members, student affairs staff, chairs, and deans must establish limits to inhospitable ways of behaving. As professionals, all educators have a moral responsibility to advance the good of their students. As William May (2001) observes,

> teachers who wield knowledge simply to dazzle, to show off, or to jangle the verger's keys of learning without opening the door to their students, malpractice, as surely as dentists who exploit their patients' ignorance to sell them expensive procedures. (p. 9)

Other educators behave inhospitably through their inaccessibility, rather than self-preoccupied performance. The academy may have attracted them precisely because its conditions of autonomy make isolation possible. Autonomy becomes problematic when it prevents reciprocity and intellectual exchange, when it works against the respectful conversations that create the collegium.

As Rosovsky and Ameer note, educational leaders, chairs, and deans need to set clear tasks and limits—limits to malpractice and inaccessibility. But they also need to do more. Setting tasks and limits takes us only part way to hospitality. Chairs and deans need to use a variety of ways to talk up, celebrate, and reward professors' pastoral duties and to emphasize institutional citizenship. Perhaps the key to finding mechanisms that best promote hospitality is to distinguish between practices and viewpoints that reflect the self as inherently related to others and potentially enriched by them from those that understand others as potential opponents and risks to individual accomplishment and security. Those who dwell in the first set see others as part of a nexus to which all contribute and from which they draw. Those in the second set of attitudes and values see others simply as a collection of competitors.

With this in mind, the hospitable leader works with colleagues to select mechanisms that welcome new faculty and staff, while also helping the old to feel useful and valued. He or she prods them to attend to the hospitality characteristic of good teaching and scholarship—to the importance of openly sharing and receiving learning, rather than separating teaching and scholarship and sequestering both. The hospitable chair works with others to nurture the curriculum as retaining the best of the past and also addressing the new. In every case strategies and techniques that recognize the self as relational rather than autonomous—as constituted by relationships with others rather than independent of them—work better in promoting effective self-regulation and in providing individual fulfillment.

In short, I suggest that it is precisely in cultivating and modeling hospitality that department chairs and others can promote the pastoral duties and citizenship for which Rosovsky and Ameer are rightly calling. Miniseminars for graduate students are fine, but we need more immediate attention to practices that right now may be ruining some lives and injuring others. Chairs are in an excellent position to lead the way in fostering more professional conduct. Deans and other midlevel leaders can facilitate their efforts.

Power

Yet, department chairs often complain about their lack of power. "Our responsibilities are incommensurate with the authority we are given" is a common lament. "How," they ask, "can we exercise leadership?" When we think of institutions of higher education in terms of organizational charts, chairs are almost always at the bottom. The budgets they control are usually quite modest; they must clear hiring and salary recommendations with others; revisions in curriculum and department mission are notoriously difficult to effect. The list goes on. Yet, chairs are located where the actual teaching, research, and service of the institution are carried out.

It appears, then, that any institutional power a chair may possess is hostage to controls effected by a number of others. However, isn't this simply the nature of work in the academy? Deans and provosts also complain about their lack of power. They too must work with others in contexts that defy the clarity of organizational charts. Faculty senate officers and student affairs personnel are also familiar with this situation. Even presidents fuss about their inability to introduce change. If an individual or a group really doesn't want to do something, or even to be generally cooperative, most campuses offer many ways to delay, resist, or actually thwart the initiatives of others. Yet, academic work does go on. Things do get done. Every campus has leaders—including chairpersons—who are known for making a difference. They must have some power, even if not the kind whose absence is frequently lamented.

Leadership means making a positive difference. Thus, academic leadership requires that chairs, deans, and others figure out what kinds of differences they want to promote and what works to promote them. Most of us are familiar with what I have been calling unilateral power—power associated with agency and control. Those seeking this kind of power want to pursue their agendas and resist the agendas of others. The more successful they are in executing their plans, and in resisting others' agendas, the more powerful they feel. The academy places a high value on controlling power. Although sometimes in a backhanded or even resentful kind of way, most of us do admire those who appear to have it—the strong, forceful, and determined sorts who get their way. It is power to control that is usually what we have in mind when we lament not having enough.

However, it is probably a good thing that others cause us to complain. We may be frustrated at times by their obstinacy, but successful leadership obviously requires others. And when it occurs, it is considerably better for having been done with and through others. Even though they need to be streamlined to allow more rapid decisions in these times of greatly increased change, the elaborate checks and balances of the academy—the intricate modes of our shared governance—usually assure that our hold on controlling power will be limited. Instead of moving quickly and unilaterally to implement our plans, we are forced to deliberate and discuss them with others. The metaphor of education as conversation comes into play. Through reflection and consultation we are helped to see things more clearly—perhaps even to change our minds and incorporate things we had not considered. In the process, we come closer to covenantal community and to relational power.

Relational power involves allowing oneself to be affected by others as well as seeking to affect them. There is strength in receptivity as well as agency. Successful leadership involves letting others make differences. We know controlling power alone is deficient when we reflect on the nature of healthy interactions—characterized by reciprocity and mutuality, they display a minimum of control. No one is regarded as self-sufficient in insight or ability; genuine openness to the perspectives and ideas of others is deemed essential for significant and enduring progress.

Relational power is central to good peer review in which honest and supportive give and take leads to growth and development. It is not a deformed kind of controlling power—weak, passive, and ineffectual. Indeed, in one sense, controlling power is a deformed kind of relational power. For in the grip of controlling power, one sees others as threats rather than as potential gifts. In the end, controlling power by itself is exhausting. Everyone is left struggling to protect himself or herself against the rest. If leadership means promoting desirable differences, it requires openness to others. It means encouraging and allowing them to play roles as well. It involves the receptivity that is part of relational power. Successful chairs and other campus leaders know how this works.

Rarely, though, does change come easily. One management professor, highly experienced in conducting professional development workshops for chairpersons, reports that fewer than one-third of the more than 4,500 chairpersons she surveyed "report any degree of success in motivating difficult colleagues or poor teachers who are tenured"—in getting faculty to pull their weight or to address conflict (Lucas, 1999, p. 3). I suspect that something like insistent individualism is afflicting the work of the other 3,000 chairpersons and no doubt tenure reinforces it. Faculty in these departments are blind to the truth that setting and pursuing shared goals can allow them to realize their own as well. Inviting them into conversation about fundamental educational commitments can help.

In fact, facilitating conversation is the best way to overcome traditional debilitating myths about academic leadership. Insistent individualism reinforces a common perception that academic leaders are but second-rate professors. Faculty who see themselves as locked in competition rather than enriched by collaboration seem naturally to view leaders as opponents who can't make it in teaching and research, despite ample evidence to the contrary. Special leadership certificates or degrees command little cachet, and prior subject-matter expertise or reputation rarely carries over to bestow leadership authority. Alternatives must be identified and cultivated.

Conversations and Teaching

Under the leadership of an energetic and hospitable chairperson, dean, or other leader, conversation provokes a broad examination of pedagogy, curricula, or policy objectives. When this happens, diversity of talent and perspective is celebrated within frameworks that are often expanded precisely because of the conversation. As a result, the unit, department, or school becomes *more* than the sum of its members. But this usually happens only when the director, department chair or dean takes the lead or encourages and allows others to do so.

The successful leader promotes a variety of conversations by all means possible. Some of these are ad hoc, reflecting shrewd use of unforeseen or unpredictable developments. Special events, award ceremonies, and faculty publications create opportunities for fostering conversation. Other opportunities are regular occurrences, part of the culture and ethos of the academy. Examples include tenure awards and promotions—as well as events welcoming new faculty and staff. The best conversations touch on teaching and learning in one way or another. Everyone gains from creating hospitable and nourishing environments and cultures, promoting collective as well as individual excellence. When leaders foster this kind of connectivity and conversation, communities of learning emerge—communities in which individuals contribute their distinctive talents to a common good marked by mutual enrichment. Even as they may debate the failures of the academy, they help to correct them.

This analysis of power and conversation should remind us of good teaching as well as leadership. The reason, of course, is that teaching is a form of leadership and vice versa. The current preference for talk about learning rather than teaching reflects the importance of relational power because teaching lends itself to controlling power. The instructor is the authority, standing above and outside others. He or she sets the agenda and decides when and how it is completed. However, when learning rather than teaching governs, students are active players. Their individual talents and past experiences become part of the process and are utilized rather than ignored in the educational experience. They are seen as having something to offer, not simply as having educational deficiencies or voids. Instructors themselves become examples of learners and learning with others, not above them. Indeed, they use their learning to become exemplary students. The parallel with successful, hospitable leadership is striking.

Selves and Structures

Effective teaching and leadership require self-insight. Appropriate subject matter or management knowledge is certainly necessary, but hardly sufficient. In the end, the importance of the person looms larger in good teaching and leadership than do pedagogical or management techniques. The role of leader and teacher alike is to bring into personal focus the impersonal theories and abstractions of knowledge—to witness and attest to why and how these things matter.

Whether in teaching or leading, practicing hospitality means understanding the self as dependent upon contributions from others as well as contributing to the self-constitution of others. Those who acknowledge this reality are more likely to contribute to the enrichment of others and to enjoy fulfilled lives. They are more likely to exercise genuine authority and to be successful as leaders, teachers, and scholars. Their leadership and their teaching reflect their interest in learning from others and in having their colleagues and students learn from each other. Students are seen as individuals, possessing different personal gifts and educational needs and talents. Colleagues are treated as those with whom one is linked in common endeavors—endeavors advanced only through mutual interest and reciprocity.

The department and school ought to be the immediate context for this linkage since they are where faculty are likely to commit to regular exchange of interests and insights. In hospitable collegia, faculty members agree to regular review of standards governing curriculum, grading, and advising as well as faculty evaluation and recommendations for hiring, promotion, and tenure. Mutual reciprocity is key, for the vibrant collegium is known as a place where members show up and attend to each other in teaching, scholarship, and service. They attend as well to their broader institutional citizenship—to working with the faculty senate and student affairs staff.

Elsewhere I explore in detail (Bennett, 1998) various strategies respecting recruitment, orientation, and mentoring that department and division chairpersons and heads can use. A key factor in the success of these tasks is clear and honest communication about both assets and problems. The point applies across the campus. Admission offices should work closely with campus tour guides to ensure that claims about the institution are accurate. Orientation programs for all new employees should provide both comprehensive and accurate information—particularly for those who have initial or frequent contact with the public. Public affairs officials need to be provided clear objectives consonant with institutional realities and hospitable relations with the publics they address—not expectations for spin or denial.

Identifying imaginative strategies for promoting greater communication is at the heart of leadership. For instance, staffing hiring committees with members from other units can advance greater understanding and relational awareness through mutual education. These cross-disciplinary and cross-institutional activities can foster both individual and institutional vitality. They can generate new research and educational projects. Likewise, involving retired faculty and staff in institutional studies and activities can provide valuable perspectives on campus ethics and spiritualities as well as operational matters.

Modeling Respectfulness

The practice of sharing information plays an important part in how academic leaders generate respect. The three parts of Stanley Fish's (2001) golden rule of administration apply to all educational leaders—to committee heads, department chairpersons, and deans, and no less, as we will see, to presidents: "Part one is, always tell the truth. Part two is, always tell more of the truth than you have to. And part three is, always tell the truth before anyone asks you to" (p. B14). Fish characterizes his rule as both moral counsel and strategy. Like knowledge, information is power, but "it is a power best exercised when it is expended, not hoarded"

(Fish, 2001, p. B14). To promote a sense of belonging to the institution, leaders must share information.

As leaders of the department or school, chairpersons, deans, and other leaders need personally to model the openness to the other, the new, and the different that hospitality involves. Attending to the other requires stepping back for the moment from policies and procedures that may be stagnant and obsolete in order to hear the new, which may be the better. Openness requires dismantling the barriers to new insight that fear of change or denial of ignorance can erect. To be engaged in the institutional pursuit of truth in a worthy manner, our common work requires this kind of attentiveness. Leaders show the way in periodic review of the old, the familiar, and the traditional in order to assess their continuing adequacy. They can delegate a number of responsibilities, because chairs, deans, and other leaders have limited time and energy. But hospitableness is not something that can be delegated, only modeled. It cannot be commended without being practiced, or enjoined without being displayed.

Hospitableness should inform all leadership efforts. Curriculum review comes immediately to mind as does faculty professional formation and evaluation. Curricula need periodic assessment, marked by members who openly, honestly, and collaboratively question whether they really serve the good of the student or just the convenience of the faculty member. Any change comes with difficulty, but fostering collective openness to alternatives and improvements to established patterns is a key part of the leader's job and points to the importance of hospitable planning and assessment as well.

Likewise, attending productively to issues of faculty formation requires both sensitivity to the individual and concern for the department and school. Conducting open, inclusive searches and welcoming the new member into the department and the institution are perhaps the most obvious examples of hospitableness. Too often, however, a kind of social Darwinism occurs and the new member is left to sink or swim alone (Boice, 1992). Opportunities for mentoring by more senior members are overlooked as are chances for mutual enrichment that come from collaborative activities. Older faculty and staff can get stuck or go backwards and it is tempting to work around them. But the continued growth of all members is important for the department and school as a whole—value achieved by one redounds to the welfare of others as well.

Personnel evaluation, in turn, provides an opportunity to support individuals in the context of their contributions to the welfare of the department, students, the school, and the institution. The effective leader is able to present evaluation activities as opportunities for individuals to identify accomplishments and strengths that might otherwise go unnoticed. Periodic evaluation also provides occasions for individuals to enlist the help of colleagues in constructing a realistic plan of professional development for future years. For the individual who no longer contributes to the academy, hospitableness requires honest and firm presentation of a plan of action (and perhaps separation) that the leader has previously discussed with the supervisor.

It is often said that the job of the chairperson is like that of herding cats or frogs. Notoriously individualistic faculty members like to go their own way and the job of the chair is to elicit a functional unity within plurality. Chairs too can be individualists, and so the job of evoking and supporting unity is bumped up to the dean's level. Longstanding traditions like academic freedom reinforce this individualism. On the one hand, it is the disciplines, the scholarly professions, that generate or warrant the worth of knowledge. On the other hand, "the strongest right of tenured professors is that of defying their professions. . . . [often] this means that, in the end, there is little collective responsibility for the program of the university" (Anderson, 1993, p. 31).

To think about hospitableness and conversation in this context is to give a new slant to the job. For far from being superficial or superfluous, hospitality and conversation are essential to the work of academic leaders. They provide for the health of the individual, the increase of learning, *and* collective responsibility for the welfare of the community and its programs. None of us is infallible or has an indisputable edge on truth. We need and depend upon others. Openness to them is an essential condition of learning and fostering learning, of knowing and doing—of passing through the inevitable trials and disappointments to the better idea. Hospitableness and conversation are prerequisites, not substitutes, for competence. They are the means whereby the covenanted collegium of scholars and learners is created and sustained, and they seem vital to the deep satisfactions we all seek as educators. Far from a counsel of perfection, hospitableness, conversation, and covenant are essential to environments of learning and the academic life. Midlevel leaders impoverish themselves and their calling when they neglect this foundation of the academy.

PRESIDENTS

Are matters different when we come to the position of institutional president? Some think so. Former university president James Fisher has written in support of a heroic model of the institutional president—a leadership form of insistent individualism. He argues for a "socially distant" president who is authorized in the strongest sense by the board. Fisher (1994) considers the egalitarian waves of the 1960s and 1970s to have undercut and "compromised the order that made our institutions work—including an effective, energetic leadership role for the president" (p. 61). In this view, an institution of vigor, capable of substantial change, cannot tolerate blurred roles for students, faculty, administrators, and trustees. In blurring roles and reducing presidential social distance, those two decades often reduced leadership to matters of ceremony and ritual.

Social Distance and Heroic Leadership

Let us examine this heroic leader in more detail. The effective leader must stand apart. Fisher regards social distance as the most significant characteristic of effective leadership. It "means being present on important occasions and appearing often, but briefly and informally, in the workplace" (Fisher, 1994, p. 64). In effect, Fisher is arguing for the importance of the appearance—but not the reality—of approachability and accessibility. Actually being approachable detracts from the power of the president, compromising his or her stature and aura of wisdom. "Day-to-day intimacy destroys illusions and makes the leader more debatable and less likely to be inspiring. Collegial contact can obscure strengths, highlight weaknesses, and eliminate perceived referent qualities" (Fisher, 1994, p. 64).

Only through the adroit use of social distance can the institutional president hope to be truly transformational and not merely transactional. Using James MacGregor Burns' (1978) now famous distinction between two schools of leadership, Fisher observes that the transactional leader is a collegial sort, perhaps first among equals, who manages the institution toward the realization of its goals. By contrast, transformers are leaders who through character and charisma give visionary direction and expression to institutional goals. As Fisher (1994) sees things, "the transformational president typically is more distant, more decisive, more assertive, and more visionary; the transactional president is more collaborative, less decisive, less assertive, and more personally engaged in institutional affairs" (p. 61). What institutions of higher education need most are presidents capable of both vision and decisiveness, not openness to others or collaboration with them.

Is Fisher on track? Are hospitality and relational power really deficits and liabilities in effective presidential leadership? One wonders about the staying power of the charisma Fisher celebrates when it is used to bolster personal, unilateral power. And his use of social distance cuts two ways. On the one hand it may prolong presidential controlling power, but on the other the leader's absence and failure to collaborate can only undercut trust and confidence. As socially distant, one is hardly modeling the fruit of education as liberated engagement. Instead, one risks the reputation, and reality, of arrogance.

The contrasts Fisher constructs appear almost oxymoronic in character. "Distance means being utterly open but always remote. . . . It is being a friendly presence: warm and genuine, concerned and interested, but never around too long and rarely getting too involved" (Fisher, 1994, p. 65). Indeed, even Fisher's description of the presidential role smacks of elitism and an amazing degree of self-aggrandizement:

> I continue to believe that the college presidency offers the grandest opportunity in the most noble of human enterprises. I believe it is the most difficult leadership role in our society, and that it takes both an extraordinary person and appropriate conditions to conduct the office effectively. (p. 60)

Rather than envisioning faculty as the key institutional resource for meeting the growing challenge to traditional higher education, Fisher argues for their exclusion from governance deliberations. Indeed, he holds that "the most intransigent group in any [university] is bound to be that which is interested in keeping it as it is . . . the faculty" (Fisher, 1994, p. 61). Overall, the flow of Fisher's position drifts toward the hubris of insistent individualism and the subtle sense that the chief executive *is* the organization.

Team Leadership

Writing in response to Fisher's position, Madeleine Green argues that the day of heroic leadership is over—in the corporate and political worlds as well as in education. Fisher is describing an ideal of the past. There are no "great" leaders now in the sense of those who control things by dint of intelligence, charisma, and other personal powers. Ours is an era of delegation and collaboration. Our times are characterized by much greater diversity and achieving consensus is often far more difficult. Leadership today must be an interactive process. "The traits of the leader become less important than the complex interrelationships among leaders, followers, context, and the tasks at hand" (Green, 1994, p. 56). Green's relational understanding of leadership emphasizes both its complexity and the unavailability of easy formulas for unilateral power and successful leadership. "For those seeking power and ego gratification, this conception of leadership seems downright wimpy" (Green, 1994, p. 56).

Green cites with favor scholars who argue that presidents do not create an institutional vision, but tap into the ideas, hopes, and dreams within the institution that are waiting to be acknowledged and renewed. Robert Greenleaf (1998) puts the issue well: "Institutions function better when the idea, the dream, is to the fore, and the person, the leader, is seen as the servant of the idea" (p. 87). It is the dream, the vision that energizes—not the leader, however socially distant. "It is not 'I,' the ultimate leader, that is moving this institution to greatness; it is the dream, the great idea" that unites and moves the institution forward (Greenleaf, 1998, p. 87). The dream must be shared so that it can evolve. Good leaders not only permit but evoke participation in the development, formation, and extension of the dream. That is, good leaders are servants to the process of conversation.

Green notes the importance of teams that enable a variety of perspectives, approaches, and strategies to emerge. Of course not every team is real—some are "illusory" teams, sharing only information but not responsibility. But real, effective teams display the characteristics of collegia. They

> benefit from the diversity of their members and enable their members to engage in meaningful dialogue, learn from one another, and benefit from their differences, rather than minimize or discount them. In this context, leadership roles are multiple. One person may keep the group on task, one may serve as its conscience, another as its emotional glue. (Green, 1994, p. 56)

Hospitality seems a critical virtue in the exercise of this kind of post-heroic leadership. Openness to others, learning from them, and addressing the others in *their* terms are essential. From this point of view, the markers of effective presidential leadership are no different from those of chairs, deans, or other educational leaders.

> Team leadership requires the ability to listen to others and to value their viewpoints, as well as to understand them. It requires letting go, giving up control as the predominant mode, and being prepared for unexpected outcomes. It

requires establishing trust, first by trusting others and then by modeling the behaviors of valuing diverse opinions and sharing leadership. (Green, 1994, p. 56)

This is a long way from the concept of heroic leadership where the model is that of the Western—a model of command and control. Heroic leadership tends to exclude others, deny them access to appropriate and relevant information, and mislead or in other ways treat them as means to an outcome rather than as valuable agents in helping to determine and achieve that outcome. Heroic leadership oversimplifies the complexities involved. Unfortunately, this type of leadership is all too common and everyone involved pays a price. This leadership severs rather than promotes the connections distinctive of a covenantal society. It illustrates a particular type of insistent individualism by modeling secrecy rather than sharing, unilateral rather than relational power.

The heroic type also neglects the fundamental teaching role of the leader. As teacher, the hospitable leader extends the educational conversation by distributing, not sequestering, information. He or she includes others in institutional decision-making, taking advantage of their special knowledge, insight, and perspective. "Leadership that teaches does not simply bend people against their will, or dazzle them out of their faculties, or manipulate them behind their backs, or indoctrinate them without illuminating" (May, 2001, p. 157). The point, rather, is to expand "the horizon against which colleagues see a given world of practice and [to enlarge their] freedom to perform in new ways" (May, 2001, p. 157).

Hospitable leadership does not mean one is unable to be decisive and make quiet decisions when necessary. But it does require ongoing attention to others—understanding their perspectives from their points of view. Informed by these viewpoints, hospitable leadership relies upon persuasion rather than command. It requires the energy and flexibility to recognize and even encourage changing coalitions. Issues change, often quite rapidly, and authority and power change as well.

Leaders must sometimes be followers themselves. Sometimes they must deliberately share their power with others by delegating it or by truly giving it away. At other times, when power is not theirs to give away, they must draw power from others by creating partnerships and alliances. (Green, 1994, p. 59)

From a more comprehensive point of view, the role of the leader is to convert social contract communities into the broader covenantal communities from which they draw their strength. It is scarcely an easy task.

> The rules of academic leadership are sufficiently ambiguous, the players sufficiently unpredictable and contentious, and the issues sufficiently intractable that the task is neither for the faint-hearted nor for the disciples of simplicity. Managing cacophony, diversity, and downright incivility requires subtlety, courage, and the self-discipline to submerge one's own ego in service of a greater accomplishment. (Green, 1994, pp. 59–60)

Overall, the task is to create and sustain a collegium or learning organization—one possessing an institutional culture of critical inquiry. The means include fostering connectivity and conversation, recognizing achievement, providing other rewards, and personally modeling espoused values.

Presidential Influence

There are differences of location—if not of leadership character—between institutional presidents and other academic leaders. Chief executive leaders can occupy positions of extraordinary prominence and visibility. Critics are quick to observe discrepancies between public pronouncements and personal behavior. Accordingly, it is almost impossible to overstate the role of the president in establishing the values and tone of an institution. His or her behaviors and decisions on issues of hospitality, conversation, and covenant are noted and have a widespread effect.

For instance, scrupulous attention to matters of hospitality and honesty sets an example for others. On the other hand, subtle messages that institutional budget or enrollment numbers reported to the public can be manipulated to institutional advantage give others in the institution permission to be dishonest. A president's refusal to acknowledge damaging news discourages honest reporting about what everyone knows to be the truth. Why fight those who control whether one continues and at what salary?

That institutional "misrepresentations" are in fact *untruths* about a particular college or university is the real issue. The very institution that identifies itself as conducting an unfettered search for truth fetters itself by these behaviors. Some institutions might claim that a doctored photograph, for instance, is actually quite representative of the campus, but the fact remains that the college or university is still lying about the photograph itself. Other institutions may defend their practice of misrepresenting data because greater competitive positioning allows them to achieve goals such as greater diversity, but desirable ends do not automatically justify means.

Instead, the untruths of education are violations of its very purpose of discovering and promoting truth. They work directly against education. They present a message at odds with the teaching of hospitable faculty and staff. They diminish the public standing of other colleges and universities that are committed to the welfare of students rather than their own status and competitive success. Providing an ethical compass is part of leadership. Job descriptions for presidents and chief academic officers should include issues of ethics and personal character as central elements.

Parallels With Faculty Ethics
There are instructive parallels with the impact of faculty misrepresentations. A celebrated controversy at the level of individual faculty ethics centered on Joseph Ellis, a history professor disclosed to have fabricated a personal past respecting his involvement in Vietnam, civil rights, and peace movements. Some of the controversy turned on why a highly regarded and successful teacher-scholar felt it necessary for at least a decade to lie in his classroom. Personal ambition seems unlikely. A well-known, respected scholar of the American colonial era, Ellis' reputation was secure. He had already won a Pulitzer prize for one of his books and a National Book Award for another. What did he stand to gain by lying? Already accomplished professionally, why did he risk personal embarrassment and professional diminishment? Persuasive answers are elusive. Most of us are left to speculate about the allure of dangerous risk-taking and/or the numbing effect of repeated, successful (that is, undetected) misrepresentations.

That the history professor embellished his teaching with stories that were simply false raises a number of questions about the ethics of teaching. As fellow historian Elliott Gorn (2001) observed,

> much is at stake: How the public perceives college faculties; our definition of proper professional conduct; the limits of freedom in the classroom; how we define our mission as faculty members; our claim to speak and write about the past with legitimacy. (p. B14)

Troubling in any case, deliberate misrepresentation of the past seems particularly so when committed by an historian.

However, the academy needs to engage in similar conversation about the behavior of institutions and their leaders. Periodically, we hear about high-ranking executives who plagiarized or otherwise falsified their credentials. Some leaders have been charged with diverting institutional funds into reimbursements for arguably personal expenses. And collegiate athletic scandals and abuses seem always to be with us. Fortunately, these kinds of abuses do receive attention, if not solution. Apparently of lesser community concern are the lower-profile, but more corrosive, matters of deliberate misrepresentation of institutional achievement and performance—and the subtle, debilitating consequences of increasing reliance upon part-time faculty as a major mechanism for providing instruction.

When presidents are heard to say that higher education institutions can "get away" with these activities, colleagues and others hear and conclude that they too need not pursue the highest levels of ethical behavior, especially when alternatives appear easier or more desirable. When presidents do not speak to the academic purposes and identity of the institution or declare what knowledge is most worth having, others in the institution conclude that it is business as usual (not academics or education) that is most important—business such as increasing enrollments, securing positive media coverage, producing winning athletic teams, or satisfying alumni and trustees.

These behaviors imply that public misrepresentations are acceptable, that even outright fabrications can be justified by some higher end they serve, and that the slow evisceration of academic substance through decreasing use of full-time faculty is permissible. Some institutions have also abandoned other aspects of a moral role they once played. Rather than grappling with broad topical issues, institutions are more frequently silent on them. I am not thinking of narrowly partisan political issues. The point is rather that universities and colleges are not providing adequate moral leadership by analyzing and speaking to issues of environmental abuse, the economics of global warming, exploitation of developing nations, teenage pregnancy, crime and incarceration, etc. Nor are they providing leadership on local issues, such as adequate compensation for their janitorial staff—or even for their own graduate students. Only when publicly pressed by student demonstrations have some institutional leaders shown the kind of moral awareness that educational institutions should *themselves* illustrate as well as promote in their students.

Society provides institutions of higher education a privileged status. Yet, colleges and universities are inherently public and communal, and have corresponding ethical responsibilities. Presidents and other leaders need to tell more, not less, about their institutions—and be forthcoming in what they do tell, instead of modeling the art of social distance. Leaders must be caring as well as knowledgeable. They must bring ethics and spirituality to their intellectual and practical concerns. And they must recognize the primary standing of relationality and their connectedness with others. As Green and others suggest, successful leadership involves dispersing, not concentrating, leadership functions.

These functions return us to the importance of academic politics— but considered now as how we engage each other in conversation, not in combat. Stanley Hauerwas (1995) reminds us that

> an appreciation of the university as a moral community requires a return to politics as essential to the university's intellectual mission, for the politics of the university must be governed and shaped by the common purpose to educate and form students to know and desire the right things rightly. (p. 36)

In this sense, politics is not the bitter contest over small stakes; it "is not the unseemly side of the university, but the essential conversation that must go on about what it is students should read and how they are best taught to read" (Hauerwas, 1995, p. 36).

Both Transactional and Transformational—or Neither

It has become increasingly clear that at least as applied to the academy, Burns' distinction between transactional and transformational divides what should be joined. In the academy, good management is a necessary condition for effective leadership, and vice versa. Further, as James Downey (2001) correctly observes, both transactional and transformational concepts

> focus too much attention on the 'leader' and encourage the erroneous belief that organizations rely on a gifted individual or two for their prosperity or even survival. This in turn bespeaks a culture of dependence and conformity which is at odds not only with how universities actually operate but with an ideal of highly distributed leadership which is the heart of the collegium. (p. 237)

The academy contains a variety of leaders—school deans, office directors, student life officers, committee heads, department chairpersons, and presidents. The most successful display the leadership philosophy of which Green, rather than Fisher, writes. They may complain that they have little power. And, indeed, any institutional power is almost always hostage to multiple controls in the hands of others. But successful leaders recognize that the clarity of organizational charts often has little correspondence with the actualities of academe. Presidents do play a key role, but I suggest that it is dependent less upon charisma than on hospitality. As Downey (2001) notes,

> visions in universities are not manufactured; they are harvested. The president's role is to take the lead in cultivating an institutional climate where openness, mutual respect, and the release of creative energies are valued as acts of leadership in themselves. (p. 237)

HOSPITALITY AS LEADERSHIP

Downey's statement provides a helpful summary of some of the themes of this book. Leadership involves "cultivating an institutional climate where openness, mutual respect, and the release of creative energies are valued as acts of leadership in themselves." That is, leadership involves practicing hospitality. But equally important, practicing hospitality is a form of leadership. Robert Greenleaf (1998) had it right: those who are committed to service, lead others. As servants they promote, support, and extend the hospitality and conversation that constitute education— and invite others to do likewise. Hospitable leaders push, cajole, arouse—and listen.

Those who make openness to others a habit seek ways to overcome the fragmentation and isolation of both individuals and institutions. They develop philosophies and ethics that promote both individual and common goods. Thus they create conditions for healthy spiritualities— understandings of self as linked with others in commitments that attend to others, advance insight into self, and promote ethical fulfillment. They draw on their different strengths to pursue the common tasks of revitalizing traditions of openness—traditions that are becoming weakened and depleted as higher education becomes more a business than a social institution.

Hospitable leaders introduce a constructive restlessness instead of a comfortable self-satisfaction. They resist the reduction of colleges and universities to the reproduction of the hierarchy of power, wealth, and authority. As a consequence, they are custodians of standards: they help others to contest dullness and the obsolete; to distinguish bold experimentation from carelessness; and to attend to others and to opposing positions. They remind us of the resources we already have—our ability in conversation to distinguish the good from the bad. They also remind us that the ideal of the better is always available for self-criticism and for the search for deeper insights and more rewarding ways of being together.

Those who practice hospitality in formal positions of leadership elicit appropriate unities out of aggregations of individualists and nurture institutional structures that integrate rather than separate. They promote organizational arrangements that display interest in individuals and their distinctive gifts, rather than indifference to their presence. They use an array of rituals, celebrations, and other symbols to create and reinforce patterns of openness—presenting these symbols as reminders of the many voices and idioms, the conversational richness of human achievements and self-understandings that constitute our inheritance. Hospitable leaders invite participation in conversation that reflects, reaffirms, and extends the underlying connectivity, not the atomistic fragmentation, that is our basic reality. They see differences as opportunities to seek both reconciliation and transformation through deeper and more inclusive concepts rather than oppositional ones.

These leaders invite others to share the responsibilities and opportunities of the collegium—to transcend the self-promotion and self-protection of insistent individualism. They authorize us to discover and develop our own talents and goods through discovering and creating the common good we share with others. They devise procedures that recognize and incorporate the voices of institutional members in institutional decisions. They use to advantage the history of their institution to cultivate campus intellectual life. That is, they draw upon the traditions of what higher education has done best, rather than imitate proprietary institutions with their unbundled faculty, their standardized curricula, and their emphasis upon production rather than conversation. They work to counteract the increasing evisceration of higher education through the growing reliance upon adjunct faculty. They devise ways to reverse the rapid dismantling of the central core and stewardship of instruction that unbundling and accelerated adjunct dependence represent.

To protect the vitality of traditional education, these leaders incorporate faculty and staff of all kinds in conversations about the future. They know that faculty priorities and commitments often rest elsewhere than in the institution, but they also realize that it is a major stretch for faculty to see administrators and boards as partners when secrecy and superficial consultation on their part are the rule. When these leaders authorize everyone to understand the collegium in terms of covenant (with different voices, traditions, texts, and people—the familiar as well as the strange) rather than social contract, they reduce the prospect that education will be seen as commodity.

These leaders help replace the metaphor of education as production with that of a commonwealth whose essential defining characteristic is conversation. They know that hospitable conversation has a self-referential character other metaphors for education do not. They also know that conversation as a defining metaphor for higher education is in retreat in the face of increasing technological and socioeconomic change. And they sense that without the centrality of conversation as its distinctive feature, higher education reduces itself to a commercial transaction. Nostalgia is always a risk, and the "good old days" never really existed. But traditional education *has* centrally engaged hospitality and conversation as ideals, however flawed the efforts might have been. When we abandon these ideals in favor of market efficiency and productivity we lose the distinctiveness of higher education.

CONCLUSION

Only when educational leaders and all who participate in higher education allow themselves to be truly *formed* as well as informed by conversation and hospitable teaching, scholarship, and service, can the academy remain true to itself. Only when we see ourselves as members of a covenantal collegium can higher education stand against the elements of anti-intellectualism that threaten our work as educators—reducing education to the transmission of information and credentialing. When pursued with genuine openness, learning makes a difference in who we are.

I have offered ways in which we might resist the seductive suggestions that comfortable routines suffice, or that business models—developing aggressive public relations, unbundling faculty, establishing for-profit subsidiaries, and loading up with adjunct faculty—are the way to go. Vital education requires engagement—a professional life full of conversation and honest reflection on ourselves, our programs, our research and teaching, and our institutions. The challenge before us is twofold—to educate others *and* ourselves; to facilitate the growth of others and ourselves. Through our learning we can release healing forces in the world and in ourselves.

I have suggested that this challenge is best met when we commit to hospitality, conversation, and covenant. These are indispensable concepts for our work as educators. They connect and illuminate our best self-understandings and actions. They are best demonstrated, however, rather than simply talked about.

REFERENCES

Anderson, C. W. (1993). *Prescribing the life of the mind: An essay on the purpose of the university, the aims of liberal education, the competence of citizens, and the cultivation of practical reason*. Madison, WI: University of Wisconsin Press.

Bennett, J. B. (1990, Winter). The dean and the department chair: Toward greater collaboration. *Educational Record, 71* (1), 24–26.

Bennett, J. B. (1998). *Collegial professionalism: The academy, individualism, and the common good*. Phoenix, AZ: American Council on Education/Oryx Press.

Boice, R. (1992). *The new faculty member: Supporting and fostering professional development*. San Francisco, CA: Jossey-Bass.

Burns, J. M. (1978). *Leadership*. New York, NY: Harper & Row.

Downey, J. (2001, Summer). Guest editor's introduction: Academic leadership and organizational change. *Innovative Higher Education, 25* (4), 235–238.

Fish, S. (2001, October 19). To thine own faculty be truthful. *The Chronicle of Higher Education*, pp. B13–B14.

Fisher, J. L. (1994, Summer). Reflections on transformational leadership. *Educational Record, 75* (3), 54, 60–65.

Gorn, E. J. (2001, July 20). Why are academics ducking the Ellis case? *The Chronicle of Higher Education*, p. B14.

Green, M. F. (1994, Summer). Not for wimps or cowards: Leadership in the post-heroic age. *Educational Record, 75* (3), 55–60.

Greenleaf, R. (1998). *The power of servant-leadership: Essays*. L. C. Spears (Ed.). San Francisco, CA: Berrett-Koehler.

Hauerwas, S. M. (1995). The morality of teaching. In A. L. DeNeef & C. D. Goodwin (Eds.), *The academic's handbook* (2nd ed.) (pp. 29–37). Durham, NC: Duke University Press.

Lucas, A. F. (1999, November). Myths that make chairs feel they are powerless: Six fallacies that stifle change—and how to overcome them. *AAHE Bulletin, 53* (3), 3–5.

May, W. F. (2001). *Beleaguered rulers: The public obligation of the professional.* Louisville, KY: Westminster John Knox Press.

Rosovsky, H., & Ameer, I.-L. (1998). A neglected topic: Professional conduct of college and university teachers. In W. G. Bowen & H. T. Shapiro (Eds.), *Universities and their leadership* (pp. 119–156). Princeton, NJ: Princeton University Press.

Bibliography

Allan, G. (1993). Process ideology and the common good. *The Journal of Speculative Philosophy, VII* (4), 266–285.

Allan, G. (1996, Fall/Winter). Playing with worlds: John Dewey, the habit of experiment, and the goods of democracy. *Soundings, 79* (3–4), 447–468.

Allan, G. (1997). *Rethinking college education.* Lawrence, KS: University Press of Kansas.

Anderson, C. W. (1993). *Prescribing the life of the mind: An essay on the purpose of the university, the aims of liberal education, the competence of citizens, and the cultivation of practical reason.* Madison, WI: University of Wisconsin Press.

Anderson, M. (1992). *Imposters in the temple: American intellectuals are destroying our universities.* New York, NY: Simon and Schuster.

Arden, E. (2001, October). When it's time to leave—leave! Mandatory retirement is good for higher education. *AAHE Bulletin, 54* (2), 8–9.

Arenson, K. W. (2002, March 17). Columbia soothes the dogs of war in its English Dept. *The New York Times,* pp. A1, 43.

Astin, A. (1991). *The unrealized potential of American higher education.* Athens, GA: The University of Georgia Institute of Higher Education.

Astin, A. (1997, September 26). Our obsession with being 'smart' is distorting intellectual life. *The Chronicle of Higher Education,* p. A60.

Bartlett, T. (2001, November 23). Colleges praise new source of data, as long as their scores stay secret. *The Chronicle of Higher Education,* p. A31.

Bass, D. (Ed.). (1997). *Practicing our faith: A way of life for a searching people.* San Francisco, CA: Jossey-Bass.

Bauerlein, M. (2001, November 16). The two cultures again: Tilting against objectivity. *The Chronicle of Higher Education,* p. B14.

Bellah, R. N. (1998). Courageous or indifferent individualism. *Ethical Perspectives, 5* (2), 92–102.

Bellah, R. N., Madsen, R., Sullivan, W. M., Swidler, A., & Tipton, S. M. (1985). *Habits of the heart: Individualism and commitment in American life.* Berkeley, CA: University of California Press.

Bellah, R. N., Madsen, R., Sullivan, W. M., Swidler, A., & Tipton, S. M. (1991). *The good society.* New York, NY: Random House.

Benhabib, S. (1992). *Situating the self: Gender, community, and postmodernism in contemporary ethics.* New York, NY: Routledge.

Bennett, J. B. (1990, Winter). The dean and the department chair: Toward greater collaboration. *Educational Record, 71* (1), 24–26.

Bennett, J. B. (1998). *Collegial professionalism: The academy, individualism, and the common good.* Phoenix, AZ: American Council on Education/Oryx Press.

Bennett, J. B., & Dreyer, E. (1994, April). On complaining about students. *AAHE Bulletin, 46* (8), 7–8.

Berube, M. (2001, September 21). Dream a little dream. *The Chronicle of Higher Education,* p. B20.

Boice, R. (1992). *The new faculty member: Supporting and fostering professional development.* San Francisco, CA: Jossey-Bass.

Booth, W. C. (1988). *The vocation of a teacher: Rhetorical occasions 1967–1988.* Chicago, IL: University of Chicago Press.

Burns, J. M. (1978). *Leadership.* New York, NY: Harper & Row.

Carlson, E., & Kimball, B. (1994, Fall). Introduction by Ralph Lundgren. Two views of the academic life. *Liberal Education, 80* (4), 4–15.

Chickering, A. W., & Kytle, J. (1999). The collegial ideal in the twenty-first century. In J. D. Toma & A. J. Kezar (Eds.), *Reconceptualizing the collegiate ideal* (pp. 109–120). San Francisco, CA: Jossey-Bass.

Clegg, R. (2000, November 24). Photographs and fraud over race. *The Chronicle of Higher Education,* p. B17.

Cobb, J. B., Jr. (1991). Theology against the disciplines. In B. G. Wheeler & E. Farley (Eds.), *Shifting boundaries: Contextual approaches to the structure of theological education* (pp. 241–258). Louisville, KY: Westminster/John Knox.

Corts, T. E. (1997, January/February). Let's stop trivializing the truth. *Trusteeship,* 6–10.

Cowan, M. A., & Lee, B J. (1997). *Conversation, risk, and conversion: The inner and public life of small Christian communities.* Maryknoll, NY: Orbis Books.

Cross, P. K. (1994, October). Academic citizenship. *AAHE Bulletin, 47* (2), 3–5, 10.

Damrosch, D. (1995). *We scholars: Changing the culture of the university.* Cambridge, MA: Harvard University Press.

Davis, L. J. (1999, June 11). The uses of fear and envy in academe. *The Chronicle of Higher Education,* p. B8.

Downey, J. (2001, Summer). Guest editor's introduction: Academic leadership and organizational change. *Innovative Higher Education, 25* (4), 235–238.

Elkins, J. (2001, November 9). The ivory tower of tearlessness. *The Chronicle of Higher Education,* pp. B7–B10.

Fairweather, J. S. (1996). *Faculty work and public trust: Restoring the value of teaching and public service in American academic life.* Boston, MA: Allyn and Bacon.

Farley, E. (1988). *The fragility of knowledge: Theological education in the church and the university.* Philadelphia, PA: Fortress Press.

Fish, S. (2001, October 19). To thine own faculty be truthful. *The Chronicle of Higher Education,* pp. B13–B14.

Fisher, J. L. (1994, Summer). Reflections on transformational leadership. *Educational Record, 75* (3), 54, 60–65.

Ford, D. F. (1999). *Self and salvation: Being transformed.* New York, NY: Cambridge University Press.

Gerdy, J. R. (2002, January/February). Athletic victories, educational defeats. *Academe, 88* (1), 32–36.

Getman, J. (1992). *In the company of scholars: The struggle for the soul of higher education.* Austin, TX: University of Texas Press.

Glassick, C. E., Huber, M. T., & Maeroff, G. I. (1997). *Scholarship assessed: Evaluation of the professoriate.* San Francisco, CA: Jossey-Bass.

Gonzalez, V., & Lopez, E. (2001, April). The age of incivility: Countering disruptive behavior in the classroom. *AAHE Bulletin, 53* (8), 3–6.

Gorn, E. J. (2001, July 20). Why are academics ducking the Ellis case? *The Chronicle of Higher Education,* p. B14.

Green, M. F. (1994, Summer). Not for wimps or cowards: Leadership in the post-heroic age. *Educational Record, 75* (3), 55–60.

Greenleaf, R. (1998). *The power of servant-leadership: Essays.* L. C. Spears (Ed.). San Francisco, CA: Berrett-Koehler.

Gregory, M. (1987, Summer). If education is a feast, why do we restrict the menu? A critique of pedagogical metaphors. *College Teaching, 35* (3), 101–106.

Habermas, J. (1984). *Theory of communicative action* (I. T. McCarthy, Trans.). Boston, MA: Beacon Press.

Hadot, P. (1995). *Philosophy as a way of life* (A. I. Davidson, Ed. & Trans.). Cambridge, MA: Blackwell.

Hartshorne, C. (1976). Beyond enlightened self-interest. In H. J. Cargas & B. Lee (Eds.), *Religious experience and process theology: The pastoral implications of a major modern movement* (pp. 301–322). New York, NY: Paulist Press.

Hauerwas, S. M. (1995). The morality of teaching. In A. L. DeNeef & C. D. Goodwin (Eds.), *The academic's handbook* (2nd ed.) (pp. 29–37). Durham, NC: Duke University Press.

Haughton, R. L. (1997). *Images for change: The transformation of society.* Mahwah, NJ: Paulist Press.

Henry, P. (1999). *The ironic Christian's companion: Finding the marks of God's grace in the world.* New York, NY: Riverhead Book.

Hunt, M. E. (1994). Commentary. In L. K. Daly (Ed.), *Feminist theological ethics* (pp. 104–107). Louisville, KY: Westminster John Knox Press.

Jacobson, J. (2001, March 16). In brochures, what you see isn't necessarily what you get: Scandals raise larger issues about how diversity is portrayed. *The Chronicle of Higher Education,* p. A41.

Jeavons, T. (1993, Spring). Humanizing doctoral education: Honoring student aspirations. *Liberal Education, 79* (2), 50–52.

Jensen, E. J. (1995, January/February). The bitter groves of academe. *Change, 27* (1), 8–11.

Kerr, C. (1994, January/February). Knowledge ethics and the new academic culture. *Change, 26* (1), 8–15.

Kerr, C. (1995). *The uses of the university* (4th ed.). Cambridge, MA: Harvard University Press.

Kimball, B. A. (1992). *The 'true professional ideal' in America: A history.* Cambridge, MA: Blackwell.

Kirp, D. L. (2002, March 15). Higher ed inc.: Avoiding the perils of outsourcing. *The Chronicle of Higher Education,* p. B13f.

Kowalsky, D. (2001, December 18). Do I have junior faculty syndrome? *The Chronicle of Higher Education.* Available: http://chronicle.com/jobs/2001/12/2001121801c.htm

Longin, T. (2002). Institutional governance: A call for collaborative decision-making in American higher education. In L. A. McMillin & W. G. Berberet (Eds.), *A new academic compact: Revisioning the relationship between faculty and their institutions* (pp. 211–221). Bolton, MA: Anker.

Loomer, B. (1976, Spring). Two kinds of power. *Process Studies, 6* (1), 5–32.

Loomer, B. (1981). Theology in the American grain. In J. B. Cobb, Jr. & W. W. Schroeder (Eds.), *Process philosophy and social thought* (pp. 141–152). Chicago, IL: Center for the Scientific Study of Religion.

Lovin, R. (1986). Social contract or a public covenant? In R. Lovin (Ed.), *Religion and American public life* (pp. 132–145). Mahwah, NJ: Paulist Press.

Lucas, A. F. (1994). *Strengthening departmental leadership: A team-building guide for chairs in colleges and universities.* San Francisco, CA: Jossey-Bass.

Lucas, A. F. (1999, November). Myths that make chairs feel they are powerless: Six fallacies that stifle change—and how to overcome them. *AAHE Bulletin, 53* (3), 3–5.

May, W. F. (1983). *The physician's covenant: Images of the healer in medical ethics.* Philadelphia, PA: The Westminster Press.

May, W. F. (1996). *Testing the medical covenant: Active euthanasia and health-care reform.* Grand Rapids, MI: Eerdmans.

May, W. F. (2001). *Beleaguered rulers: The public obligation of the professional.* Louisville, KY: Westminster John Knox Press.

McMillin, L. A., & Berberet. W. G. (2002). *A new academic compact: Revisioning the relationship between faculty and their institutions.* Bolton, MA: Anker.

McMurtrie, B. (2001, January 12). Regional accreditors punish colleges rarely and inconsistently. *The Chronicle of Higher Education,* pp. A27–A28.

Miller, J. (1994, July). Joy and gravity: A meditation on the will to live. *Second Opinion, 20* (1), 57–69.

Moran, G. (1997). *Showing how: The act of teaching.* Valley Forge, PA: Trinity Press.

Muller, S. (1994). Presidential leadership. In J. R. Cole, E. G. Barber, & S. R. Graubard (Eds.), *The research university in a time of discontent* (pp. 115–130). Baltimore, MD: Johns Hopkins University Press.

Murdoch, I. (1970). *The sovereignty of good.* New York, NY: Routledge.

Nouwen, H. M. (1975). *Reaching out: Three movements of the spiritual life.* Garden City, NJ: Doubleday and Company.

Oakeshott, M. (1989). *The voice of liberal learning* (T. Fuller, Ed.). New Haven, CT: Yale University Press.

Oakeshott, M. (1991). *Rationalism in politics and other essays.* Indianapolis, IN: Liberty Press.

O'Brien, G. D. (1998). *All the essential half-truths about higher education.* Chicago, IL: University of Chicago Press.

Ong, W. J. (1981). *Fighting for life.* Ithaca, NY: Cornell University Press.

Palmer, P. J. (1983). *To know as we are known: Education as a spiritual journey.* San Francisco, CA: Harper and Row.

Palmer, P. J. (1990). 'All the way down': A spirituality of public life. In P. J. Parker, B. G. Wheeler, & J. W. Fowler (Eds.), *Caring for the commonweal: Education for religious and public life* (pp. 147–163). Macon, GA: Mercer University Press.

Palmer, P. J. (1992a, September). Community and commitment in higher education: An interview with Russell Edgerton. *AAHE Bulletin, 45* (1), 3–7.

Palmer, P. J. (1992b). *Reflections on a program for 'the formation of teachers.'* Kalamazoo, MI: The Fetzer Institute.

Palmer, P. J. (1993, November/December). Good talk about good teaching: Improving teaching through conversation and community. *Change, 25* (6) 8–13.

Palmer, P. J. (1997, September). The grace of great things: Reclaiming the sacred in knowing, teaching, and learning. *The Holistic Education Review, 10* (3), 8–16.

Palmer, P. J. (1998). *The courage to teach: Exploring the inner landscape of a teacher's life.* San Francisco, CA: Jossey-Bass.

Palmer, P. J. (2000). *Let your life speak: Listening for the voice of vocation.* San Francisco, CA: Jossey-Bass.

Pascarella, E. T., & Terenzini, P. T. (1991). *How college affects students: Findings and insights from twenty years of research.* San Francisco, CA: Jossey-Bass.

Pattyn, B. (1998). Introduction: Courageous or indifferent individualism. *Ethical Perspectives, 5* (2), 85–88.

Paulsell, S. (2002). Writing as a spiritual discipline. In L. G. Jones & S. Paulsell (Eds.), *The scope of our art: The vocation of the theological teacher* (pp. 17–31). Grand Rapids, MI: Eerdmans.

Payne, H. C. (1996, Fall). Can or should a college teach virtue? *Liberal Education, 82* (4), 18–25.

Pelikan, J. (1992). *The idea of the university: A reexamination.* New Haven, CT: Yale University Press.

Plante, P. (1990, Winter). An administrator will yearn for the classroom: Myth or reality? *Educational Record, 71* (1), 27–30.

Readings, B. (1996). *The university in ruins.* Cambridge, MA: Harvard University Press.

Rhodes, F. H. T. (1998). The university and its critics. In W. G. Bowen & H. T. Shapiro (Eds.), *Universities and their leadership* (pp. 3–14). Princeton, NJ: Princeton University Press.

Rivkin, J. (1993, Spring). Beyond the prestige economy of graduate education. *Liberal Education, 79* (2), 16–19.

Rosovsky, H. (1990). *The university: An owner's manual.* New York, NY: W. W. Norton.

Rosovsky, H., & Ameer, I.-L. (1998). A neglected topic: Professional conduct of college and university teachers. In W. G. Bowen & H. T. Shapiro (Eds.), *Universities and their leadership* (pp. 119–156). Princeton, NJ: Princeton University Press.

Ruddick, L. (2001, November 23). The near enemy of the humanities is professionalism. *The Chronicle of Higher Education*, pp. B7–B9.

Schneider, A. (1998, March 27). Insubordination and intimidation signal the end of decorum in many classrooms. *The Chronicle of Higher Education*, p. A12.

Shils, E. (1984). *The academic ethic.* Chicago, IL: University of Chicago Press.

Simpson, R. D. (1999, Summer). The importance of being a nobody in higher education. *Innovative Higher Education, 23* (4), 237–240.

Slaughter, S., & Leslie, L. (1997). *Academic capitalism: Politics, policies, and the entrepreneurial university.* Baltimore, MD: Johns Hopkins University Press.

Smith, B. H. (1989, May). Presidential address 1988. Limelight: Reflections on a public year. *Publications of the Modern Language Association of America, 104* (3), 285–293.

Smith, J. E. (1982, Winter). Community, cooperation, and the adventure of learning. *Soundings, LXV* (4), 447–455.

Stecklow, S. (1995, April 5). Cheat sheets: Colleges inflate SATs and graduation rates in popular guidebooks. *The Wall Street Journal, CCXXV* (66), pp. A1, 8.

Sturm, D. (1998a). *Community and alienation: Essays on process thought and public life.* Notre Dame, IN: University of Notre Dame Press.

Sturm, D. (1998b). *Solidarity and suffering: Toward a politics of relationality.* Albany, NY: State University of New York Press.

Sullivan, W. M. (1995). *Work and integrity: The crisis and promise of professionalism in America.* New York, NY: HarperBusiness.

Tannen, D. (1998). *The argument culture.* New York, NY: Random House.

Tannen, D. (2000, March 31). Agonism in the academy: Surviving higher learning's argument culture. *The Chronicle of Higher Education*, p. B7.

Taylor, C. (1992). The politics of recognition. In A. Gutman (Ed.), *Multiculturalism and the politics of recognition* (pp. 25–73). Princeton, NJ: Princeton University Press.

Tompkins, J. (1992). *West of everything: The inner life of westerns.* New York, NY: Oxford University Press.

Tompkins, J. (1996). *A life in school: What the teacher learned.* Reading, MA: Addison Wesley.

Trout, P. A. (1998, July 24). Incivility in the classroom breeds 'education lite.' *The Chronicle of Higher Education*, p. A40.

Veysey, L. (1965). *The emergence of the American university.* Chicago, IL: University of Chicago Press.

Weil, S. (1951). *Waiting for God* (E. Craufurd, Trans.). New York, NY: Harper and Row.

Whitehead, A. N. (1933). *Adventures of ideas.* New York, NY: Macmillan.

Whitehead, A. N. (1936). Harvard: The future. *The Atlantic Monthly, 138* (3), 260–270.

Whitehead, A. N. (1967a). *Science and the modern world.* New York, NY: The Free Press.

Whitehead, A. N. (1967b). *The aims of education and other essays.* New York, NY: The Free Press.

Whitehead, A. N. (1978). *Process and reality* (corrected ed.) (D. W. Sherburne & D. R. Griffin, Eds.). New York, NY: The Free Press.

Williams, R. (2000). *Lost Icons: Reflections on cultural bereavement.* Edinburgh, Scotland: T & T Clark.

Wilshire, B. (1990). *The moral collapse of the university: Professionalism, purity, and alienation.* Albany, NY: State University of New York Press.

Wittgenstein, L. (1963). *Philosophical investigations* (G. E. M. Anscombe, Trans.). New York, NY: Macmillan.

Wolfe, A. (1998, December 4). How a for-profit university can be invaluable to the traditional liberal arts. *The Chronicle of Higher Education,* p. B4.

Wolff, R. P. (1969). The ideal of the university. Boston, MA: Beacon Press.

Worsfold, V. L. (2000, Fall). Faculty excellence. *Perspectives, 30* (2), 113–127.

Young, L. (2002, January 29). Losing status: A former faculty member takes a staff job. *The Chronicle of Higher Education Career Network.* Available: http://chronicle.com/jobs

Index